Shakespearean Pragmatism

Shakespearean Pragmatism

MARKET OF HIS TIME

LARS ENGLE

THE UNIVERSITY OF CHICAGO PRESS
CHICAGO AND LONDON

Lars Engle is associate professor of English at the University of Tulsa.

The University of Chicago Press, Chicago 60637
The University of Chicago Press, Ltd., London
© 1993 by The University of Chicago
All rights reserved. Published 1993
Printed in the United States of America

02 01 00 99 98 97 96 95 94 93   1 2 3 4 5
ISBN: 0-226-20942-3

Library of Congress Cataloging-in-Publication Data

Engle, Lars.
    Shakespearean pragmatism : market of his time / Lars Engle.
        p.   cm.
    Includes bibliographical references and index.
    1. Shakespeare, William, 1564–1616—Philosophy.   2. Pragmatism
in literature.   I. Title.
PR3001.E64   1993
822.3'3—dc20   93-140
                                                                             CIP

For my parents, who made it possible,
and Holly, who made it actual

Contents

Acknowledgments

An earlier and shorter version of chapter 2 appeared as "Afloat in Thick Deeps: Shakespeare's Sonnets on Certainty," in *PMLA* 104 (October 1989). Material from that version is reprinted here by permission of the copyright owner, The Modern Language Association of America. About half of chapter 3 appeared as "Discourse, Agency, and Therapy in *Hamlet*" in *Exemplaria* 4, no. 2 (Fall 1992) and is reprinted here by permission of the copyright owner, the Center for Medieval and Early Renaissance Studies, SUNY Binghamton. An earlier and shorter version of chapter 4 appeared as "'Thrift Is Blessing': Exchange and Explanation in *The Merchant of Venice*" in *Shakespeare Quarterly* 37 (Spring 1986). I have also taken some paragraphs in the introduction from a book review in *Shakespeare Quarterly* 40 (Fall 1989). I am grateful for permission to reprint.

I am also grateful to audiences at Yale, the Universities of British Columbia, Virginia, Tulsa, Kansas, and Stellenbosch, the Folger Shakespeare Library, New College, and several Modern Language Association sessions, who have listened to versions of parts of this book and improved it by their questions. Versions of chapters were circulated among the members of seminars at the past four Shakespeare Association meetings, and I thank them for their comments; Victoria Kahn and Paul Yachnin were particularly acute respondents.

Many friends and colleagues have read and commented on chapters in draft or article form: let me take this opportunity to thank Marie Borroff, Jonathan Crewe, Heather Dubrow, Alan Engle, Margaret Ferguson, Donald Foster, Michiel Heyns, George Hunter, Clare Kinney, Dan Kinney, Arthur Kirsch, Michael Mosher, Jerome McGann, David Schalkwyk, Bob Spoo, Gordon Taylor, James Watson, Paul Yachnin.

David Bevington, Stephen Curtis, Mark Edmundson, Jay Engle, Michael Goldman, Norman Grabo, Peter Holbrook, Bridget Murnaghan, Richard Rorty, and two anonymous reviewers for the Press read the entire manuscript in its penultimate version and gave me warning, encouragement, and many particular suggestions, some of which I have taken. Peter Rudnytsky offered detailed marginal commentary on the entire manuscript and substantially improved it. Holly

Laird edited the entire manuscript at two different stages and also read most of its chapters when they first appeared.

My thanks to the Andrew Mellon Foundation and the English Department at the University of Virginia for a Mellon Junior Scholarship at the Center for Advanced Study of the University of Virginia, which gave me time to get started on this project, and to the University of Tulsa for a series of summer grants that have enabled me to finish it. Thanks also to the National Endowment for the Humanities, which funded my attendance of Michael Goldman's seminar at the Folger Library in 1987.

It has been a pleasure to work with Alan Thomas and John Grossman of the University of Chicago Press.

My chief personal debts are suggested by the dedication.

1

Introduction

ɤ̆

This book argues that the contingency of evaluation served as a recurrent enabling irritant for Shakespeare's creativity. Problems of worth, price, and value everywhere vex his texts—at least as much, in my opinion, as the related issues of linguistic *différence* and psychological non-self-identity more often brought to bear on Shakespeare by contemporary theoretically oriented criticism.

Shakespeare's theater, itself subject to varied contemporary evaluations and occasionally threatened with closure by the more adverse of them, produced plays for money; the plays so produced were subjected to immediate evaluation from audiences; through them actors strove to please. The plays subjected actions, persons, and motives to evaluative trial. Shakespeare—actor, playwright, and shareholder—invested and prospered.

That such a market-like theater might provide a model for how humans decide whether something is true and how much it is worth has long been a demonized other for serious thought. The antitheatrical prejudice stems from fear of the idea that life, like theater, may consist of nothing more solid than human descriptions and human assessments of those descriptions. In chapters 2 and 3 I develop this idea in relation to both Shakespeare's sonnets and his life in the theater, and I argue that it is Shakespeare's philosophy, which means that he was what would until quite recently have been considered a non- or antiphilosopher. I believe he assessed the ethical, ontological, social, or religious commitments available to his experience and imagination by submitting them to stress and seeing how well they worked; in this sense, interpretation of his texts consists partly in deciding how they function as machines or systems for evaluation. They entertain partly because watching success and failure happen is entertaining; they instruct because this is a topic on which people wish to be instructed. Seeing the stabilities and pitfalls of an economy is as useful as it would be to see absolute truths delineated, were such truths available.

My title suggests how closely I think Shakespeare's work resembles a market in performing this kind of assessment—a market which gives a local window on the larger economy of which it is part. The analogy did not escape Shakespeare, and in a number of chapters I show how subtly his plays, in particular, work with the idea of the

1

market. Local markets were a familiar phenomenon (Stratford was a market town), and to a perceptibly accelerating degree all of English society was being penetrated by a placeless national market which sent commodities and people from one site to another seeking an environment in which they would achieve greater value. Shakespeare moved from Stratford to London in such a search, and finding or failing to find a value-enhancing environment is a recurrent motive in the plots of his plays.

The existence of a large-scale invisible market economy disconcerted early modern Britons more than it reassured them: prior to Adam Smith, the market had little of its contemporary ideological valence as a normalizer or harmonizer of needs and capacities. Shakespearean pragmatism works with the same reduction of human nature as Smith's—the idea that we can assign to each agent's interaction with his or her environment the motive of increasing the value of his or her situation. But Shakespeare's drama complicates this supposition (and makes it nonreductive) by recognizing the variation of value environments and the plurality of value systems converging on any particular agent, and also by recognizing that destructive expenditure of the sort emphasized by Georges Bataille may be part of a subject's "profit" not accounted for in bourgeois balance sheets.[1] Thus Shakespearean "profit" is immensely complex by comparison with the profit of Enlightenment rational economists. It is also complex, arguably at least, by comparison with some of his contemporaries who see a profit-motive driving their characters—Middleton and Jonson, for instance, in whose plays of urban economic life the idea of the market, and money-profit and social ascent as drives, serve to demystify and undercut more expansive-sounding motives. For Shakespeare possibilities of describing oneself in dignified or even in transcendent terms are themselves part of the value economy available to an agent; such possibilities act on experience even as they are acted upon by it, and under some conditions will be reinforced rather than undermined. "What is a man / If his chief good and market of his time / Be but to sleep and feed" (4.4.33), asks Hamlet, signalling that for him at least the idea of living in a marketplace does not reduce life to concentration on its material conditions and comforts.

This is not to say, however, that a view of the world as shaped by economic constraints and economic exchanges is the exclusive property or characteristic of theater. On the contrary, the sonnets—frequently associated though they are with claims to transcendence, permanence, and ideality—offer a crucial example of Shakespeare's attitude toward contingency in evaluation, and thus a step toward claims for a Shakespearean pragmatism which crosses over generic boundaries. Theater is an especially fertile ground for pragmatic thinking; but the poems show that certainty cannot be obtained even a genre hospitable to gestures of transcendence.

This study, then, attributes to Shakespeare both a view of social interaction as an economy, a diffuse network of discursive transactions which hang together according to humanly established (and thus mutable) patterns of exchange, and a tendency to treat truth, knowledge, and certainty as relatively stable goods in such an economy rather than gateways out of it. In other words, the book claims that Shakespeare's literary economism is pragmatism, and that pragmatism is a kind of generalization of economism.

I take the central move of pragmatists to be the substitution of a mutable economy of value, action, and belief for what the philosophic tradition has tried to establish as a fixed structure of fact, truth, and knowledge. This is most evident when pragmatists work in areas where fixed structures of fact seem thicker on the ground than they do in literary studies. W. V. O. Quine's argument that the "certainty" of an empirical observation is a product of commitment to central beliefs which would be disturbed if it were seen otherwise redescribes physical science as such an economy;[2] Thomas Kuhn offers a history of science that is basically a history of the substitution of one set of values, activities, and beliefs in particular expert communities for another.[3] Similarly, Donald Davidson's attack on scheme/content distinctions as absolute or inherent characteristics of fields of knowledge insists that what might seem a fixed law of systems is actually a feature of potentially mutable economies.[4] John von Neumann's suggestion that early computers be redesigned so that instructions and data were no longer kept separate from one another (so that, in other words, instructions could become data for other instructions, producing feedback loops) launched computer science and the most significant technological revolution of our time, and this too is a substitution of an economy for a fixed structure.

I cite these tendencies toward pragmatism in analytic philosophy and the history of science and technology because I want to stress that the obvious substitutions of dynamic economies for fixed structures in literary theory of the past several decades are part of a general tendency occurring outside as well as within literature departments. I want to make clear here at the outset, too, that what I am calling pragmatism is not the attempt to apply an absolute denial of scheme-content distinctions to the intellectual realm: it is not pragmatism, as I see it, to say that since there are no eternally binding schemes we should all

stop theorizing (the sort of thing Steven Knapp and Walter Benn
Michaels did on a limited scale in their "Against Theory" article).[5] In
redescribing Shakespeare's texts I invoke rather a recurrent theme of
pragmatists: a recognition of the fallibility, mutability, and interdependence of the provisional scheme-content relations which give some
shape and thus intelligibility to particular forms of life. Of course we
scheme; of course our schemes have consequences. Of course we try
to understand our situations; and of course it matters what terms of
understanding are afoot in the world. Just saying this in this way puts
me in conflict with Stanley Fish, one of the most prominent pragmatic
thinkers in literary criticism, and I take up this difference in some
detail below. Since I am presenting pragmatism as the substitution of
dynamic economies for fixed structures, I also see an affinity between
pragmatism and poststructuralism; in this I am influenced not only by
the past two decades in literary theory, which have focused on the
ways structures that guided criticism in the past are fluid, splintered,
or self-dissolving in literary texts, but also by the efforts of philosophers like Richard Rorty to see Derrida, Heidegger, Wittgenstein, and
Dewey in a common light.

  Pragmatism began by substituting economic terms for essentialist
concepts. William James spoke of pragmatism as the philosophy which
sought to "bring out of each word its practical cash-value."[6] But with
the major exception of Barbara Herrnstein Smith (whose book I discuss
in detail in chapter 2), contemporary pragmatists have underplayed the
extent to which their philosophic position sets all values and truth-
claims in a market. Richard Rorty (the leading contemporary exponent
of pragmatism and an important influence on this study) tends to make
"conversation" a master metaphor for the endless process of exchange,
but he nonetheless suggests the appropriateness of calling the general
environment of such exchanges a "market" in response to a challenge
from Clifford Geertz. Geertz, reacting against the conversational view
and against Rorty's endorsement of "anti-anti-ethnocentrism," comments that the contemporary world is more like a Kuwaiti bazaar than
an English gentlemen's club. Rorty replies by appropriating Geertz's
simile as an image of pragmatic civil society:

> Like Geertz, I have never been in a Kuwaiti bazaar (nor in an English
> gentlemen's club). So I can give free rein to my fantasies. I picture many
> of the people in such a bazaar as preferring to die rather than share the
> beliefs of many of those with whom they are haggling, yet as haggling
> profitably away nevertheless. Such a bazaar is, obviously, not a commu-
> nity, in the strong approbative sense of "community" used by critics of
> liberalism like Alasdair MacIntyre and Robert Bellah. You cannot have

an old-timey *Gemeinschaft* unless everybody pretty well agrees on who counts as a decent human being and who does not. But you *can* have a civil society of the bourgeois democratic sort.[7]

Rorty and other avowed contemporary pragmatists might be less than happy, however, with the overarching definition I offer of pragmatism as an economism. Ever since James chose to use the hardheaded Yankee rhetoric of "cash value" to convey his view of truth, pragmatism has been attacked as a theory that colludes with capitalism, especially the free-market capitalism of late-nineteenth-century America. But to substitute economy for structure is not to assert that one form of economic organization is necessarily superior to another, and pragmatism is antithetical to the idea that one form of economic organization, the so-called free market, is natural and therefore fundamental to optimal social forms. Rather, pragmatism moves us to interrogate the complex relations between modes of economic organization and the ways people are shaped by them, even, indeed especially, how their thought is shaped. Pragmatists have thus sought to open the way for social experiment, but also to impede or undercut fanaticism.

Pragmatism, then, is a theory with ideological and genealogical affinities to American democracy, but it is not bound to any particular strand: it can be mobilized against capitalism and, for that matter, against individualism, since pragmatists argue that the mental activity of selves is conditioned and partly constructed by the economies in which they live—by familial developmental economies, whose contingent shapes are the province of psychology, and by social and intellectual economies whose contingent shapes are the province of the rest of the human sciences. The ideas of exchange, interdependence, nurturance, and feedback cut all ways. From this viewpoint also, as Frank Lentricchia puts it, William James "out-Marxes Marx."[8] It is when Marx seeks to supply necessary steps in an inevitable historical process that pragmatism parts ways with Marxism. "Always contextualize" and "always historicize" are as much pragmatic as Marxist slogans; pragmatists, however, are skeptical that there is a single History to elicit any more than there are universal conditions for the possibility of knowledge or absolute ideals.

Rorty's remarks about the Kuwaiti bazaar also hint at, but do not pursue, the important question of difference in pragmatism. In addition to being associated (erroneously, as I have argued) with right-wing American capitalists, pragmatists are sometimes chided, from both left and right, for postulating too comfortable a universe, one in which all differences are negotiable and the role of domination, denial, and institutionalized cruelty is underplayed. "Economy" again seems to me a better term than, say, "conversation" for the metadescription which underpins pragmatic accounts of things, partly because no one denies that economies both run on difference and maintain it, and no one thinks it ipso facto comforting to be part of an economy. All actual economies we know of are cruel for someone, and many have been cruel to most; the attempt to imagine economies without losers, and the unsuccessful sporadic attempts to institute such economies both locally and nationally, have been a central preoccupation of social thought since at least the Enlightenment.[9] But as suggested above by instances from philosophy of science and philosophy of language, the idea of an economy, the notion of a system of exchanges responsive to both difference and consensus in collective valuation, can be powerful as a descriptive idea in areas not directly concerned with money or goods. Viewing reality as an economy allows one to assert the interconnectedness of everything without claiming that everything can be centered or unified, or that particular parts or values can be made commensurable with each other; economies are set in motion to take advantage of difference through exchange, but they do not function to ensure that all parts can be exchanged for all others.[10] And the idea of an economy stresses some of the ways intellectual change and social change may be interrelated. Marketlike economies are explored more directly in some chapters than in others; indeed, economy is not always or everywhere the most useful metaphor for pragmatic description. But economy operates as an important metaphor—one to which I will often return in this book—for the kind of pragmatic "world" that Shakespeare worried over, redescribed, and helped to produce.

Pragmatism, the market view, sets the attempt to haggle profitably in conditions of cultural asymmetry at the center of human social life. I suggest in this book that Shakespeare's texts act as instruments for the explanation and investigation both of such haggling and of the value-shaping economic environments in which it takes place.

One might link Shakespeare historically with pragmatism in two ways. The first, which I sketch here but do not seriously attempt, would be to argue that one of the ways Shakespeare's texts have worked through English and American history is to further pragmatic ways of looking at things, or, more plausibly, pragmatic ways of talking about a great many different things at once. The historical argument might run like this: Emerson saw Shakespeare as representative of a kind of fluid and developing communal thought; Emersonian understanding of the free individual as a creative source of revaluations in a matrix of communal understanding passes into the American philosophical projects of C. S. Pierce and William James and there gets dubbed "pragmatism"; and, finally, for some contemporary critics it is the existence and power of Shakespearean description which enable us to take pragmatism seriously.[11] Harold Bloom, for instance, after calling himself (possibly with tongue in cheek) "nothing but a critical pragmatist," comments in *Ruin the Sacred Truths* that Shakespeare "was a mortal god . . . because his art was not a mimesis at all. A mode of representation that is always out ahead of any historically unfolding reality necessarily contains us more than we can contain it."[12] This makes the existence of an Emersonian kind of Shakespeare sound like a necessary precondition for the existence of a Bloomian kind of contemporary critical pragmatism.

Both the genealogy I have just sketched and the claim I have just quoted, however, surely overestimate the intellectual role of even the most canonical of literary authors. One might attack the genealogy at its American root by observing that Emerson manages to make Plato sound just about as protopragmatic as Shakespeare and that one would be hard put to argue that either author was nearly as important for Emerson as Emerson's understanding of the peculiarly American opportunity to refashion inherited thoughts in a context of new social and economic relations.[13]

The second way of connecting Shakespeare and pragmatism, and the one I follow in this book, is to take seriously William James's designation of pragmatism as "a new name for some old ways of thinking":[14] to argue, as I have done already, that pragmatism is a general redescription of fixed systems as dynamic economies and to show that this is a useful way to think about Shakespeare. However, even if the plausibility of my redescription of Shakespeare were granted by an unusually compliant reader without further demonstration, it might be held that there can be no *historical* sense in which such an anachronistic description could truly hold. (We owe a developed sense of the word "pragmatism" to the late nineteenth century and a developed sense of the word "economy" to the late eighteenth.) Can Shakespeare's way of dealing with the world be something which modern pragmatists are *recovering*? I think so.

[margin handwritten note: P is a general redesc. of fixed systems]

The historical claim that Shakespeare is a kind of pragmatist rests on two aspects of his moment. First, Shakespeare lived at a time of expanding economic development, the extension of market economies, the ever-increasing importance of London as a center of exchanges. This book presupposes that a general and partly visible transition from medieval to early modern ways of thinking about things, and from feudal to early capitalist modes of economic organization, was taking place all around Shakespeare. Thus what we might call an actual econ-

omy was visible to Shakespeare as a social and political force for the
deconsecration and, often, destabilization of hierarchies. Shakespeare's
interest in figuring various processes in economic terms might therefore
very plausibly arise from his immediate experience of life. I can both
imagine and recall good books partly about Shakespeare which document and argue for local connections between Shakespeare and this
broad historical process, and several chapters below make such connections. But on the whole, since this general shift has been argued
for effectively by many others, my book takes it for granted and
offers instead readings of Shakespeare's plays as exploratory redescriptions in their own right, redescriptions that attempt to account for the
meaning-giving forms of his world as features in a human economy
rather than the necessary structures of reality. Shakespeare's plays
themselves enact, embody, and articulate the pragmatic substitution
of economies for fixed structures.

What is equally salient, indeed more so from our retrospective viewpoint, is a second aspect of Shakespeare's historical moment: that he
lived immediately *before* Descartes and Galileo launched the great certainty project of modernity—the project to which modern pragmatism
is a reaction. Pragmatism, as a philosophical movement, constitutes a
reaction to what James and Dewey perceived as the excesses of theory
or pure rationality in philosophy. Thus they intended pragmatism as
a critique of a period in thought whose beginning can be fairly precisely
located to the 1630s, with the inauguration of a project in the sciences
and philosophy in which the most abstract way of posing problems is
seen as most likely to yield solutions to them. The kind of complex
and socially specific exploration of problems we get in an essay by
Montaigne or a play by Shakespeare ceases to be a model for intellectu-
ally serious investigation, and this, as Stephen Toulmin argues, creates
a gap between, on the one hand, philosophy and science, and, on the
other hand, literature and what he calls humanism.

In choosing as the goals of Modernity an intellectual and practical agenda
that set aside the tolerant, skeptical attitude of the 16th-century humanists, and focussed on the 17th-century pursuit of mathematical exactitude
and logical rigor, intellectual certainty and moral purity, Europe set
itself on a cultural and political road that has led both to its most striking
technical successes and to its deepest human failures. If we have any
lesson to learn from the experience of the 1960s and '70s [i.e. the critiques
of modernity and rationality that arose then], this (I have come to believe)
is our need to reappropriate the wisdom of the 16th-century humanists,
and develop a point of view that combines the abstract rigor and exacti-

tude of the 17th-century "new philosophy" with a practical concern for human life in its concrete detail.[15]

Toulmin's historical argument seems to me very right, though, in my opinion, he makes humanistic culture sound rather more like a warm bath than he should. Stanley Cavell's claim that Shakespearean tragedy registers the terrifying consequences of proto-Cartesian skepticism, which will not take solace either in God or in rationality projects, might be applied as a corrective. But Cavell also goes too far in making Shakespeare into a Descartes:

> My intuition is that the advent of skepticism as manifested in Descartes's *Meditations* is already in full existence in Shakespeare, from the time of the great tragedies in the first years of the seventeenth century, in the generation preceding that of Descartes. However strong the presence of Montaigne and Montaigne's skepticism is in various of Shakespeare's plays, the skeptical problematic I have in mind is given its philosophical refinement in Descartes's way of raising the questions of God's existence and of the immortality of the soul (I assume as, among other things, preparations for, or against, the credibility of the new science of the external world). The issue posed is no longer, or not alone, as with earlier skepticism, how to conduct oneself best in an uncertain world; the issue suggested is how to live at all in a groundless world. Our skepticism is a function of our now illimitable desire. In Descartes's thinking, the ground, one gathers, still exists, in the assurance of God. But Descartes's very clarity about the necessity of God's assurance in establishing a rough adequation or collaboration between our everyday judgments and the world (however the matter may stand in natural science) means that if assurance in God will be shaken, the ground of the everyday is thereby shaken.
>
> . . . Shakespeare's plays . . . find no stable solution to skepticism, in particular no rest in what we know of God.[16]

While I agree with Cavell that Shakespeare's plays do not invoke God to solve skepticism, and am happy to enlist such a reputable ally in the attempt to read Shakespeare as an accoucheur at the birth of modern philosophy, I follow Toulmin in invoking "skeptical humanists" against Descartes's radical skepticism rather than Cavell in seeing Shakespeare as Descartes minus God.[17] In arguing that Shakespeare's texts tend to pose problems in collective economic terms, I move them out of the arena of radical skepticism (the solitary knower's difficulties with certainty) and into that of pragmatism (the involved participant's struggle to maintain a satisfactory position in an ongoing pattern of exchanges).

Rorty has also endorsed the notion that I have attributed to Toulmin of an important philosophical road not taken in the early seventeenth century:

> One can . . . attribute Descartes' role as "founder of modern philosophy" to his development of what I earlier called "an overzealous philosophy of science"—the sort of philosophy of science which saw Galilean mechanics, analytic geometry, mathematical optics, and the like, as having more spiritual significance than they in fact have. By taking the ability to do such science as a mark of something deep and essential to human nature, as the place where we got closest to our true selves, Descartes preserved just those themes in ancient thought which Bacon had tried to obliterate. The preservation of the Platonic idea that our most distinctively human faculty was our ability to manipulate "clear and distinct ideas," rather than to accomplish feats of social engineering, was Descartes' most important and most unfortunate contribution to what we now think of as "modern philosophy." Had Bacon—the prophet of self-assertion, as opposed to self-grounding—been taken more seriously, we might not have been struck ["stuck"?] with a canon of "great modern philosophers" who took "subjectivity" as their theme. . . . We might thereby see what Blumenberg calls "self-assertion"—the willingness to center our hopes on the future of the race, on the unpredictable successes of our descendants—as the "principle of the modern."[18]

Though Shakespeare has relatively little to say about science, he obviously offers one of the great treatments of subjectivity and self-assertion. What I take from Toulmin and Rorty, then, is the idea that Shakespeare, living at a moment when economic and cultural developments had put various religious and social institutions within a visible economic frame—Henri IV said "Paris vaut bien une messe" in 1594— also lived at a moment when serious intellectual culture was about to take up the abstraction of fixed structures from the flux of experience as its major project. Shakespearean pragmatism thus substitutes economies for various more or less medieval stabilizing structures like divine kingship, but also exemplifies a way of figuring intellectual issues in economic terms to which pragmatists have returned in our time.

So far the characteristic of pragmatism on which I have insisted is its dynamism: the potential alteration of even the most central or most basic features of a form of life. One of the chief corollary aims of this book will be to show that even the most rigid dualisms of intellectual and theoretical discourse are subject to change and should be redescribed pragmatically as opposed "directions" on various continua. This point leads me to an important area of disagreement with Stanley Fish. Fish practices a variant of pragmatism which turns it into a

continual hunt for other writers' essentialism and objectivism and a
continual critical assertion of context relativism and interpretationism.
He is less interested in dynamics than in conditions of possibility, and
at times he seems to regard the effort of human beings to develop
desirable generalities on which to base their activities as sentimen-
tality. It should already be clear that I think anti-essentialist theory
leaves room for respectful redescription of human efforts at long-term
grounding or stabilization (a view that I elaborate more fully in a discussion of Shakespeare's sonnets in chapter 2). I want to sketch more
fully here, however, my sense of difference from Fish—a difference
within kinship, certainly, from the point of view of readers who look to
Shakespeare and Shakespeare criticism for transcendence claims—but
quite an important difference, I think, focusing on the important problems of both essentialist and dualistic terminologies.

For Fish, the "grounding" efforts of the past, or of the current
disciplines which have essentialist goals, must fall away when the error
of their presuppositions—of a formalist stance toward meaning, for
instance—is seen. Thus he begins *Doing What Comes Naturally* with a
typically trenchant account of a book by Ruth Kempson, a semanticist,
on semantics. Semanticists try to specify meaning as a function of
observable formal features of language. Kempson, then, when consid-
ering the possibility that meaning cannot be specified without taking
into account the intentions and situations of speakers, decides that
speakers' intentions cannot be a necessary part of sentence meaning
because, if they were, the whole project of semantics would have
failed. She is writing for other semanticists, to whom this argument is
presumably convincing rather than self-betraying.[19]

Fish sees Kempson as paradigmatic of how professional objectivist
argument takes place within interpretive communities. Thus he does
not imagine that, because of his illustration, semantics will shrivel up
and die or even register pain. But he does think his critique of semantics is on target given the terms he regards as the right ones (those
shared by his interpretive community), and the impression he leaves
is that semantics only stays alive by excluding the kind of argument
he makes from the charmed circle of its interpretive community. Thus
on the one hand Fish's lucid demonstration of circular thinking suggests, in the quasi-Darwinian view of intellectual history favored by
pragmatists,[20] that perhaps in the fullness of time semantics will go the
way of phrenology. Semantics was developed as a discipline when the
human sciences were trying to be like physics, after all, but thanks to
people like Fish and Rorty the discipline whose vocabularies are currently being borrowed on all sides is literary theory. This seems bad

news for semantics. So in the evolving economy of the human sciences, Fish's argument and the existence of lots of other arguments like it surely threaten semanticists.

Yet Fish claims rather bafflingly that theory—his as well as others'—has no consequences.[21] Fish applies a sociology of knowledge (an economics, if you will) to subsystems like semantics in order to establish the idea of shared values in communities, but he will not allow this sociology or economics full scope in terms of the consequences through time of general arguments. Semanticists' arguments may be contingently true for a particular community, but to have "consequences," Fish thinks, they would have to be "necessary" independent of context, and nothing is that. For pragmatists, however, the idea of "consequences" surely involves engagement with the real, and the real for pragmatists is always and everywhere contingent. Thus Fish's "no consequences" claim seems perverse, and numerous fellow pragmatists have felt that it cuts against his own grain.[22]

This might also be said of Fish's style—one which, however, I must say as a reader I thoroughly enjoy. Fish is an adversarial stylist, pugnacious, agonistic, and thereby instructive and entertaining. He loves knockdown arguments, and he tends constantly to turn the issues he deals with into open and shut cases with on-off switches, and into I'm right–you're wrong demonstrations. Having fought well and awarded himself the palm, he then turns on his own victories and declares them inconsequential. He regards them as inconsequential because of his overall commitment to a kind of holism which makes broad changes in institutions and habits unlikely to depend on particular intellectual controversies. Particular arguments about particular issues are always referred to a general intellectual context (the shared beliefs of an interpretive community, in Fish's case), and a holistic view of how intellectual communities work is not one which favors progress by means of argumentative knockdowns. Richard Rorty, describing John Dewey's ships-passing-in-the-night relation to Bertrand Russell and Bernard Williams (and implicitly alluding to his own relation to Williams) writes on philosophical style in a way that is helpful here:

> Williams is what Janice Moulton has called an 'adversarial' philosopher, in the tradition of Ayer and Russell. (Russell once told Sidney Hook that his first question on meeting a man of outstanding intellectual reputation was 'Can I take him, or can he take me?') This way of doing philosophy, which has survived the death of logical empiricism and still sets the tone of analytic philosophy in both Britain and America, makes

much of the goal of 'getting it right,' and of the need for knock-down arguments. Dewey, by contrast, was non-adversarial, in the sense that he almost never gave a head-on reply to criticism. He exasperated his opponents by trying to move out of the range of their vocabulary, by dissolving their problems rather than offering solutions to them, and by transferring issues to the fuzzy, hard-to-discuss area of conflicting values. . . . The non-adversarial stance . . . is in part responsible for his widespread neglect.[23]

In the terms of this passage, Fish combines Russell's argumentative style with Dewey's beliefs—a combination which may suggest why he often seems at odds with himself. Of course no one neglects Fish, who may indeed feel he has the best of both worlds. But his style is in implicit conflict with his message, as he knocks his opponents down and then retrospectively redescribes the gladiatorial encounter as unimportant since only large fuzzy shifts in value really matter. And in general Fish's noneconomic approach to pragmatism does not stress the ways argument about value can further desired shifts; he treats such shifts as though argument has no purchase on them, partly because the kind of wrestler's hold he wants on things he talks about is difficult to obtain when values are in question.

Fish's chief target is essentialism (a.k.a. foundationalism and objectivism), and he goes around stamping it out wherever he sees it. But "essentialism," like "realism," is of course itself not an absolute but a relative term: there is no essence of essentialism. Among philosophers who take on these issues directly, Kant is less essentialist than Plato, but more so than Hegel; Nietzsche less essentialist than Hegel, but more so than Heidegger; Heidegger accuses Sartre of covert essentialism and is in turn accused of it by Derrida, and so on.

One of the strengths of pragmatism as an explanatory style is in my opinion its capacity to redescribe foundational structures as contingent structures based on strata of social or intellectual embeddedness—as in Quine or late Wittgenstein. I have called this the redescription of fixed structures as economies. One of its central intellectual moves is the conversion of binary oppositions into continua, for instance, the conversion of the opposition "necessary/contingent" into a continuum with "more stable" and "more fluid" as its directions, and no end point imagined either way.[24] On this view, it does make sense to look for what is basic in some area of inquiry, but what is basic is so because more depends on it; what is basic to communities in which one lives has so much hanging on it that it cannot easily be discussed or questioned. The metaphoric topsy-turviness of this dynamic is nicely captured in a famous remark from Wittgenstein's *On Certainty* to which I will return in the next chapter:

> 248. I have arrived at the rock bottom of my convictions. And one might almost say that these foundation-walls are carried by the whole house. (33e)

Fish seems categorically unwilling to redeem or redescribe certainty projects as embeddedness projects which may well retain a great deal of social usefulness even outside the interpretive communities which share specific foundational convictions.

Why, or how, then, is this book not a Stanley Fishian project? In one sense, of course, it is: as will become increasingly apparent, it is like Fish in situating itself, in the name of pragmatism, between foundationalist conservatism on the one hand and negative critique on the other. But it is unlike Fish in that it generally favors a way of describing the situation of human beings that Fish consistently attacks: it seeks to redescribe certainty projects as embeddedness projects. In addition, it favors redescribing—and, at times, finding more pragmatic analogues to—inherited dualisms such as fact and value, truth and opinion, reality and appearance, logos and nomos, as pointing to continua on which human activities can usefully be mapped, rather than as pathways to heavenly certainties on the one hand and a nasty flux of human error on the other. Fish is himself, as already discussed, stylistically committed to one kind of dualism ("I'm right, you're wrong"), yet he at various points contests the kind of redescription I'm proposing as if it were always an apology for foundationalism.[25] But Fish is also much more prone than I would be, or than I think pragmatists should be, categorically to oppose leftist claims that conceptual critique can bring about social changes. This is related, I believe, to his reluctance to permit redescribed versions of essentialist distinctions to have any validity. An important example (which will bear on the arguments of my final chapter) arises when he contests Roberto Unger's attempt to lay out social arrangements on a continuum derived from unfolding one of the most important and contested of our inherited essentializing dualisms, that of freedom and necessity.

Fish quotes Unger's *Passion:*

> "Contexts of representation or relationship . . . differ in the severity of the limits they impose upon our activity," and "the more entrenched against revision a social plan becomes, the more it enacts and imposes an intolerably restricted picture of our fundamental identity and our opportunities for practical or passionate connection" (p. 25). Through the continual and expanded practice of critique "we can create institu-

tions and conceptions that go ever further in denying . . . immunity to themselves and to the routines they help shape" and by such means, Unger concludes, "we can break through the false necessities that enmesh exchange and production in rigid hierarchies and that hold each individual's experiments in association and self-expression within frozen social forms" (266).[26]

Fish concludes from this that Unger's radical socio-intellectual project involves a covert essentialism:

> Here in more explicit language than any we have yet seen are the key components of the critical scenario, past, present, and future: first there is a self conceived of as a quantity of energy and vision that can either be left free to discover and nourish its "fundamental identity" or continue to be constrained in its activities by external forces that keep it from realizing its own true nature; second, there are the institutions and conceptions that are complicit with, because they are extensions of, these tyrannous constraints; but, third, even amid these enslaving forces there is always a measure of freedom left somewhere (often in the greatest works of art and in the best impulses of philosophy and religion), and if that measure can be increased by the exercise of critical self-reflection, we can, step by step, transform the material conditions of our existence so that the structures we inhabit are less and less constraining until finally we will have transformed ourselves and realized our true destiny.[27]

I think this mischaracterizes Unger, not only with respect to the larger picture (considerably enlarged by the three volumes of *Politics* published in 1987 and not discussed by Fish, who is reprinting earlier essays in *Doing What Comes Naturally*), but even with respect to the passages Fish himself cites. Unger after all talks about the variable degree of constraint on our *activity* that social contexts exert. He is not addressing the epistemological question of whether minds can attain a space free of historical constraints, but rather raising questions in political economy, questions like: How free are people to associate in new ways they dream up? How free to talk about ways of behaving different from those to which most of their contemporaries or compatriots conform? And the factor according to which Unger wants to differentiate "social plans" is "entrenchment against revision," which again refers to social, educational, and political arrangements and the degree to which they foster change, not to an abstract necessity.

Fish wants to read Unger here as imagining that some societies could be less "constrained" *in an absolute sense* than others: he comments that "there is no continuum [of social arrangements with respect to degrees of freedom] because the degree of constraint—at least with

respect to *an ideal condition of freedom*—is always the same and always
total."[28] But what Unger is talking about are degrees of openness to
social experiment—Unger believes no more than Fish that absolute
constraints or absolute freedoms exist. Fish makes a puppet out of
Unger, making him sound like a foundationalist with his left hand so
that he can slap him around for it with his right—not, alas, an unfamil-
iar mode of current theoretical writing where someone else's essentialism is the bone of contention.

The same thing happens when Fish talks about Unger's view of
human nature. Unger inveighs against entrenched arrangements which
impose "an intolerably restricted picture of our fundamental identity,"
and Fish pounces upon "fundamental" and attacks Unger for romantic
essentialism: "there is a self conceived of as a quantity of energy and
vision that can either be left free to discover and nourish its 'fundamental identity' or continue to be constrained in its activities by external
forces that keep it from realizing its own true nature." But Unger did
not say we possessed a fundamental identity (by reference to whose
imperatives social arrangements could be judged); he said that entrenched arrangements give us an intolerably restricted *picture* of our
fundamental identity—part of the restriction being the fostered belief
that we are (as human beings) just this and not something else. Unger
does not like social arrangements which purport to tell us what our
fundamental identity is. He wants social arrangements which urge us
to imagine and realize new potentials. This is romantic, but it is romantic pragmatism, not romantic essentialism, and Fish is misreading it.
Unger may leave himself open by using words like "fundamental,"
but Unger's project is not to purify our vocabularies from essentialist
remnants; it is to reform our society by redeeming some essentialist
projects (emancipatory liberalism and Marxism, for instance), through
assaulting parts of their method while applauding parts of their analysis
and their general social aims.

To put the issue more generally: the move toward decontextualized
generalization or abstraction by way of dialectic—Plato's philosophic
path toward truth—is a rhetorical one which aims at persuasion, but
it is also a move that can be pragmatically understood as a praiseworthy
attempt toward persuading a larger community (or different communities for different purposes) of something that is widely useful to believe.
Fish treats this generalizing move as though it were the pragmatist's
duty always to debunk it, because he feels it always retains a residual
claim to a context-independent truth. I do not think it constitutes such
a claim, and I think pragmatism would be the poorer if it excluded such
moves as not part of its plan. Indeed, it is the pragmatist's challenge to

redescribe this move toward social generality so that its unquestionable force is not lost even while its meaning is seen to be different.

The sort of point Fish constantly makes is based on three theses: (1) there are no objective absolute constraints on practice or thought (i.e., practice and thought are cultural activities), and so "conservative" attempts to ground practice on certainty are doomed; (2) practice and thought are, however, entirely and ineluctably constrained by beliefs (i.e., by inherited thoughts and practices); (3) shared beliefs mark professional communities. Thesis 1 marks Fish as a pragmatist, perspectivalist, antifoundationalist, and so forth and puts him on the currently ascendent side of a very old quarrel in which respectability has usually been on the other side (the side of available certainties). Thesis 1 also seems a valid basis for moving from fixed structures to economies as paradigms of description. Theses 2 and 3 mark Fish as Fish and separate him from many people who share or think they share thesis 1. Fish treats thesis 2 as a corollary of thesis 1; that is, he treats arguments for thesis 1 as if they counted also as arguments for thesis 2. In fact he rarely argues specifically for thesis 2, which, on the face of it, does not seem to need much argument (perhaps less than thesis 1). Thesis 3 he has argued vigorously for many years.

Despite its innocuous appearance, however, thesis 2 plays a central and questionable role for Fish. The claim that all practice is entirely and ineluctably constrained by belief supplies the starch in Fish's arguments by giving him a coercive certainty, a piece of absolute knowledge about the way things are, which he feels his sentimental opponents are trying to soften. Thesis 2 is especially important when Fish turns on emancipatory theorists on the left (like Unger); one cannot be emancipatory without asserting that some people are or could be freer than others, and Fish tends to treat this as a contradiction of thesis 2. But for pragmatists, words like "freedom" and "constraint" work very nicely as relative terms, and one can use them (of both social and intellectual processes) happily in a relative way. Beliefs work on each other, I am suggesting, in a fluid economy whose dynamism Fish's thesis 2 disallows.

Fish, then, while policing discourse in the name of antifoundationalism, retains a style of argument suited for foundational discourse. He himself almost admits this toward the end of the introduction of *Doing What Comes Naturally:*

> Of course, there are distinctions between the ways in which the objective knowledge that flows from one's beliefs might be urged on others, styles of self-presentation that are often thought of wrongly as

styles of knowing. I might say to you, for example, "what you have just said is obviously false for the following indisputable reasons" (this is, in fact, my style), or I might say, "I see your point, and it is certainly an important one, but I wonder if we might make room for this other perspective," and, depending on your sense of decorum and on the conventions in place in the arena of our discussion, the conversation between us would unfold differently.[29]

My preceding argument suggests why I think, despite Fish's dismissal of the idea, that Fish's "style of self-presentation" says something important about his "style of knowing."

Fish, however, returns to the question I am trying to raise here—the question whether his intellectual style is one appropriate to what I consider a pragmatist redescription of the world—in what amounts to an apologetic admission that one's style of self-presentation *does* have an impact on what one can know or find out, and then he goes on to offer a persuasive pragmatist justification of his style; but it is a justification that also has an impact on some of his previous assertions, moving Fish toward a different and, in my view, better and more pragmatic stance. He begins by addressing the problem I have been discussing of "being embedded":

> Being embedded means just that, being embedded *always*, and one does not escape embeddedness by acknowledging, as I do, that it is itself a fractured, fissured, volatile condition.

He then leaves a blank space, presumably to elicit at least a raised eyebrow, and proceeds:

> But why, one might ask, is there so little of that acknowledgement in your work? Why are these key terms ["constraint," "belief," "community," "practice"] almost always employed in a way that implies the seamlessness and closure you now repudiate? The answer to this (really) final question is that everything in discourse depends on what I call the "angle of lean," the direction you are facing as you begin your discursive task. In these essays there are characteristically two: either I am facing those who wish to identify a rationality to which beliefs or community practices would be submitted for judgment, or I am facing those who find in the deconstruction of that rationality the possibility of throwing off those beliefs and practices that now define us. When I argue against the first group, beliefs are forever escaping the constraints that rationality would impose; when I argue against the second group, beliefs are themselves constraints that cannot be escaped. Neither stance delivers a finely tuned picture of the operations of belief (or community or practice) because that is not my task, and indeed it is a task which, if taken seriously (as it certainly should be), would prevent me from doing what I have here tried to do.[30]

This is an admirable and disarming piece of self-contextualization, in effect a kind of apology to fellow pragmatists who largely agree with him about how things are but feel that his style of argument fits that state of things poorly, combined with a characteristically aggressive assault on the wrongness of those who disagree. Moreover, as a recontextualizion, it modifies some stated positions of Fish's substantially: Fish situates himself in a contemporary critical economy as a force for change.

To some extent, as Fish has shown of Unger and as I believe I have shown of Fish, theoretical elaborations of pragmatism are liable to fall into the kinds of reductive essentialism, on the one hand, and the equally reductive negation of all positive claims, on the other, that pragmatists want to protest and to situate themselves between. For a theory is partly a bunch of intellectual habits, and these habits include some key beliefs (which may easily become parts of a creed, and thus be subject to someone else's critique as "essentialist") and some key articles of disbelief (which may easily become the dead horses one is always kicking); both of these tendencies may rigidify, channel one's thinking, and eventually reduce the usefulness of one's theory as a tool for understanding or changing how things are. No one could accuse Stanley Fish of intellectual narrowness; his zest, clarity, and industry are extraordinary. But his version of pragmatism is too much of a dead horse roundup (roping in the occasional live lion like Unger by mistake) to suit my sense of pragmatism's political importance.

Saying this nudges us back toward Shakespeare by suggesting how plays and poems may be more suitable in some ways for the central pragmatic and economic enterprise of delivering finely tuned pictures of social operation and social change than is theoretical debate of the kind Fish provides, debate in which there must be absolute winners and losers. But, as I have argued, this is, finally, a stylistic choice Fish makes rather than a necessary attribute of a particular kind—or genre—of discourse. In both Shakespeare's poems and plays—in what I call Shakespearean pragmatism—it is among other things the evolution of degrees of lean that we are shown.

ৼ

Much recent writing on Shakespeare suggests that it is fruitful to think of his texts as both participating in and evoking a complex economy. Without using the words "market" or "economy" prominently, and with some resistance to the association of these terms with totalizing concepts that are inappropriate, in his view, to such a fissured phenomenon, Stephen Greenblatt comments in the introduction to *Shakespearean Negotiations* that he has learned to replace the dream of "finding an originary moment" of Shakespearean creativity with glimpses of "something that seems at first far less spectacular: a subtle, elusive set of exchanges, a network of trades and trade-offs, a jostling of competing representations, a negotiation between joint stock companies."[31] This is clearly a view of a market economy at work, and I believe that if we can set aside Adam Smith's rationalized view of how markets function (to say nothing of Ronald Reagan's fantasies on the subject), the idea of the market and the invisible large economy on which it is a window offer the kind of general illumination of Shakespeare's work that justifies calling it a Shakespearean philosophy, however opposed to Platonic or Cartesian philosophy this may be.

In calling his literary activity "Shakespearean pragmatism," as in insisting on his vision of a social market, I draw, finally, on recent writing on Shakespeare which suggests the philosophic complexity of Shakespeare's treatment of value and certainty. I think "pragmatism" a good, that is, useful, redescription of what, for instance, Graham Bradshaw (thinking of Montaigne rather than Descartes) calls "radical scepticism" in Shakespeare. Bradshaw, claiming a more or less constructive side to Shakespearean scepticism, draws our attention to "the crucial distinction between *dogmatic* scepticism, as represented by the terminal, materialistic nihilism of a Thersites, Iago or Edmund, and *radical* scepticism, which turns on itself—weighing the human need to affirm values against the inherently problematic nature of all acts of valuing."[32] Shakespeare's perspectivism about the construction of value amounts to pragmatism, and the holism which undergirds this perspectivism—the way particular attributions of value are linked to larger environments which favor some values or persons and hinder others—amounts to the recognition of the ubiquity of economy.

Tudor-Stuart markets and theaters have been persuasively linked by Jean-Christophe Agnew as agents and manifestations of a general liquefaction of social identity in the period. He writes (perhaps too readily crediting the Renaissance with a massive change in consciousness from an imaginary stable medieval synthesis) of early modern Britons experiencing their social situations not as secure states but rather as thresholds:

> With the emergence of a placeless market [in the late 1500s], the threshold experience threatened to become coextensive with all that a deritualized commodity exchange touched. Life now resembled an infinite series of thresholds, a profusion of potential passages or opportunity costs running alongside experience as a constant reminder of the selves not taken. And just as London's Exchange enforced an ideal of financial liquidity, so London's theaters enacted a vision of this new sociological

and psychological fluidity. And why not, since the world was at once a market and a stage?[33]

It is interesting to set Agnew's arguments alongside the question asked by Fernand Braudel in one of his accounts of early modern exchange patterns:

> is it possible to 'locate' the market in its proper place? This is not as easy as it might look, because the word 'market' is itself equivocal. On one hand it is used, in a very loose sense, of all types of exchange that go beyond self-sufficiency, of all the wheels of trade, large and small, that we have described, of all the categories relating to trading areas (urban market, national market) or to a given product (the market in sugar, precious metals, spices etc.). In this sense the word is the equivalent of exchange, circulation, distribution. On the other hand, the word 'market' is often applied to a rather large broad form of exchange, also known as the *market economy*, that is, to a system.
>
> The difficulty is first, that the market complex can only be understood when it is replaced within the context of an economic life and no less a *social* life that changes over the years; and secondly that this complex is itself constantly evolving and changing; it never has the same meaning or significance from one minute to the next.[34]

Agnew's book argues that the very difficulty of this Braudelian question suggests a kind of answer to it: that the market has no "proper place" and that its ubiquity or penetrativeness shows that no social or intellectual "proper place," no firm ground or radiant center, can remain separate or sacrosanct. Theater, Agnew shows, has this same quality, with the added feature that it is both a social activity and a reflective discourse.

My own book works out more precisely than Agnew does the implications for Shakespeare's career of this concatenation. I take the historic and economic idea of the market, the historic and literary phenomenon of drama, and the theoretical vocabulary of contemporary pragmatism and mobilize them in a series of readings of plays and poems by Shakespeare.

Chapters 2 and 3 develop the book's major premises through theoretical and critical arguments, first about the sonnets, and then about the theater. In chapter 2 I argue from a reading of the sonnets that Shakespeare thought of value, whether stable long-term value or unstable short-term value, in economic and pragmatic terms, as a product of the needs of communities rather than as arising from some source of certainty beyond community. I adapt cognate passages from Wittgenstein and from Barbara Herrnstein Smith to clarify and extend this argument. Chapter 3 develops the salient parallels between this attitude toward value and the theater's characteristic mode of operation and argues for the special role that theater—and especially Shakespeare's theater—plays in pragmatic investigation and interrogation of social "truths." (It is no accident that foundationalists have repeatedly pitted themselves against both theater and pragmatist philosophizing.) I then illustrate how pragmatism works in the theater by turning to a reading of *Hamlet* as an economics of agency amid discursive constraints— Hamlet must constantly test the worth of his own and others' beliefs in theatricalized situations. I develop here also the usefulness of "agency" and "discourse" as terms for the particular kind of pragmatic haggling over personal identity that goes on continually in plays.

Part I of the book, then, sets out the two related modes of pragmatic redescription I attribute to Shakespeare: first, a transactional analysis of human social behavior as moves or bids in a market economy of contingent values, and second, the negotiation of apparently essential oppositions as differences on a spectrum of possible responses to a social or intellectual problem. Shakespeare brings opposed forces into play in a complex arena of multiple contingencies; in his marketlike theater there are no noncontingent outcomes and few opposites that remain uncontaminated by each other.

Part II introduces three important contexts which are subject to pragmatic analysis as shaping forces in a dynamic economy: marriage and friendship, royal succession and legitimation, and literary influence. In chapter 4 *The Merchant of Venice* is read as a remarkably precise audit of a large transaction, using the homosocial terms with which Eve Sedgwick has enriched our vocabularies to discuss what seems to me a qualified triumph for female subjectivity (that is, for Portia) over normally male-dominated circuits of exchange. Chapter 5 does the same sort of thing on a larger scale with Shakespeare's second Lancastrian tetralogy; in it I describe intergenerational flows of emotional and political credit which tend to profit Hal in the same ways that those in *The Merchant of Venice* profited Portia, but which he exploits in the service of victories more nearly final. In the course of this discussion, Falstaff's promotion of Bakhtinian transition to carnival is treated as a market-linked phenomenon, and to some extent the whole *Henriad* is presented as a contest between two opposed strategies for the repudiation of debt. Chapter 6 discusses a case of hitherto-unremarked influence on Shakespeare; it attempts to redescribe literary influence in pragmatic terms (and thus to discuss why Shakespeare seems to feel its anxiety less than others). It also suggests that Chaucer anticipates a number of the pragmatic tendencies I attribute to Shakespeare and may have helped teach Shakespeare how to write about social relations in pragmatic ways.

Thus part II demonstrates how Shakespeare takes up the market economy both as a social concept useful in describing the complex erotic and economic circuits which bind the parties in a single short-term transaction, and as a historical metaphor useful in keeping track of the wider set of transactions involved in a long-term process of dynastic change and legitimation. I then turn to a pragmatic description of intertextual relations between two canonical authors.

Part III explores in some detail a central problem for contemporary pragmatism by investigating the relation of Shakespearean pragmatism to politics in three plays set in the pre-Christian world. While pragmatism refers all questions to a communal arena of agreement and disagreement, and thus claims that there are no nonpolitical issues, contemporary pragmatism has often been seen as having difficulty with political commitment, as not offering terms in which to argue for or against different kinds of political arrangements. In one (self-invalidating) sense this criticism sticks: pragmatism does not make absolute moral claims and thus does not think that any science will distinguish one social system as objectively better than another (so it says to such critics: Do not expect theorists to solve such problems; they can't). But in another sense, as a way of describing political and intellectual life which stresses analysis in terms of value-claims, pragmatism helps to tease out the value-affiliations involved in political conflicts and thus to redescribe them in terms which show which values we demonstrate in siding one way or another. Shakespeare shows how Trojan and Roman politics lend themselves to discussion in terms of exchanges, markets, and returns, and *Troilus and Cressida*, *Coriolanus*, and *Antony and Cleopatra* suggest that it is in fact possible to distinguish poorer and richer forms of political give and take, more or less effective forms of leadership, and more or less hopeful or inclusive forms of governance.

In chapter 7 I discuss market evaluation under historical stress in *Troilus and Cressida*, arguing that both aesthetic evaluations of the two major sources, Homer's *Iliad* and Chaucer's *Troilus and Criseyde*, and personal evaluations within the play are subjected to a forceful thought experiment in perspective reversal. Like Troilus watching Cressida negotiate with Diomede, we as readers or audience members are pushed by witnessing the degradation of something we value to reflect on what kinds of social stability underly the high long-term value of literary classics, and how such communal valuations resemble fragile individual erotic choices. *Troilus and Cressida* imagines a political world in which every decision is explicitly thought of (and often formally discussed) in market terms, and in which people do very little besides bargaining to bid up their own values and those of commodities they temporarily possess. The richly plural environment of stable customary values that surrounds most transactions is absent, and the play thus enacts, I argue, a narrower and poorer market than most for political and personal interactions. The last two chapters, on the two late Roman plays, show Shakespeare giving a pragmatic account of individual leaders shaping and being shaped by history. In chapter 8 I discuss *Coriolanus* as a clash of different moral economies: that of the self-regarding noble hero and that of the Roman crowd. Both Coriolanus and the plebeians, I suggest, find that the remarkably modern dynamic of the Roman market economy makes their stabilizing expectations fail. Coriolanus lives in a way which might support an essentialist view of human excellence, but he refuses even the minimal negotiations which would give that view social power. In chapter 9, on *Antony and Cleopatra*, Roberto Unger's vocabulary of formative contexts and context revision is examined as a way of looking at human constraint and freedom with respect to history. I discuss the Machiavellian view of world-historical individuals in Marlowe's *Tamburlaine* and Marvell's "Horatian Ode" and use those accounts of context revising figures to frame an account of *Antony and Cleopatra* as a contest between different modes of context revision, one Machiavellian (and thus pragmatist in a relatively narrow sense), associated with Octavian, the other committed to a constant process of context softening, a permanent historical plasticity, associated with Cleopatra and Antony.

The readings in this book as a whole, then, analyze Shakespeare's enterprise as the substitution of dynamic economies for fixed systems, and show Shakespeare anticipating many of the features of a contemporary pragmatist view of the world. In the pragmatic theory it advocates, it is a book which seeks, finally, to renegotiate some of the current disputes between humanists and poststructuralists, to resist fundamentalist stances, on the one hand, and reductionist critique, on the other, and to redefine old terms and reanalyze old texts in a (relatively) new pragmatic way. I begin my particular analysis with the treatment of value and duration in the sonnets.

I

Toward Shakespearean Pragmatism

2

Certainty and Uncertainty
in the Sonnets

From fairest creatures we desire increase,
That thereby beauty's rose might never die . . .

❦

The opening lines of Shakespeare's first sonnet state a double premise
that turns out to suggest major thematic features of the entire sequence.
The first clause proposes an imaginative or erotic economy, introducing what Thomas Greene has called "the anxiety of cosmic or existen-
tial economics which haunts the Sonnets."[1] The second explains this
economy by referring to a general social hope or purpose: to achieve a
permanence or stability in beauty that will successfully oppose death.
In isolation, we might unpack them as follows. The first clause claims
that "we"—human beings, or right-thinking observers (it will soon be
clear that the "we" is male, but this is not yet evident)—respond to
beauty by desiring a profit of some sort from it, that beauty engenders
desire for more. The second, relative, clause tells us that the desired
return from beauty, the desired result of the implied transactions it
evokes, is a permanence or stability in beauty which opposes itself to
death. The continuance of beauty against death, then, is presented as
a shared social goal, spurred by a shared fear of loss. This curious
response to beauty reflects neither a desire to possess or share it (the
response we might expect of a lover), nor a wish to replicate it for
profit (the response we expect from a stock-breeder): it is more the
response of a conservationist. It might be the voice-over of a Sierra
Club film in which California condors soar over their eggless nest. It
speaks from within a recognizably economic frame of reference about
a span of time longer than that which figures in normal economic
arguments.

These inaugural hints point toward the sonnets' transactive analysis
of human value in time, and it is this anti-essentialist or anti-Platonic
analysis of value that gives the poems modernity, even contemporane-
ity, and establishes their status as breakthrough documents toward and
beyond literary "inwardness" or "poetic subjectivity." The sonnets to
the young man enact an affluent or generative economy of human
value. They thus approximate in their results, while differing crucially

in their methods from, Petrarchan sonnets in which market-exchange is rejected and poetic value is linked to claims of transcendence.[2] The sonnets to the dark lady enact a poor, and consequently a naked and self-critical economy of human value, in which reflection on the love exchange and the needs from which it all-too-locally and directly arises promotes a deflationary perspective on idealization of all sorts. By emphasizing the ways love fuels and is fuelled by social economies of human value, the sonnets explore both the stability and the instability—the long idyllic bull markets and the catastrophic crashes—of a peculiarly de-idealized or anti-Platonic notion of how things hang together: a world-view in which truth and lasting value are simply that which a mutable community, for a variety of discussable reasons, chooses to regard as good for a long time.

This description makes Shakespeare's sonnets sound very up to date, since it views their meditations on human value as simultaneous meditations on the social mechanisms by which value is maintained or lost. Claims that the sonnets approach a modern perspective are not unusual in recent criticism, and my analysis builds on some of these, though it differs in the way it explains the modernity of Shakespearean subjectivity. In the past decade, Anne Ferry and the late Joel Fineman have independently put forward arguments that Shakespeare in effect invents or anticipates modern subjectivity, though they have somewhat different notions of what counts as modern. Ferry comments that "one would have to look to John Locke's *An Essay Concerning Humane Understanding*, published in 1689, eighty years after Shakespeare's sonnets, for the earliest use of a vocabulary that defines in systematic philosophic terms something like the kind of modern consciousness we identify in Shakespeare's speakers."[3] And she then gives a precise account of the evolution of an inward language in sixteenth-century English poetry, seeing Shakespeare's reading of Sidney's *Astrophil and Stella* as a key factor in this development in the sonnets and seeing the sonnets themselves as Shakespeare's own preparation for writing *Hamlet*, a famous milestone in the representation of an inward self.[4] Fineman, who sees in the dark-lady sonnets a reflexive turn on the idealizing poetics of the young-man sonnets (so that the sequence as a whole replicates a Lacanian story in which, by accepting that meanings and emotions and values are matters of language rather than sight, one can break through the imaginary to the symbolic), comments at the end of the introduction of *Shakespeare's Perjured Eye*:

there is at least the possibility that modernist—and, for that matter, post-modernist—theories of the self are not so much a theoretical ac-

count or explanation of subjectivity as they are the conclusion of the
literary subjectivity initially invented in the Renaissance. If this is the
case, we might want to say that Shakespeare marks the beginning of
the modernist self and Freud . . . its end, the two of them together thus
bracketing an epoch of subjectivity.[5]

The tentativeness of this claim, which stands out amid the general
audacity of Fineman's prose, may be accounted for in one of two ways.
Either the historical sweep of Fineman's conception here daunts even
its author, so that he has to advance it as a possibility (or as something
subtly more—"at least the possibility") or Fineman was poised between more important alternatives. In this passage Fineman seems
uncertain whether he is arguing, with Ferry, and with the book he
"originally conceived,"[6] that Shakespeare is a pioneer or inventor of
interiority of consciousness and thus of the possibility of literary "character" (Shakespeare as Locke, Freud, and other mapmaking explorers
of inner space), or arguing that Shakespeare not only invents but also
deconstructs the modern self (Shakespeare as a transgressive modernist
or "postmodernist," as Heidegger or Derrida).[7] The issue is encapsu-
lated in the odd offhandedness of the phrase "modernist—and, for that
matter, postmodernist—theories of the self." The wording suggests
either that the "post" marks no real break, that postmodernists are
simply pursuing the ineluctable consequences of the "end" marked by
Freud, or that Shakespeare is modern, modernist, and postmodern all
at once, so that the choice of historical argument can be left to the
sprezzatura of the critic.

My own argument, like Ferry's and Fineman's, backdates certain
explicit modern philosophical issues by finding them implicitly treated
in Shakespeare's sonnets. But the modern issue that concerns me here
is the dispute about certainty. As I argued in chapter 1, Shakespeare
stands just prior to the great certainty projects of Descartes and Galileo, projects to which modern pragmatists have reacted by, in effect,
returning to Renaissance modes of social contextualization and specificity. I see Shakespeare as having taken up in the sonnets the issue of
how to understand permanence in economic terms.

The dispute about certainty among modern philosophers has been
waged between conventionalists and objectivists over the seductive Platonic offer to build a world-system on solid and indisputable founda-
tions. At the MLA, if not the NSF, conventionalists seem these days
to have won the war of theory; the burden of my argument is that
their account of things has long been in circulation. Shakespeare's
sonnets seem to me anti-foundationalist both when they are asserting

enduring value and when they are denying it. Thus alongside Ferry's
Lockean Shakespeare and Fineman's Lacanian Shakespeare, I offer a
Shakespeare who anticipates the pragmatism of late Wittgenstein or
Richard Rorty. Like Ferry and Fineman, I also base my interpretation
on Shakespeare's development of certain aspects of the sonnet tradition:
the turn toward subjectivity and inwardness, the potential solipsism
in evaluation that emerges when the will to praise is closely connected
with personal rather than public ends, and the tradition of "eternizing,"
with its necessary claims to define or predict public values. My general
argument includes three further claims: first, that Shakespeare's sonnets embrace a fundamentally economic idea of value; second, that they
endorse a notion of utility through change which suggests a pragmatic
account of human continuity and thus a nonessentialist idea of human
nature; and finally, that these assertions suggest, in part, why the
sonnets maintain their peculiarly canonical status.

It is quite easy to see how a poem may have an "economic" function
in addressing or praising a beloved, the imagined context that domi-
nates Renaissance sonnet sequences. An expression of praise is a bid
in a market as well as an announcement of a state of feeling; it enhances
the worth of the recipient, often by declaring the enhanced worth of
the sender, sometimes in an explicit context of profit and loss: "but
if the while I think on thee, dear friend, / All losses are restored, and
sorrows end" (30).[8] In romantic love, says Freud, the lover overvalues
the beloved;[9] in Shakespeare's sonnets this overvaluation is markedly
self-conscious, involving acute sensitivity to the processes of evaluation
that surround and underwrite the activity of praise. The sonnets are
in advance of most criticism of them in discussing larger contexts in
which their use value emerges: they contain many important indications of their own utility.

This argument aligns me with Fineman and John Bernard in maintaining that Shakespeare's sonnets initiate a new and un-Petrarchan
working problem for praise poets, but the processes I identify are
different.[10] I am suggesting that Shakespeare's sonnets present local,
even momentary vicissitudes of value in a dynamic market as an important element in their treatment of evaluation, overestimation, investment in another, and resultant vulnerability and self-questioning in
love. The special subjectivity in the sonnets is mainly, I think, a consequence of emotional recognition that no ascription of value, even between two people who defy the rest of the world, is independent of
the ever-changing economies of value around it. The figures used to
characterize the love of the poet and the young man—trafficking, selling, shopping, worth, profit and loss, leasing, thriving, failing, spend-

ing, auditing, bankruptcy, wealth, and so on—might be considered aspects of a microeconomics of human value. The sequence gives recurrent attention to the contingency of lovers' feelings in local and immediate social circumstances, an attention which, by the playful complexity that Stephen Booth extensively celebrates, almost never sacrifices semantic or erotic or aural suggestion to clarity.

But the sonnets are also, perhaps even more notably and famously, concerned with what the Annalistes have taught us to call the *longue durée*, with the ways human patterns change slowly over generations and with the ways love or poetry can survive the bodies and emotions that gave them birth. The sonnets' repeated assertions that love and poetry can defeat time hardly seem economic. Nor does their own value—their capacity to fulfill some of their own prophecies—seem easy to explain as the product of a particular value-creating context. As Adena Rosmarin notes, the sonnets consistently extend that context into the distant future: "by expecting the future readers they find, the sonnets prefigure our retrospective confirmation of their excellence."[11] Market economics does not allow for ventures that defer the profitable return indefinitely.[12]

From this point of view, it is not surprising to find critics arguing that Shakespeare presents triumph over time as a matter of transcendence, the necessary result of poetry's access to ideal properties outside time altogether, properties giving poems absolute value that time cannot touch.[13] But does Shakespeare in fact idealize the power of poetry over circumstance, or does he treat this triumph as a *contingent* process, the result of the interplay of different forces and needs which maintains the value of some things (e.g., poems and some of the emotional gestures they embody) while destroying many others (empires, monuments, individual lives, personal beauty, summer's honey breath, etc.)? Does Shakespeare treat the survival of "classics" as, so to speak, a macroeconomic phenomenon? This question also casts doubt on the consistency of the sequence, if one accepts the economic character of the sonnets more directly addressed to the young man and the dark lady. Is Shakespeare an economist or pragmatist about local social and sexual relations, but an idealist in the long term? Such a position, though incoherent, would be familiar, like being an Epicurean toward pleasure and a stoic toward pain, and one to some extent supported by Renaissance cosmological beliefs and Christian theories of universal history.

In my view, however, Shakespeare treats value that defies time and death as contingent, subject to the same general explanations as the local immediate value of a particular person at a particular time. This

treatment is often obscured by his tendency to express the high value
of a given personal gesture or action as a burst of golden relief which
allows escape from calculations of profit and loss:

> Ah, but those tears are pearl which thy love sheeds,
> And they are rich, and ransom all ill deeds. (34)[14]

But such bursts of relief are momentary; their mood of expansive assurance never lasts long.

A number of the sonnets seem to me to suggest Shakespeare's position on value over the *longue durée*. In sonnet 108, for instance, the poet
worries that there is nothing new under the sun.

> What's in the brain that ink may character,
> Which hath not figured to thee my true spirit?
> What's new to speak, what now to register,
> That may express my love, or thy dear merit?
> Nothing, sweet boy, but yet, like prayers divine,
> I must each day say o'er the very same;
> Counting no old thing old, thou mine, I thine,
> Ev'n as when first I hallowed thy fair name.
> So that eternal love in love's fresh case
> Weighs not the dust and injury of age,
> Nor gives to necessary wrinkles place,
> But makes antiquity for aye his page,
> > Finding the first conceit of love there bred,
> > Where time and outward form would show it dead. (108)

Poems and loving gestures are iterable like prayer in spiritual discipline, and by this process of continued and repeated use, "eternal love
in love's fresh case" can "make antiquity for aye his page" and turn
signs of death into the sources of ever-renewed love. The pun on
"page" ("servant" or "leaf of a book") empowers my sense that the
survival of poems beyond their originating context is treated alongside—as subsidiary to—the survival of love beyond its initial response
to beauty's stimulus. Here, "Time and outward form" are defeated not
by transcendence but by continued repetition of something that does
not easily grow stale: reciprocal affection and its expression, "thou
mine, I thine."[15] Wilson Knight generalizes this survival beyond the
particular relation involved: "The youth . . . will exist in poetry for
ages to come, as he existed in ages past; almost, we may add, irrespec-
tive of whether Shakespeare's poetry survives or not, since there will
be other poets at work, and the theme is immortal."[16] This "immortal"
means "eternally recurrent," as Knight also notes, but he then characteristically goes on to insist that poetry must not be content with publi-

cation and perpetuity but must "focus . . . a supernal reality, or truth."[17] I cannot accept this last step. Nor, I believe, does Shakespeare take it. Sonnet 108 triumphs over time by offering a repeatable gesture that will serve recurrent human needs.

Similarly, sonnet 123 challenges time by making a claim not to independence but, rather, to continually recovered contingent success:

> No! Time, thou shalt not boast that I do change.
> Thy pyramids built up with newer might
> To me are nothing novel, nothing strange;
> They are but dressings of a former sight.
> Our dates are brief, and therefore we admire
> What thou dost foist upon us that is old,
> And rather make them born to our desire
> Than think that we before have heard them told.
> Thy registers and thee I both defy,
> Not wond'ring at the present, nor the past;
> For thy recórds, and what we see, doth lie,
> Made more or less by thy continual haste.
>   This I do vow, and this shall ever be,
>   I will be true despite thy scythe and thee. (123)

The poem has puzzled commentators: Booth notes that "as the poem progresses, obvious opposites blend into one another; change looks like constancy and constancy like change."[18] To my mind, the poem treats these pairs as false opposites and meditates on the relative continuity of cultural use that monuments (new or old), poems, and emotional gestures of wide currency can attain. It goes on to suggest that a triumphant relation to time rewards any gesture or attitude which, once struck, may be again and again "born to our desire," or that of our successors, since both past and present gestures are subject to vagaries of value over time: "Made more or less by thy continual haste." The sonnet's world-weary suggestions that nothing is really new, and that our own briefness makes us prone to confusion and susceptible to artificial novelty, would seem cynical and limited were they not combined with opening and closing vows that suggest constancy as a prudential response to change over time. Overvaluation of both past and present results from our fear of time; understanding time leads us to value the gestures that enable us to align ourselves with it and that may someday be re-offered by others to others. Some fine comments of Heather Dubrow's on closure in the sonnets offer support for this view:

> if the nature of experience renders closure problematic, the character
> of this particular speaker renders it virtually impossible. Attracted

though he may be to absolutes, he is . . . involved to the point of obsession with doubts and fears about what is to come. . . . Shakespeare's couplets . . . embody both the all-too-human desire to seek finality and certainty and the all-too-human difficulties of doing so. Hence they trouble us—and teach us—more *through what they do (or fail to do) than through what they say.*[19]

An interest in the survival value of the time-bound gesture, in what the sonnets "do (or fail to do)," is rewarded in the following sonnet 124, where the poet's love seems to distinguish itself sharply from contingency, but turns out to triumph in a more expansive commitment to a long-term policy that emerges as contingency writ large. As Murray Krieger points out, in this sonnet "the only terms available [to celebrate love] are those of the world"—of "state"—and the meaning of "state" spreads out "to envelop the contingencies of the human condition":[20]

> If my dear love were but the child of state,
> It might for fortune's bastard be unfathered,
> As subject to time's love, or to time's hate,
> Weeds among weeds, or flow'rs with flowers gathered.
> No, it was builded far from accident;
> It suffers not in smiling pomp, nor falls
> Under the blow of thrallèd discontent,
> Whereto th'inviting time our fashion calls.
> It fears not policy, that heretic
> Which works on leases of short numb'red hours,
> But all alone stands hugely politic,
> That it nor grows with heat, nor drowns with show'rs.
>   To this I witness call the fools of time,
>   Which die for goodness, who have lived for crime. (124)

To be "hugely politic" is precisely to grasp that success in the *longue durée* is the result of a more far-sighted understanding of contingency and time, not the result of some absolute escape from time's hold altogether. To be "hugely politic" is to be contingent on the stablest external factors available.[21] I take the enigmatic final couplet to refer, as Booth suggests, to the way approaching death tends to revise attitudes toward time and eternity; death itself becomes a contingency affecting temporal attitudes. Booth cites instances of deathbed conversions from Protestantism to Catholicism and vice versa: one might add Donne's "as Atheists at their dying houre / Call, what they cannot name, an unknowne power," which gives perhaps more precisely the sense that death refocuses the whole topic for those who suddenly find themselves near it, sponsoring a sudden intense interest in the possibility of endurance or transcendence, and therby recontextualizing (as "crime") past living habits.[22] Donne's couplet makes this a matter of a sudden vague theism, whereas Shakespeare claims for his love a "hugely politic" expertise in endurance.

That the sonnets thus make endurance claims at moments when they seem, and are often taken, to make transcendence claims, is, I believe, part of a general Shakespearean relocation of the human urge for certainty, knowledge, and permanence within the boundaries of human community over time, a relocation we are more accustomed to think of as the characteristic activity of our own moment in intellectual history rather than his (even allowing for the description of Shakespeare's lifetime I offered in the preceding chapter).[23] Consider, for instance, the similarity between what I have been arguing for in the sonnets and the following remarks from Wittgenstein's *On Certainty*, the collection of his final writings on the question of how we can know anything for sure when we find no fixed ground upon which our knowledge rests. I should say in advance that the sort of "certainty" Wittgenstein is discussing has less reach than, say, "Love's not Time's fool" or "Everything that grows / Holds in perfection but a little moment"; Wittgenstein is thinking above all of G. E. Moore's comically limited claim to know "here is my right hand, here is my left" and is taking part in Moore's attempt to answer Descartes' skeptical demon. Wittgenstein himself, moreover, did not seem to feel that his investigation was over when he turned up the wonderful, rather Ovidian metaphors which follow. He kept on writing fragments of argument, most of them much more prosaic than these.

94. . . . I did not get my picture of the world by satisfying myself of its correctness; nor do I have it because I am satisfied of its correctness. No: it is the inherited background against which I distinguish between true and false.

95. The propositions describing this world-picture might be part of a kind of mythology . . . .

96. It might be imagined that some propositions, of the form of empirical propositions, were hardened and functioned as channels for such empirical propositions as were not hardened but fluid; and that this relation altered with time, in that fluid propositions hardened, and hard ones became fluid.

97. The mythology may change back into a state of flux, the river-bed of thoughts may shift. But I distinguish between the movement of the waters on the river-bed and the shift of the bed itself; though there is not a sharp division of the one from the other.

99. And the bank of that river consists partly of hard rock, subject

to no alteration or only to an imperceptible one, partly of sand, which now in one place now in another gets washed away, or deposited.

248. I have arrived at the rock bottom of my convictions. And one might almost say that these foundation-walls are carried by the whole house.[24]

Thus our experience flows in the relatively firm channels defined by the objects of our knowledge, but that channel too is part of a slower flow of erosion and deposit, discovery, maturation, commitment, abandonment. Some of that slower flow we can experience within a single lifetime, but it is much clearer when we survey the sweep of the past, and especially the succession of belief systems which, since Hegel, we have seen as remaking the world in successive generations. The more or less coherent structure of convictions we inhabit can be stable and feel well founded without having a particular point of grounding or centering, either transcendental or logical; instead of such possible anchors for the individual sensorium, we turn to a relative continuity of community support for basic knowledge: "Knowledge is in the end based on acknowledgement" (On Certainty, 49e). This continuity is no absolute assurance of the permanence of anything, but it offers a kind of deeply stable contingency, like a rocky channel conducting more fluid aspects of our experience.[25]

What is exciting in these comments is their suggestion that, like geological strata, levels of contingency themselves may have a recoverable and stable, if not inalterable or grounded, structure. (They hint, that is, at some recovery of Wittgenstein's life-long interest in building from simple toward complex forms in the face of his acknowledgment that nothing absolutely simple to build on will be found. One could argue along these lines, for instance, that dialectic is better at getting at stable areas of our experience than rhetoric, even though dialectic cannot promise access to truths beyond negotiation and thus cannot be absolutely opposed to rhetoric.) Thus, in describing structures of human experience, our alternatives need not be limited to "necessary" structures grounded on imaginary essences on one hand and vertigo or fleeting fictions on the other. Some "temporary historical resting places," to use Richard Rorty's deliberately disconcerting description of successive philosophical vocabularies,[26] are less temporary than others, and may be so because they grapple better with mortality, love, social inequality, discontent with conditions of life, and other stably contingent (or contingently stable) factors in human self-description. Obviously we should not be passive or acquiescent in the face of such recognition, or imagine that such continuities confer sanctity on any particular status quo. But the notion that strata of stable contingency underlie and shape the liquid flow of experience and the volatility of thought suggests that parts of a Kantian/Platonic grounding project may be recuperable without belief in bedrock objective truths. Shakespeare, his melancholy sitting in brood over varieties of love and over the long survival of beautiful forms of speech, suggests in the poems I have cited that the survival of vestiges of the self beyond a particular life span may be attained by doing something useful for others. He has suggested further that the usefulness of poetry involves intimacy with the deposits of past experience and the creation of further accessible shapes for the experience of others. That is, he both believes in and contributes to continuity in communal experience. Perhaps, in this light, we need to rethink the key architectural metaphor of "grounding": Shakespeare's poetry, like Frank Lloyd Wright's Imperial Hotel in Tokyo, does not anchor itself on an essential bedrock from which it can be shaken by metaphysical earthquakes but instead floats deep in a thickly liquid deposit of human behaviors and desires.[27]

Before moving to a discussion of Barbara Herrnstein Smith's *Contingencies of Value*, the book which has most explicitly argued that we see canonical stability as well as market vicissitude in economic terms, I shall discuss the contingency of value in two of the most famous sonnets, 55 and 116. Both are often considered sonnets of idealization (as Shakespeare's sonnets go); both appear to claim that time can be transcended, either through poetry (55) or unilateral commitment (116). Both, I shall argue, locate the immortality of love poetry and poetic love in the kind of stable or deep contingency I have been (with Wittgenstein's help) attempting to define. I should say at the outset, however, that these two poems are also bound to immediate contingencies, since their contexts in the sequence are highly qualifying: sonnet 56, "Sweet love, renew thy force," is about impotence, and sonnet 117, "Accuse me thus," about faithlessness. But both 55 and 116 refer to themselves and thus invite consideration of their separate activities.

> Not marble nor the gilded monuments
> Of princes shall outlive this pow'rful rhyme,
> But you shall shine more bright in these conténts
> Than unswept stone, besmeared with sluttish time.
> When wasteful war shall statues overturn,
> And broils root out the work of masonry,
> Nor Mars his sword nor war's quick fire shall burn
> The living record of your memory.
> 'Gainst death and all oblivious enmity
> Shall you pace forth; your praise shall still find room,

> Ev'n in the eyes of all posterity
> That wear this world out to the ending doom.
>   So, till the judgement that yourself arise,
>   You live in this, and dwell in lovers' eyes. (55)

This sonnet draws on and appropriates two often-invoked classical passages. Horace claims in *Odes* 3:30 to have

> finished a monument more lasting than bronze and loftier than the Pyramids' royal pile, one that no wasting rain, no furious north wind can destroy, or the countless chain of years and the ages' flight. I shall not altogether die, but a mighty part of me shall escape the death-goddess. On and on shall I grow, ever fresh with the glory of after time.[28]

And Ovid claims at the end of the *Metamorphoses* (here given in Golding's translation) that

> Now have I brought a woork too end which neither *Joves* feerce wrath
> Nor swoord, nor fyre, nor freating age with all the force it hath
> Are able too abolish quyght . . . .
>   And all the world shall never
> Be able for too quench my name. For looke how farre so ever
> The Romane Empyre by the ryght of conquest shall extend,
> So farre shall all folke reade this woork. And tyme without all end
> (If Poets as by prophesie about the truth may ame)
> My lyfe shall everlastingly bee lengthened still by fame.[29]

The difference—that Shakespeare offers immortality to another, while Horace and Ovid claim it for themselves—is signal, but the similarities of image and aspiration are inescapable. A reader's recognition of the allusions, of course, reinforces the initially improbable statement that "this pow'rful rhyme" will outlive other kinds of monuments: Ovid and Horace live on in the Renaissance curriculum, their value maintained in the imitative exercises and tingling elite backsides of scholarly generations, while the ruins of Rome crumble. By echoing them, Shakespeare makes his own claim to transcend time into an acutely historical one: canonical literary works *have* outlasted monuments— that is how history has turned out. Their survival may say something about the distinctive individual greatness of Ovid and Horace, but it says more about the continuity of human community, particularly since Shakespeare's poem uses Ovid and Horace without naming them.[30] The allusions, then, are evidential, not just self-aggrandizing: they offer contingent historical justification for the ambitions the sonnet articulates.

The survival of Latin classics also, of course, says something about the survival strategies of a literate elite and thus of the system of social divisions which favors it, and this Shakespeare does not comment on directly in the sonnets. Indeed, his frequent contrasts between poems and gilded monuments, tyrants' crests, and other appurtenances of rulers' self-glorification, combined with his occasional pungent registration of his own social inconsequence, make the survival of poetry seem like the revenge of the socially humble against their oppressors. If for "socially humble" in my last sentence we read "emergent bourgeoisie," then we may see the sonnets (especially if we accept them as economic discourse) participating in a covert struggle for the vocabulary in which social values are negotiated. But appeals to sentiments like "thou mine, I thine" cut across social divisions, and this cutting or bridging power also helps explain poetry's endurance.

The personification of time in sonnet 55, as in many of the other sonnets, dramatizes the consequences of contingency: meaning slips away from monuments through slovenliness or unreliability of "sluttish time"—as contexts change, meanings change or vanish with them. People stop caring or paying attention. This happens dramatically when war or revolution destroys or reverses value and structure ("broils root out the work of masonry"), slowly when nature erodes or obscures the surface of a statue. So when the sonnet promises that it itself—or the book or manuscript containing it—will survive and give permanence, it seems to claim absolute victory over time. But poetry, which lives "where breath most breathes, ev'n in the mouths of men" (81), survives according to sonnet 55 not by monumental resistance but by a kind of relative activity. It manages to keep a space for the beloved and for assertions of his value in the corrosive public gaze ("the eyes of all posterity / That wear this world out to the ending doom"). With a subdued allusion to the rhythmic activity of prosody, the beloved marches through time: "'Gainst death, and all oblivious enmity / Shall you pace forth.". Poetry's survival value, then, is not a matter of fixity—Booth notes, for instance, that "even as [lines 7–8] assert the immortality of the poem [they] remind a reader of the flimsiness and vulnerability of anything written on paper."[31]

Clearly the "living record of your memory" is not a physical book. Rather, poetry survives by being useful to the living, hence participating in a continuous ongoing economy of invocation: "you live in this, and dwell in lovers' eyes." By making the beloved a token of value, and part of a system by which love is both valued and made, the poet can triumph over the threat of his own and his beloved's contingency and make the sonnet itself something of contingent value to future lovers. It is a confirming, though perhaps unintended, fact that the male beloved exists only as defined by this particular emotional relation in the sequence: he has no name, no actions, no historical existence, and Donald Foster denies him even his initials.[32] He exists only as part of a system of loving praise, as a varyingly assessed locus of emotional value, in a collection which suggests strongly that this is how all of us can best endure.

Poems last better than beauty or deeds; they are less vulnerable to time and the contingency of immediate circumstances; this is true because of the cultural forces or habits that make us preserve, value, and transmit some poems, and which put them in a privileged relation to long-lasting, stably contingent natural/cultural phenomena like love, friendship, and praise.[33] Insofar as this claim concerns canonicity, it has to do more with poetry as a cultural activity than with this particular poem in competition with others.

Sonnet 55's couplet may seem to contrast earthly judgment, which is contingent, with the Last Judgment, which is absolute. But the couplet makes clear that poetry lives in time, in contingency, not beyond it: "So, *till* the judgement that yourself arise / You live in this, and dwell in lovers' eyes." There is a hint of poetic weariness—the yearning to get done with all the contingent values which are poetry's substance and subject and on to a time when poetry will be unnecessary—the sentiment of the last two stanzas of Spenser's *Mutability*. But there is no assertion that poetry *transcends* contingency. I cannot agree with Ferry that 55 and other relatively early sonnets make claims "above all for the poet's power to create verbal constructs which may alter the laws of nature, arrest change, exclude 'Devouring time,' and so preserve the ideal eternally, a power which is, by metaphorical definition, not natural or human or even prophetic but miraculous."[34] In the sonnets, poetry's life is a contingent life, remade to fit new situations, as we see in sonnet 106:

> When in the chronicle of wasted time
> I see descriptions of the fairest wights
> And beauty making beautiful old rhyme
> In praise of ladies dead and lovely knights,
> Then in the blazon of sweet beauty's best,
> Of hand, of foot, of lip, of eye, of brow,
> I see their ántique pen would have expressed
> Ev'n such a beauty as you master now.
> So all their praises are but prophecies
> Of this our time, all you prefiguring,
> And for they looked but with divining eyes,
> They had not skill enough your worth to sing;
> > For we which now behold these present days,
> > Have eyes to wonder, but lack tongues to praise. (106)

Without meaning to, perhaps, these lines give a pattern for the use of Shakespeare's own verse in the future, when lovers resurrect the emotions, situations, or descriptions of the past to serve their own purposes. The next sonnet, at any rate, takes up the question of what will become of Shakespeare's love:

> Not mine own fears nor the prophetic soul
> Of the wide world dreaming on things to come
> Can yet the lease of my true love control,
> Supposed as forfeit to a cónfined doom. (107)

The future for his love consists, at least in part, in the posthumous life his sonnets provide for the lovers: the couplet of 107 asserts that "thou in this shalt find thy monument, / When tyrants' crests and tombs of brass are spent." Poetry is a gift that goes on giving.

Sonnet 116, perhaps the most famous and surely one of the most beautiful in the sequence, in frequent if unquantifiable use at weddings, does for the relation between love and contingency what sonnet 55 does for the relation between poetry and contingency.

> Let me not to the marriage of true minds
> Admit impediments. Love is not love
> Which alters when it alteration finds,
> Or bends with the remover to remove.
> O no, it is an ever-fixèd mark
> That looks on tempests and is never shaken;
> It is the star to every wand'ring bark,
> Whose worth's unknown, although his height be taken.
> Love's not time's fool, though rosy lips and cheeks
> Within his bending sickle's compass come.
> Love alters not with his brief hours and weeks,
> But bears it out ev'n to the edge of doom
>   If this be error and upon me proved,
>   I never writ, nor no man ever loved. (116)

Love here is in an unusually paradoxical relation to knowledge: it knows what it is not without being able to say what it is. Obviously this kind of uncertainty can be presented as an enhancer of value: in Donne's "A Valediction: forbidding mourning," for instance, it supports the assertion of an intimacy that defies categories:

> But we by a love, so much refin'd
>   That our selves know not what it is,
> Inter-assured of the mind,
>   Care lesse, eyes, lips, and hands to misse.[35]

But in Shakespeare the context is entirely different. The first two lines echo the part of the marriage service designed to accommodate the possibility of error:

> "I require and charge you (as you will answer at the dreadful day of judgment, when the secrets of all hearts shall be disclosed) that if either of you do know any impediment why ye may not be lawfully joined together in matrimony, that ye confess it."[36]

"Let me not admit" may mean, then, "may I never have to admit" or "Lord, strengthen me that I may never admit" or even "let me somehow say what I have to say without admitting"; it may also mean, "even on the dreadful day of judgment, when all secrets are out, let it not come from *me* that . . ." Since one ordinarily "admits" something with reluctance, as a breakthrough from elsewhere (from one's private thoughts into speech, or from another's mind into one's own discourse), the phrase suggests an effort to maintain discursive purity under duress, either from evident public experience or from private misgivings. If the opening sentence is taken as a vow—this is Booth's suggestion—then it is clearly a vow *against* a probable kind of breakdown or failure of meaning. The exclusionary force is also present, at least potentially, in "the marriage of true minds," something which may be a daily event at every village vestry or as rare as phoenix feathers. The question hangs on what it takes for minds, or love, to be "true" and on whether the marriage of minds is meant as an alternative to the marriage of bodies, goods, and futures that any ceremony includes. From the first quatrain the speaker describing this truth finds himself between an idealized concept ("the marriage of true minds") and familiar failed approximations of it.

As I noted above, love is in a paradoxical relation to knowledge here. In happier sonnets, the particular love of the young man is an object of knowledge and a source of value, consoling in difficulties: "For thy sweet love rememb'red such wealth brings, / That then I scorn to change my state with kings" (29). Sonnet 116, however, provides considerable detail about what love must set aside: "Love is not love / Which alters when it alteration finds / Or bends with the remover to remove." Yet these lines powerfully evoke the experience of a changeable love: both sound and syntax enact sensitivity to circumstance and an acceptance of one's contingency, since the words themselves change form with their grammatical situation in "alters . . . alteration" and "remover . . . remove." The sonnet touches base in collective experience here, soliciting our recognition that love is contingent, on beauty, for instance, or presence, or mutual availability. For most people this is an easy recognition, one that is based on firsthand knowledge and one for which the sonnets offer much evidence, especially in the nearby groups 92–96, in which the friend is deceptive, and 109–112, in which the poet has made himself a motley to the view, gored his own thoughts, sold cheap what is most dear, and so on. Both parties to the male-male relation in the sonnets have altered or bent with circumstances. Looking ahead to the dark-lady sonnets, of course, we find yet more confirmation of this. Sonnet 116 solicits our experience of this sort of vicissitude so thoroughly that it does not effectively exclude that experience by saying "love is not love which . . . " The marriage of true minds is familiar with love's failures, is sensitive to alteration and aware of removal, and these failures emerge as a direction to be avoided rather than as an area of experience which can be altogether excluded in favor of a transcendent alternative.

In the second quatrain, the sonnet arrives at positive statements by way of forthright denial:

> Oh no, it is an ever-fixèd mark
> That looks on tempests and is never shaken;
> It is the star to every wand'ring bark,
> Whose worth's unknown, although his height be taken.

To serve as models of love or marriage, these images need to be assimilated, to be converted into humanly available likenesses. The seamark and the polestar, apparently transcendent metaphors, are directional indicators, both literally and in their figurative action. The seamark's very name fastens it to an economy of use: by being relatively steadfast, it guides men through tempests. The polestar, which is too far off to be assigned a contingent or relational value (its "worth's unknown"), still has a clear use occasioned by vicissitude. Once again the speaker, who may be trying not to be a wandering bark, cannot appropriate the metaphors, but must situate himself between what he rejects ("love which is not love") and what he may seek to resemble or at any rate use as a model (unshakable beacons, immutable stars).[37]

In the third quatrain we see the pattern of the first two quatrains writ small. "Love's not time's fool" incorporates not only the denial of love's mortality and of love's jester-like dependence on time noted by Booth,[38] but also a denial that time regards love with intimate affectionate pity.[39] But once again these denials are immediately undercut as "rosy lips and cheeks / Within [time's] bending sickle's compass come." The sickle's dynamic enclosure of rosy lips is not only grotesquely intimate; it is also uncannily responsive, since a bending sickle can either smile or frown depending how it is held. Because beauty fades, we want to believe that love does not, but the quatrain defines this belief by negatives, presenting it as held against experience: "Love's not . . . Love alters not."[40] "Bears it out" can mean "carries on playing the part," as well as simply "endures."[41] For my argument it is also important to note that "love" apparently cannot "bear it out" unless it is in close and continual association with its opposite. Opposites of this sort need each other, since the marriage of true minds can evidently only sustain itself by situating commitment between an experienced dissatisfaction and an unrealizable perfection. Seen in this way, the evocation of such a marriage is useful for almost anyone. The sonnet leads readers to discriminate familiar failure from unreachable success and locate their own loving somewhere between these poles.

The couplet, like the sonnet's opening statement, has a clear performative aspect: we might sum up these lines by calling them a garbled vow. "If this be error and upon me proved, / I never writ, nor no man ever loved." The peculiar defensive logic is formally self-validating and hence formally empty: since we cannot read the couplet without knowing that the conclusion is false (because the sonnet exists, we know that the poet "writ"), the entire if-then proposition cannot be true unless the premise is also false. In reading the sonnet, we prove either that its claims are not erroneous or that its error cannot be proved upon the poet. In a less strictly logical way, the couplet suggests that the speaker so values the sonnet's claims that he will give up all his writing and sacrifice the collective experience of love if those claims turn out to be unfounded. But no single poet is in a position to make such universal sacrifices. In any case, as in sonnet 55, the couplet reminds us that we are reading the poem—that it was written, that it has survived, and that therefore its sentiments must have continued use. This peculiar meaning, which has grown with the poem's distance from the original context, serves as both a feature and a cause of the poem's further survival through time.

The sonnets, then, are not only preoccupied with social dynamics of human value; they propose in some detail the mechanisms of their own survival, and they do this by suggesting contingent but enduring general circumstances in which they may prove valuable by being useful. Wittgenstein's metaphors for individual certainty thus lend themselves to a general description of stabilities in the history of literature. But they cut two ways. When literary canons are reified, and especially when they are sacralized, they harden to form a rocky channel through which literary experience—and thus the reading of other less communally endorsed works—must flow. Canons at such times seem fixed and firm, and some people think them absolute. But this flow is also reshaping them, and at times they will melt, thaw, and form anew. At such times, indeed, they rise from thick deeps to be interrogated, and what seemed rock proves sand.

In the sonnets of the *longue durée* I have been discussing, the elusive particulars of Shakespeare's loves fall into general shapes which are enduringly appropriable. I have argued that this involves not an art of rising to transcendent certainties but an art of sinking to contingent stabilities, and that the sonnets appear to recognize this pragmatic difference.

Yet this argument hardly exhausts the subject. The sonnets I have discussed make the most apparently transcendent and evidently far-reaching claims for themselves, and I have ventured to generalize from them about the endurance claims readers make for the sequence as a whole. In so doing, I have said almost nothing about the dark-lady sonnets, little about the particular economic dynamic of the poet's relation to the young man, and thus little about the immediate textual matrix in which the sonnets of the *longue durée* are embedded or the historical context in which they were written—the local time-bound expectations about love and social relations that then prevailed. Value of any kind is painfully bought in the sonnets, and in concentrating on relatively optimistic poems I do not mean to suggest otherwise. Nor do I want to divert attention from what I take to be a major reason for general interest in the sonnets: the obscure glimpses they give of Shakespeare's subjectivity and of the circumstances which constrained or guided it. But the economic analysis I have made of assertions of long-term value in Shakespeare's more affirmative sonnets can readily be extended to the darker sonnets, engrossed as they are with the problem of transience, instability, and uncertainty of value. In turning to the sonnets to the dark lady, and to an explicit discussion of the major current theorist who claims that aesthetic issues are really economic ones, Barbara Herrnstein Smith, I will also be turning toward sonnets which speak more directly to local contingencies of Shakespeare's experience. In reading sonnet 138 in terms Herrnstein Smith suggests, I shall try to say something about Shakespeare's idiosyncrasies. But my particular concern in what follows is to diminish the perceived gulf between the young man and dark lady sonnets and to emphasize that the same economic or pragmatic description of evaluation can account for the value relations in both.

Wordsworth's claim that "with this key / Shakespeare unlocked his heart" may be anatomically unfashionable,[42] but the critical community continues to use the sonnets to underwrite assertions about Shakespeare's sexuality (e.g., in Joseph Pequigney's *Such Is My Love*),[43] to chart discoveries in his exploration of homosociality (Eve Sedgwick's chapter "Swan in Love" from *Between Men*),[44] or as discussed above to describe his breakthroughs toward the representation/creation of modern reflexive subjectivity (Joel Fineman and Anne Ferry). Pequigney's aside, such accounts of the sonnets are not so much claims about Shakespeare's underlying nature or covert intentions or personal disposition—a partial unpacking of what Wordsworth might mean by "his heart"—as they are claims about his productive poetic interaction with various systems of explanation or hierarchies of value he inherits, either from the specific literary tradition of praise poetry or from more generally constitutive social systems such as patriarchy. In all these cases, not excluding Pequigney's, the sonnets are made to tell a distinctively twentieth-century story of *destabilization*, and I largely agree with this story and have found these redescriptions of the sonnets and thereby of Shakespeare to be useful ones. According to this narrative, the sequence shows the breakdown of the poet's ideological assumptions about how sex should be divided from friendship, the first to be heterosexually channeled, the second homosocially, about how subjects should identify with their social situations, about how visually ascertainable binary oppositions like white/black, fair/dark, male/female, beautiful/ugly should guide one to a reliable hierarchy of value and map of desire. These ideological assumptions prove unreliable, and the resultant distress marks philosophic growth as well as personal confusion.[45]

Some kinds of historical investigation of the sequence are awkward for the argument of Fineman, which is also shared by Sedgwick, that the dark-lady sonnets represent a kind of revision, even a change in style of thought, from the young-man sonnets—that Shakespeare begins with homosocial idealization and ends in heterosexual reflexivity. Recent evidence, as summarized for instance in John Kerrigan's 1986 New Penguin edition of the sonnets,[46] suggests that sonnets 127–154 were probably written before many of sonnets 1–126. But the order of composition need not dictate the meaning of the sequence (as, if Kerrigan is right, it did not dictate its order). In any case, since I agree that in historical context the sonnets represent a destabilizing, reflexive perspective on love, praise, and human value generally, and also agree that this destabilization is particularly marked in many of sonnets 127–154, I am not the person to raise these objections. I want instead to propose that the perspective Shakespeare takes in the sonnets can be characterized in terms which I think are even more general and basic than those advanced by Fineman and Sedgwick, and that according to this categorization the dark-lady sonnets and the young-man sonnets offer the same kind of analysis of value in human circumstances.

I have discussed above the sonnets' Wittgensteinian perspective on the retention of value through time. I want now to discuss the extent to which Barbara Herrnstein Smith's recent account of an economic position, in *Contingencies of Value*, can be invoked in describing the perspective of the sonnets. Let me briefly summarize the position Herrnstein Smith presents and argues for, quoting her often aphoristic formulations as I go. Her main idea may be simply stated: there is no absolute value, and all attempts to define value with certainty as arising from fixed characteristics in the universe, the human subject, or human society always fail. Such attempts are especially prevalent in discussions of aesthetic value (and of moral value, though she makes less of this): in her view aesthetic value is *just like* economic value, in fact *is* economic value, and thus the academic defence of the temple of culture against the marketplace, though it may have political meaning, does not ever succeed in insulating art objects from the contingency of market evaluation. Aesthetics and economics are inseparable, and attempts to segregate aesthetic value (as eternal, disinterested, specially representative of human nature, or whatever) become themselves participants in the contingent circumstances affecting valuation of the objects or texts to which such values are assigned.

Herrnstein Smith's economism extends further than this, however. She sees evaluation as ubiquitous: "for responsive creatures, to exist is to evaluate."[47] And she points out, in arguments similar to those I have made above, that an economic analysis of general social value accounts both for stability *and* for instability in value according to the same theory. To be bought, praised, read, reproduced, and encouraged to survive at all, works must perform a desirable function for some set of subjects. In the case of aesthetic objects like poems or paintings, nonsurvival beyond an initial audience can usually be explained easily (needs and desires themselves are changeable, new poems and paintings keep being made in close consultation with the desires of new audiences), and the failure of an artwork to last forever need not be considered its failure really to *be* art. In the case of artworks that do survive, they survive by continuing, under the interpretation of different communities, to meet needs which will also be changing; they will eventually begin to perform the cultural functions of a "classic" simply through having endured: "Nothing endures like endurance" (*Contingencies* 50).

Herrnstein Smith stresses the "crucially relevant *continuities* between evaluative and other types of discourse" (96) and proposes that we think of communication in general not as the transmission of knowledge from an active sender to a passive receiver, but rather as a process of

> *differentially consequential interaction:* that is, an interaction in which each party acts in relation to the other differently—in different, asymmetric ways and in accord with different specific motives—and also with different consequences for each. . . . the structure of interests that motivates and governs all verbal interactions makes it inevitable that there will also be differences—sometimes very great ones—between the particular goods offered for purchase and those that the customer/thief actually makes off with, and also between the price apparently asked for those goods and what the customer/gull ends up paying. *Caveat emptor, caveat vendor.* (109)

Herrnstein Smith's formulation of what we should expect from conversation has the same de-idealizing consequences that an economic account of the production and reception of artworks has. Thus, she further argues, not only Gricean rules for proper conversation, but most of subsequent speech-act theory, deal misleadingly with human speech by ignoring the difference (and thus potential conflict) of interests, experience, vocabulary, or authority which is to be expected in social encounters. Herrnstein Smith seeks to correct such theories by providing a paradigm of human interaction which acknowledges the contingency of all factors, while tying things together by asserting the omnipresence of evaluation and of the desire on the part of subjects to maximize their own value.

This is not the same, it must quickly be said, as universalizing the profit motive or the idea of human beings as rational economic actors; Herrnstein Smith stresses the variance of particular value systems, whether those of individuals or of communities within societies. Indeed, in denying distinctions between aesthetic and economic realms, Herrnstein Smith widens the set of factors potentially taken into account in any subject's value calculations beyond the sphere of money and commodities. Potlatch, Roman suicide, and masochism are as susceptible to her enlarged form of economic analysis as shopping or flattery. She responds to Georges Bataille's presentation of apparently anti-economic practices in primitive societies with a ringing claim for the transhistorical validity of her own antitranscendent paradigm:

> all human (and not only human) activity could be seen to consist of a continuous exchange or expenditure (whether as payment, donation, sacrifice, loss, or destruction) of goods of some (but any) kind, whereby goods of some other (but, again, any) kind are secured, enhanced, or

produced. Thus, money or material provisions are expended whereby power is enlarged and status confirmed, sumptuary goods are donated or destroyed, whereby social or symbolic value is marked and maintained, bodily comfort and life are sacrificed, whereby exhilaration and glory are gained, "hours of dross" are sold to buy "terms divine," and so forth—and also, for *any* of these exchanges, vice versa: money is hoarded whereby status is risked, glory is foregone whereby comfort is secured, terms divine are sacrificed whereby hours of dross are gilded—everywhere, in every archaic tribe and "modern era," *endlessly.* (145)[48]

I do not offer this as a comprehensive account—some of the best parts of Herrnstein Smith's book are given over to replies to standard criticisms of relativism, economism, and pragmatism—but what I have said should be enough to reinforce my argument regarding the ubiquity of the contingency of value in the sonnets, from those which touch on the lastingness of aesthetic objects to those which confront the inconstancy of human attitudes. One might note here that *Contingencies of Value* begins with a discussion of sonnet 116 and uses sonnet 146 as epigraph for a key chapter (though otherwise it does not discuss Shakespeare or indeed any literary author very much) and surmise that it is no accident that Herrnstein Smith herself has moved from being professionally preoccupied with Shakespeare's sonnets to being professionally preoccupied with the contingency of value.[49] But Herrnstein Smith offers an explicit and elaborate account of an insight into the mechanisms of social value which is not only applicable to, but available in some form within, any society in which evaluative exchanges take place—that is, any society: arguably late sixteenth-century England as well as late twentieth-century North America. Following Rorty and Toulmin, I suggested in the introduction that late sixteenth-century England and late twentieth-century America may be akin in that both cultures were hospitable to skepticism about the truths provided by certainty-producing institutions. Historicizing observations such as this matter less to Herrnstein Smith, who is concerned not with any particular sociocultural moment or author but with developing a more general, logical, and practical rationale for a pragmatic economics and with justifying this as the best way to describe all evaluation everywhere.

We might now ask how Herrnstein Smith's economism explains the difference between the young-man and dark-lady sonnets, a difference that so many interpreters have proposed. As I suggested above, I see the difference as economic: the sonnets to the young man enact an affluent or generative economy of human value, and the sonnets to the dark lady enact a depressed, and consequently an exposed and

self-critical, economy of human value. Thus I characterize the instability and reflexivity of the entire sonnet sequence as an illustration of
contingency and vulnerability in erotic evaluation, and this description
does not at all depend on an imagined order of composition or on the
idea that the dark-lady sonnets represent an advance in knowledge or
experience from the young-man sonnets. The sonnets turn on themselves by describing two relations (or one complex trilateral relation)
in a variety of lights but according to two contrasting dominant moods
with respect to the availability of value, one of copious abundance (in
which the young man, given his relation to the poet and to others,
generates social value and ennobles even bad relations with him) and
one of poverty, irony, and negation (in which the dark lady, given her
relation to the poet and to others, consumes social value and casts
doubt even on the relation with the young man). The same words
or gestures often take on more or less completely transformed meanings when undertaken differently in different social circumstances.
An account of the sonnets in these terms—as both descriptions and
objects of exchange in an unstable economic system—might also
discuss Shakespeare's regular invocation of value-upholding and value-
corroding economic environments in the sequence. This is not a direction I pursue here, but one such environmental factor is precisely the
general social acceptance of the dark/fair binary opposition the poet
variously disputes and endorses as the contingencies of personal attraction move him one way and another.

To illustrate further the presence in the sequence of a pragmatic
analysis of erotic economies, here focusing on their unstable side, I
will end this chapter by discussing an unaddressed sonnet of reflection
by the poet on his relation to the dark lady.

> When my love swears that she is made of truth,
> I do believe her though I know she lies,
> That she might think me some untutored youth,
> Unlearnèd in the world's false subtleties.
> Thus vainly thinking that she thinks me young,
> Although she knows my days are past the best,
> Simply I credit her false-speaking tongue:
> On both sides thus is simple truth suppressed.
> But wherefore says she not she is unjust?
> And wherefore say not I that I am old?
> O love's best habit is in seeming trust,
> And age in love loves not to have years told.
> > Therefore I lie with her, and she with me,
> > And in our faults by lies we flattered be. (138)

Interpretation of this sonnet can and indeed must take a variety of directions, all with a family resemblance, since it is so obviously concerned with overturning expectations about meaning and relationship. Fineman, for instance, finds in it an exploration of what it means to "give the lie to my true sight" and thus, in line with his general idea of the destabilization taking place in the sonnets, says (with some local implausibility),

> By the convention of the sonneteering mode, the dark lady is as much the poet's Muse as she is his love, and so the old lover who admits he feigns his youth is equally the voice of an old poetics that "knows my days are past the best" . . . [T]he sonnet adduces a poetry as well as a desire whose "best habit" is in "seeming trust . . . " (*Shakespeare's Perjured Eye*, 166–67)

"There is," he concludes, "a transition from a poetry of praise to a poetry of epideictic paradox" (167). Thus 138 confirms Fineman's governing idea of a Lacanian fall (or rise) into linguistic reflexivity from the Platonizing visual certainties of the tradition of praise poetry.

I propose to redescribe 138 in order to avoid this dualistic contrast between nostalgically remembered certainty and an exciting but disconcerting new science of indeterminacy; that is, as Herrnstein Smith urges, I wish to distinguish discourses "not absolutely . . . by virtue of their radically opposed claims to 'truth' or 'objective validity,' but as occupying different positions along a number of relevant continua" (101). According to the economic/pragmatic idea of what both stability and instability consist of, in which the same paradigm of human exchange covers a variety of different-seeming cases successfully, we can see 138 as a sonnet which maps self-consciously an extreme case of the "differentially consequential interaction" discussed above. The sonnet shows with unusual clarity a combination of interests: the poet's interest in "seeming young" and perhaps in behaving like a young lover; the dark lady's interest in preserving the appearance of virtue with respect to the poet; the interest both evidently have in continuing the sexual relation and not rocking a boat that, at least temporarily, is going in a direction they both think (for different and doubtless asymmetrical reasons) worth maintaining or at any rate not worth disrupting.

The objectivist duality of "truth" and "lie" (as on-off states of accuracy or virtue which point to incontestable states of the world and thus to a way out of contingency) is shown increasingly in the poem to be ill-suited to this particular situation, a poor description of how language and gesture mediate the two participants' sets of purposes. The moral complexity of language users is better described by the kind of economic description we get in "simply I credit her false-speaking tongue" and by references to governing contingencies of value and desire: "O love's best habit is in seeming trust, / And age in love loves not to have years told." Finally the lie/lie pun in the couplet, like the assonantal pairing of "simple truth" with "seeming trust," can acknowledge a kind of kinship rather than point up a sharp paradox. How can we distinguish truth from agreement? How can we claim for sexual union a complete meeting of minds in which dissimulation has no part? Is this sonnet not simply an extreme, and thus revealing, case of any love arrangement, which will involve compromise, the negotiation of asymmetrical desires and commitments, and the recognition of asymmetrical gains? Obviously here we are dealing with a relation in which the stabilizing contingencies seem frail and the destabilizing ones strong; but we are not dealing with a different kind of relation, nor, in my opinion (pace Fineman), with a different kind of language use, from those we find in the sonnets to the young man. Rather, as I have already suggested, we are dealing with a poor and self-critical local *economy* as opposed to the (on the whole) rich and generative economy of sonnets 1–126.

Although the sonnets of the *longue durée* sacrifice subjective particularity to appropriable form, other sonnets to the young man as well as to the dark lady amply suggest, too, Shakespeare's fascination with (and resentment of) his own obsession—whether sexual obsession in relation to the dark lady or a more comprehensive homosocial obsession in relation to the young man. There is a difference between poems about short-term and long-term contingencies, obviously, but both illustrate what it is like to live with an awareness of contingency. The obsessions and the awareness are, in useful terms recently proposed by David Simpson, at once "idiosyncratic" and "intersubjective" effects—thus suitable for explorations both of Shakespeare's personal particularity and the particularity of the intersection of historical subcultures he inhabited.[50] As it happens, these knit-together obsessions remain phenomenona of importance in contemporary intersubjectivity and address the idiosyncrasies of many of us directly. Moreover, our intellectual culture as a whole seems to be moving toward a deeper awareness of the contingency of its structures and beliefs. The project of poetic self-generalization I have described gains interest, rather than losing it, from our recognition that Shakespeare is generalizing about particulars that for a variety of reasons fascinate us.

The sonnets are consistent with the plays in charting the powers and perils of an antifoundationalist, untranscendent, economic or pragmatic idea of the creation and loss of value. At the same time the focus of some of the sonnets on certitude enables them to be to some extent self-conserving, in that they offer an argument about how they might last; they inhere because they lend themselves to the continual recreation of kinds of experience which are deep in our cultural matrix. They float stably in a very thick liquid—in as certain a situation as the world affords. Shakespeare's plays also touch recurrently on possibilities for endurance and affiliate themselves with with lasting texts by other authors (a fact that I address explicitly in chapters 6 and 7), but the more prevalent concern of the rest of this book is with the plays' examination of the value-conferring environments in which all human agents sink or swim.

3

Dramatic Pragmatism in
Hamlet

ళ

Theater, not lyric poetry, was Shakespeare's primary mode of interaction with the market of his time. The following chapter argues in general terms for the appropriateness of a contemporary pragmatist vocabulary in describing theater and what Shakespeare did (or took part in doing) within it. It then becomes possible, using this vocabulary, to offer a reading of *Hamlet* that focuses on the crucial pragmatic issue of the constitution of individual agents in discursive environments. Theater emerges in *Hamlet* as a market where ideas or forms of life can be evaluated, tested, adapted, or condemned. In this way, Shakespeare may be regarded as meditating on social markets as arenas of competing discourses as well as of competing persons. When thus redescribed, *Hamlet* not only takes up but offers a way to renegotiate the conflict between a residual humanism and a currently dominant Foucauldian poststructuralism.

Theory, Performance, Pragmatism

> Truth in acting, defined as coherence within the role, leads us to Stanislavsky's linking of truth and belief. "Truth cannot be separated from belief, nor belief from truth" may seem dangerous advice to give for dealing with a treacherous world, but "in the part" or "on the stage" (as he always added or implied), this is curiously the case. . . . Stanislavsky was notorious in the Art Theatre for calling from the auditorium during rehearsals, "I don't believe it." (David Richard Jones, *Great Directors at Work*)

> The true is the name of whatever proves itself to be good in the way of belief. (William James, *Pragmatism*)

> "Let it work." (Hamlet, in *Hamlet*)

These epigraphs suggest an affinity between theatrical practice and American pragmatism, a kind of philosophical writing which has increasingly influenced literary theory and counts today either as a strand of theory or as an oppositional alternative to it. Both performers and pragmatists focus on what works, on what can be made visible, and on the way human purposes pan out or display their values as they encounter diverse circumstances. Pragmatic theater is not so much a social mirror as an instrument for social investigation. Theater does not simply show audiences themselves, it explains them to themselves by allowing them to witness and to partake in an experiment in the active evaluation of ideas, habits, and institutions. It makes economies—theirs and others'—visible. This orientation toward the evaluation in action of ideas is a hallmark of pragmatism.

Pragmatists reject the Platonic distinction between truth—objective and scientific or transcendent—and opinion, and deny that any truth-claim can be founded in ways which make it immune to changes in climates of opinion. Pragmatists are antifoundationalist, even, in Richard Rorty's phrase, "anti-representationalist,"[1] and an alternative to a foundational mode of adjudicating truth-claims is, I want to suggest, a theatrical one, one which turns on the capacity of a given speaker or event to please, persuade, or change an audience. John Dewey argued—and contemporary pragmatists follow him in this—that the worth of ideas or institutions becomes known and may be gauged through evaluating their practical effects: "What is needed is intelligent examination of the consequences that are actually effected by inherited institutions and customs, in order that there may be intelligent consideration of the ways in which they are to be intentionally modified in behalf of generation of different consequences."[2] This is what theater does or can do, especially when a public theater (as Shakespeare's largely was) is conceived as a literal arena of public evaluation, thriving only as it pleases a public. Shakespeare's theater, shaped by the contingencies of performance, is a peculiarly powerful species of pragmatic social "therapy" (a term to which I will return). Its attempts to show its audiences themselves are unmatched in effect.

Boldness, however, is required when attributing any philosophy to Shakespeare, whether or not it is antimetaphysical. Most traditional authorities who have broached the subject have praised, or occasionally blamed, Shakespeare for not having a nameable philosophy, seen in traditional terms as a set of essentialist commitments. Thus Coleridge on myriad-mindedness, Keats on negative capability, Arnold on Shakespeare's freedom from our questions, and Eliot on Shakespeare's inferiority to Dante. To call Shakespeare a pragmatist (and mean something more, or other, than that he was not philosophical) is also, as I mentioned in the introduction to this book, anachronistic. Though Bacon used the word "pragmaticall" in something like an anticipation of its modern sense, Shakespeare never uses any version of the word;

its philosophic use was inaugurated by Peirce in the 1870s and rescued from oblivion by William James in 1901 to describe the philosophy then being vigorously put forward by F. C. S. Schiller and himself. Pragmatism was further developed by John Dewey, of course, and Dewey's thought dominated American philosophy in the first quarter of this century, remaining, notably in the work of Richard Rorty, highly influential in revised versions today. Cornel West's recent account of modern pragmatism suggests how close it nonetheless is to the theatrical situation:

> American pragmatism is less a philosophical tradition putting forward solutions to perennial problems in the Western philosophical conversation initiated by Plato and more a continuous cultural commentary or set of interpretations that attempt to explain America to itself at a particular historical moment.
>
> The pragmatists' preoccupation with power, provocation, and personality—in contrast, say, to grounding knowledge, regulating instruction, and promoting tradition—signifies an intellectual calling to administer to a confused populace caught in the whirlwinds of societal crisis . . .[3]

Shakespeare's theater—and, indeed, theater generally—attempts to explain the audience to itself in much this provocative way, and so it becomes interpretively useful to describe theater as a pragmatic institution.

If there is a family resemblance between how theater works and how pragmatists think a nonmetaphysical philosophy should function, there is also an even closer relationship between the kinds of hostility pragmatism and theatricality arouse. Theater has, of course, endured millenia of suspicion and abuse from foundationalists, starting with Plato himself. The antitheatrical prejudice, insofar as it is philosophic, is in large part philosophy's fear (a fear so deep and *toujours déjà* that it might be felt to be constitutive of philosophy) of pragmatism and of social practices which embody it, as theater does. Plato's objections to Homer and the tragedians are intimately related to his objections to the Sophists: sophists fail to commit themselves to the vital distinction between *nomos* and *logos*, between customary opinion and truth; and poets fail consistently to endorse or confine themselves to the disciplinary practices that might make this vital distinction flourish.[4] Pragmatists repudiate this distinction, and theater and poetry undermine it. This root connection between pragmatism and theatricality has not, however, to my knowledge been explored extensively by either pragmatists or performance critics.

To the extent that theater purveys knowledge, it does so pragmatically through dramatic action: ideas and public institutions—social, philosophic, religious, or whatever—all exist in theater as mediated by dramatic action. This claim about the theatrical production of communal opinion is well illustrated by Brecht's practice as a director. As David Jones writes:

> Brecht spent hours on . . . any activity that materialized a character's relation to the world. And these hours were spent not talking but trying: "Brecht would say that he wanted no discussions in rehearsal—it would have to be tried."
> . . . If Stanislavsky's rehearsal cliché was "I don't believe it," Brecht's was "What's the position?" and it was just as revealing of his nature. He might ask "What's the position" about subjects as diverse as emotion and class relations, but his question always required a physical response. How could actors make a particular point physically, so that it became apparent or visible on the stage?[5]

Brecht here makes explicit—as part of the esprit de corps of his company—a potential that inheres in the theatrical situation. Theater presents social "truths" (what Brecht, stressing their contingency, called "positions") with emphasis on the capacity of drama to judge them by making visible the surrounding economy, to draw out their consequences, and to make their social value obvious. Any "truth" that we learn from Brecht will be a pragmatic one, something that we are persuaded is "good in the way of belief, and good, too, for definite, assignable reasons," to quote James again.[6] Brecht, of course, also had a value-laden explanatory theory, Marxism, to help him decide both what positions were and what they were worth, but his theater, like Shakespeare's, holds up ideology for judgment even as it may at times serve it. Brecht himself comments that "an epic way of acting isn't equally valid for every classical work. It seems to be most easily applicable, i.e. to hold most promise of results, in works like Shakespeare's. . . . It depends on their attitude to their social function: representation of reality with a view to influencing it."[7] Shakespeare's capacity to bring abstraction up against an event or situation which tests it suggests that he also uses the play as an instrument both for "influence" and investigation. Discourse is actually tested in his plays, as I argue below about *Hamlet*, by the uses agents make of it, or the consequences in which discursive situations enmesh agents.

If dramatic action is peculiarly pragmatic, so also are the two most influential modern accounts of the philosophy of acting, Stanislavsky's and Brecht's. Stanislavsky divides plays into a set of nested human purposes or objectives whose practical accomplishment the actor-as-character desires. Ideas in the theater are conveyed to us by way of the particular purposes they serve. Brecht insists more globally that theatrical practice must make manifest the consequences of operating social assumptions and that, unless it affects its audience, it is doing nothing. (One might cite Dewey here: "all moral judgments are about changes to be made."[8]) Those consequences must include pleasure, as Brecht acknowledged to an ever-greater extent during his career. But complex pleasures include an awareness of changes to be made, as he points out—using suspect Platonic distinctions—in the last paragraph of his *Short Organum for the Theatre:*

> our representations must take second place to what is represented, men's life together in society; and the pleasure felt in their perfection must be converted into the higher pleasure felt when the rules emerging from this life in society are treated as imperfect and provisional. In this way the theatre leaves its spectators productively disposed even after the spectacle is over.[9]

Both Stanislavski and Brecht want a theater brimming with purposes which in their working out enable us to evaluate ideas, institutions, and personal strategies.

The views of Stanislavski and Brecht could be distinguished (though by no means absolutely) by their different emphases on whether an audience *believes* a successful ("true" in Stanislavski's terms) theatrical performance, or whether it *changes* or *learns* in response to a successful performance (the point of Brecht's A-effect).[10] Yet even these different ideas about moral or political impact echo a central dialogue within American pragmatism: James, Quine, and Rorty, for instance, are somewhat more like Stanislavski in emphasising the way the intellectual habits of a community encourage stabilities of belief we call truths; Dewey or West are more like Brecht in being committed to the necessity of mobilizing the discursive community toward change or self-radicalization. The differences between these thinkers are differences primarily in the "degree of lean" in their attitudes toward social change—in the degree to which they discuss relative stability, on the one hand, or relative change, on the other, and in the ratio between reassurance and confrontation they offer.

The parallels between theater and pragmatic evaluative processes are further indicated by the theatrically oriented criticism which has recently attained prominence, if not dominance, among Shakespeareans and which seeks to remind everyone that plays have their most authentic being in a space of action structured by a set of practical circumstances that readers of plays can only incompletely imagine.[11] It reminds us, that is, that to a reader, two salient features of a play text—the agency of particular characters as they speak and the textuality of the whole—are contained and nuanced in theatrical action by other structuring factors or aimed-at effects. This is not to say that characters and texts do not matter on the stage, but they operate dynamically as actors (and agents) and as uttered speech (and discourse) rather than as static representational portraits and unconditioned aesthetic wholes. The context of human purposes involved is both richer and tighter in performance than it seems in the study.

Given the strength of the parallel I have been suggesting, Shakespeare might seem condemned to pragmatism by career choice, as, say, an investment banker is willy-nilly a practical capitalist or an archbishop a practical theist. This is true, I think, but there are plenty of playwrights among Shakespeare's contemporaries who articulate big ideas in their plays without tracing their practical consequences very far or at all. Such ideas may exist purely as covers for undignified local motives in the character who expresses them (this might almost be said to be Jonson's system for incorporating intellectual materials in his comedies) or may simply float into plays in no precise relation to the working out of their action. Part of Shakespeare's excellence, indeed, may be captured in the observation that notions in his plays receive a particularly rigorous working-out in action, however difficult it may be when the dust has settled to describe what the precise practical consequences of each have turned out to be. Indeed, the famous comments from Coleridge, Keats, Arnold, and Eliot alluded to above (comments which could easily be multiplied were one to survey Shakespearean criticism on this matter) about Shakespearean impartiality or negative capability or lack of a definite philosophy are, I would suggest, comments which.approve or disapprove of Shakespeare's willingness to let thought-experiments take their course without overt reference to extradramatic certainties that could put a stop to them or impose a predetermined shape on them.

It would be romantic exaggeration to say that *no* social certainties appear in Shakespeare's plays which are not acted upon by them, and thus subjected to their critical experiment, but it is hard to find any which are not. (This is another way of saying that it is hard to fix Shakespeare ideologically without ignoring areas of critical experimentalism in his work.[12]) Shakespeare's plays refuse the Kantian distinctions between a world of ideas, a world of practical action, and a world of aesthetic experiences, distinctions which have underlain much of the critical thinking about his plays; in this they are far better suited to the political emphases of contemporary criticism. Yet they also resist the heuristic subordination of art and entertainment to the political. Everything works on everything else in a complex economy of mutual influence.

Individual persons in such an economy, however, will obviously emerge with very different senses of the meaning of the whole, depending on where they are placed; in a class-divided economy, for example, some have leisure to contemplate such wholes, while others grunt and sweat under a weary life. Thus far I have been addressing the pragmatic tendency in drama to test ideas against action, and I have suggested that the foundationalist attack on theater focuses on the same targets as its attack on pragmatism: neither theater nor pragmatism offers up truths in the decontextualized form that foundationalists seek. I move now to a vocabulary useful to both a performance model of theater and pragmatic philosophy: that of discourse and agency. In the contained spaces of theater, actor-agents must haggle not only with each other for recognition, influence, belief, and so forth, but also with the constraints and possibilities of competing discourses. A discussion of this dynamic in *Hamlet* will enable me, first, to address a current theoretical debate about the status of the subject in social discourses and, second, to use a pragmatic stance toward agency to reread *Hamlet* as a useful experiment in the possibilities of therapeutic (that is, both investigative and influential) action. I begin with some general observations about discourse and agency as critical categories.

Discourse, Agency, and Therapy in *Hamlet*

The traditions of Shakespeare criticism, as of literary criticism generally, have in the past enormously privileged individual agency, that is, powers of responsible intentional action vested in persons regarded as the initiators of their acts. Character criticism celebrated the presence in Shakespeare's plays of convincingly real people choosing their fates in convincingly real milieux. Thematic criticism celebrated the wholeness of particular plays as integrated products and thus the integrity of Shakespeare's poetic acts. Textual criticism sought to purify the lines of transmission from Shakespeare's workplace to the modern page in order to let his words be as uncorruptedly his own as possible. Since unviolated wholeness and unalienated freedom are key terms in the traditional (though not the pragmatist) construction of the modern liberal bourgeois subject, and at the same time key qualities of the finished masterpiece under modern humanist traditions of literary description, it is easy to see valorised agency as a bridge between the explicit politics of social liberalism and the often tacit politics of humanist literary criticism.

One clear if partial way to describe the impact of theory on Shakespeare criticism in the last twenty years is to say that literary theory has consistently exposed, challenged, discredited, incriminated, and rendered hokey and passé the largely unselfconscious reliance on individual autonomy as a value category in previous scholarship. I use this array of verbs to try to describe a shift which is partly the result of important and powerful arguments but partly the unargued product of change in fashion, interest, and attention among a community of taste-makers. This critique of agency is by now extremely familiar, although it is rarely phrased as a critique of agency per se. As part of a general demystifying effort, the autonomy of the self, the preeminence of the rational mind, and the freedom of individual choice have come under attack as deconstructable or self-deconstructing modes of stabilization and centralization which are tied to the maintenance of suspect political structures. Under this critique, the "I" which subjugates verbs is a grammatical function; the "I" which knows is a function of the field of knowledge. Neither literature nor philosophy can work out from what man essentially or individually *is* to what human life ought to be or is capable of being, because the surrounding fields of discourse, power, and knowledge are prior to the human subject.

In what follows I am going to take familiarity with the main lines of antihumanist argument pretty much for granted. The terms of this argument can, in my view should, and to some extent already are being renegotiated in pragmatic terms. Let me begin by offering some definitions of the key terms in the title of this section, associating them in an allusive rather than argumentative way with Foucault, Bakhtin, and Freud.

By "discourse" I mean the collection of preexistent constitutive linguistic social and cultural modes, forms, or codes, themselves evolving and interacting, which surround, condition, and interpret the activity of subjects. Language is the most embracing and general of these, but I want to call institutions, systems of classification and coercion, and so on "discursive formations." I associate a strong view of the dominance of discourses with Foucault's lifelong attempt to rearticulate the human sciences in terms of networks of power/knowledge and of discursive institutions, which classify, divide, define, consign, and confine—which in short determine the conditions of meaning and activity, making certain techniques of selfhood available to some and denying them to others. It is relevant to note that Foucault says "it is not power but the subject which is the general theme in my work."[13] Bakhtin nudges us closer than Foucault, however, to a pragmatic definition of discourse. He also maps society in discursive terms, but espouses a looser view of the dominance of discourse. Bakhtin denies the autonomy of individuals with less emphasis on the ubiquity of constraint and more on the omnipresence of dialogic encounters: "A person has no internal sovereign territory, he is wholly and always on the boundary; looking inside himself he looks *into the eyes of another* or *with the eyes of another.*"[14] Bakhtin describes human consciousness as a kind of boundary condition between areas of discourse which are composed of many acts of volition, and sees human selfhood as a form of answering and as thus taking responsibility for one's responses to surrounding discourse. He recognizes the immense variety of discursive habits and communities, though his map of them is simpler as well as less deterministic than Foucault's; Bakhtin celebrates sociolinguistic diversity as something like an index of available possibility even under conditions of monological imposition.

"Agency" has traditionally been thought of as the power of individual persons to take meaningful action in the world. But "agency" has reemerged in recent theorizing about the constraints on the subject, where it is construed as the position a subject must take up between contradictory discourses. My initial description of agency in this section as "the powers of responsible intentional action vested in persons" suggests how easy it used to be to talk about meaningful action in the world and how much harder it becomes in a discursive or textualized environment for the subject. No one is incapable of making a mental switch to such a vocabulary of responsible intentional action, and few are the people who do not at some level (when morally condemning or praising other human beings they know personally, for instance) resort to it.[15] My purpose here in reintroducing agency is not, however, to reinstate a humanist vocabulary, but rather to point to a need to negotiate between extreme stances on this concept.

In "therapy," finally, we have a term which takes as its definition the goal of mediation between the impaired agency of the individual, now regarded as a patient, and the general and particular discursive conditions in which the patient acts or fails to act. Invoking Freud here, I should note that both Bakhtin and Foucault offer critiques of Freud's general simplification of the discursive situation of the classic patient, and that Freud's legacy has itself been divided between object-relations analysts (mostly practitioners) who aim to strengthen agency in their patients and Lacanians (often theorists) who focus rather on the inevitable fractures in discursive construction of the subject. "Normalization" is a goal for the first group and a suspect idea for the second. But in what follows I will be using "therapy" in ways that stress neither a goal of stabilized "normality" nor of fissured consciousness, but rather a dynamic process of mutual reflection and challenge between agents and the discursive situations in which they find themselves.

I realize that these definitions may sound Humpty-Dumptyish in their tendentiousness. But they allow me to advance a theoretical argument succinctly: we have by now reached a point in theoretical debate where discourse and agency need not be polemically opposed but should rather be recognized as collaborative factors in any useful description of the situation of the human subject or person. The critique of essentialist humanism that was emergent in the early 1970s is now dominant; what was dominant is now residual and terribly anxious (though still strong). I want to argue for a qualified reemergence of agency as a valorized category. This is, again, partly what I think should happen and partly what I think is, generally speaking, happening already.[16]

As my discussion of *Hamlet* will suggest, I believe that reference also to models of the theater as performance can help us toward an empowering description of agency. In the following pages, I read *Hamlet* as a meditation on the balance between the power of circumambient discourses and the capacity of an exemplary (and, in this case, privileged) human subject to find his way therapeutically among them toward a pragmatic kind of agency. As I make this transition, I might add that theories of agency have peculiar relevance in discussions of Renaissance artists, since from Burckhardt on, students of the period have represented it as a time of enhanced personal agency—as we have recently been reminded by William Kerrigan and Gordon Braden—even as the impossibility of sorting out individual agency from discourse has been a continuing theme for Stephen Greenblatt.[17] Readings specifically of *Hamlet* have, however, focused as much on the protagonist's "inwardness" as on the boundaries he sees impeding his agency. So my analysis will begin by arguing that interiority in *Hamlet* is not and cannot be separated from the exterior discourses to which it is answerable and in terms of which it finds expression.

ع

Hamlet's congeniality to the nineteenth century and continuing hold on the twentieth may possibly be explained by its exploration of the boundaries of sanity and its treatment of the problems involved in fathoming the interior of one's own mind and in imagining the interior mind of another. In no other Shakespeare play is there such concentration on hidden interiors of the mind and the way puzzles about them seem to empty out the world.

Coleridge remarks that Hamlet is "a person, in whose view the external world, and all its incidents and objects, were comparatively dim" until "reflected in the mirror of his mind," and goes on to note that "such a mind as Hamlet's is near akin to madness."[18] While it is wrong (in ways I will shortly discuss) to make such confident distinctions between mental life and the external world—and, as Bradley noted, this comment makes the hyper-active Hamlet sound incongruously like the dreamy addict Coleridge—it does remind us how much of the action of the play is devoted to characters' attempts to determine the hidden mental life of others.[19] Claudius pursues Hamlet, and Hamlet pursues Claudius and interrogates Gertrude. In each case the interrogator is after "that within which passes show" (1.2.85),[20] that is, an inner secret: Claudius seeks that "something in [Hamlet's] soul / O'er which his melancholy sits on brood" (3.1.166); Hamlet sets a trap for "the conscience of the king" (2.2.601) and exposes "the inmost part" (3.4.19) of Gertrude, her "very soul," where she sees "such . . . spots / As will not leave their tinct" (3.4.90). Influential aphorisms of interiority spring from the play: "a mote it is to trouble the mind's eye" (1.1.115); "the pale cast of thought" (3.1.85); "the heart of my mystery" (3.2.356). Moreover, the play repeatedly testifies to the uncontrollability of mental life, its weird sources, its unavailability for rational interrogation. Hamlet says he "could be bounded by a nutshell and count myself a king of infinite space—were it not that I have bad dreams" (2.2.254). Claudius tells Laertes apologetically, as one male to another, that without knowing why he finds Gertrude "so conjunctive to my life and soul," he could not move without her (4.7.14). Claudius is driven to meditate on the unavailability of proper intentions when he cannot command himself to repent, and he and the Player-King both dilate, in famous speeches, on the vulnerability of human intention to time.

Insofar as this interiority is taken (as it is by Coleridge) to constitute a privileged internal space, it is easy to turn on it in light of the discursivity theories I have sketched above. After all, the entities having these putative interiors are textual: none of these interiors remains inside (else we would not know about them); most are produced by well-defined discourses (e.g., Claudius's inability to repent, which arises from theological knowledge that he cannot "be pardon'd and retain th'offence" [3.3.56], or Hamlet's self-reproaches which stem from the family-vengeance ethic invoked by the Ghost); and several interiority effects are locally contingent, such as Gertrude's soul-spots, which seem more produced than disclosed by Hamlet's moral discourse in the closet scene.

The play's fascination with interior life is thus also a fascination with the inseparability of interiority from discursive context. Hamlet resolves to "speak daggers" to Gertrude but to use none (3.2.387); after confronting her he is urged by the Ghost to "step between her and her fighting soul" (3.4.113); and in each case he does so by offering Gertrude discursive portraits of her own behavior. He holds up a mirror to her, he says, but it is one which strongly recontextualizes her in terms of loyalties she wishes to forget and Hamlet intensely remembers: "You are the Queen, your husband's brother's wife . . ." (3.4.14).

This last observation, however, allows us to move from a description of the play's alertness to the oppositional relations between interiority and discourse to a discussion of the operation of agency within discursive contexts. The play shows Hamlet in the process of discovery or acceptance of his own characteristic mode of agency: he learns to show other people what they are doing by demonstrating to them what discursive fields they have entered, how they can plausibly be described, what script they are following. At times this involves mirrors and thus the fiction of mechanical representation ("You go not till I set you up a glass" [3.4.18]; "the purpose of playing . . . to hold . . . the mirror up to nature" [3.2.20]), but usually it takes more dramatic or didactic forms. Thus Hamlet to Guildenstern:

> Will you play upon this pipe?
> . . . Why, look you now, how unworthy a thing you make of me. You would play upon me, you would seem to know my stops, you would pluck out the heart of my mystery, you would sound me from my lowest note to the top of my compass; and there is much music, excellent voice, in this little organ, yet cannot you make it speak. 'Sblood, do you think I am easier to be played on than a pipe? Call me what instrument you will, though you fret me, you cannot play upon me. (3.2.341)

Hamlet creates a little play in which Guildenstern must confess his incompetence, then interprets the example for him, saying in effect: "this is what you are doing; surely you cannot like it." Occasionally Hamlet's moral portraiture affirms the value of its object: "Horatio, thou art e'en as just a man / As e'er my conversation cop'd withal" (3.2.54). More usually, however, it is satirical, as in the elaborate interactive mimicry of Osric, in which Hamlet temporarily adopts the discourse of foppery to confront Osric with self-comparisons (5.2.80–180). Often Hamlet makes it clear that whomever he is mirroring has fallen victim to a discursive stereotype, in some cases an explicitly textual one:

> POLONIUS: What is the matter, my lord?
> HAMLET: Between who?
> POLONIUS: I mean the matter that you read, my lord.
> HAMLET: Slanders, sir. For the satirical rogue says here that old men have grey beards, that their faces are wrinkled, their eyes purging thick amber and plum-tree gum, and that they have a plentiful lack of wit, together with most weak hams. (2.2.193)

The same thing happens when Hamlet faces Laertes over Ophelia's grave, and shows him by angry parody what a mechanically exaggerated histrionic mode Laertes has entered:

> Woo't weep, woo't fight, woo't fast, woo't tear thyself,
> Woo't drink up eisel, eat a crocodile?
>   . . . Nay, an thou'lt mouth,
> I'll rant as well as thou. (5.1.270)

Instances could be multiplied to demonstrate Hamlet's preoccupation with a kind of representation which involves reenactment for others of their being as Hamlet sees it, accentuating the extent to which *they* are caught in a discursive field that predetermines meaning and value and thus makes their agency illusory. The nunnery scene, where Hamlet advises Ophelia to escape from the deformative discourses of male desire and female provocation, offers a particularly interesting instance. It follows the "To be or not to be" soliloquy—itself a double meditation on the discursive environment's control over the ordinary male agent (obviously not entirely to be identified with Prince Hamlet himself), who can neither live as he wishes nor die when he likes, bound in as he is by class ("Th' oppressor's wrong, the proud man's contumely"), institutions ("the law's delay, / The insolence of office"), and a suicide-inhibiting "conscience" that consists partly of "the dread of something after death" reinforced by religious discourse (3.1.56–88).[21] Ophelia enters, then, a situation in which Hamlet is focused on the subject's entrapment in determining discourses. When she confronts him with past actions, he denies his own agency:

> OPHELIA: My lord, I have remembrances of yours
>   That I have longed long to redeliver.
>   I pray you now receive them.
> HAMLET: No, not I.
>   I never gave you aught. (3.1.92)

When Ophelia perseveres, invoking her own conventional moral discourse, Hamlet responds by exploring the disjunction of two discursive systems both of which Ophelia tries to inhabit:

OPHELIA: Take these again; for to the noble mind
  Rich gifts wax poor when givers prove unkind.
  There, my lord.
HAMLET: Ha, ha! Are you honest?
OPHELIA: My lord?
HAMLET: Are you fair?
OPHELIA: What means your lordship?
HAMLET: That if you be honest and fair, your honesty should admit no discourse to your beauty. (3.1.100)

Hamlet here invokes as separate discursive codes two attributes Ophelia would surely acknowledge (were it not that her modesty forces dissimulation): the beauty which engages male desire and the chastity which maintains social decorum. Ophelia's beauty alters those around her by evoking the deforming discourse of masculine desire, a discourse which made Hamlet into something other than himself (as both Laertes and Polonius warned Ophelia earlier), and which in turn, Hamlet says, "will . . . transform honesty from what it is to a bawd" (3.1.111). What is confusing here—certainly it confuses Ophelia, and it seems also to confuse most actors, who bluster their way through the scene by becoming very angry at Ophelia without being sure why—is that Hamlet is both condemning and not condemning Ophelia and condemning and not condemning himself. This happens because what he is talking about is the discursive control which preempts agency, so that it both is and is not Hamlet who loved Ophelia and both is and is not Ophelia who instigates male desire:[22]

HAMLET: I did love you once.
OPHELIA: Indeed, my lord, you made me believe so.
HAMLET: You should not have believed me; for virtue cannot so inoculate our old stock but we shall relish of it. I loved you not.
OPHELIA: I was the more deceived.
HAMLET: Get thee to a nunnery. Why, wouldst thou be a breeder of sinners? (3.1.115)

Only in a nunnery will Ophelia be free of the deformations wrought by male desire. On this reading we must accept the arguments of Harold Jenkins that "nunnery" primarily means "convent," though if we assume that Hamlet puns on the historically questionable sense of "brothel," he might be paraphrased as saying, "either remove yourself from male desire entirely (in a convent) or be entirely its creature (in a brothel)."[23] Male desire is seen here not merely as sinful individual proclivities (the "relish" of "our old stock" [3.1.118]) but as a circumambient discourse which can enter and transform any consciousness and reinterpret any action: "be thou as chaste as ice, as pure as snow, thou shalt not escape calumny" (3.1.137).

Hamlet goes on to list the various infectious tendencies which either surround or inhabit him, or both:

> I am myself indifferent honest, but yet I could accuse me of such things that it were better my mother had not borne me. I am very proud, revengeful, ambitious, with more offences at my beck than I have thoughts to put them in, imagination to give them shape, or time to act them in. (3.1.122)

The weird oscillation of inner and outer "offences" here can only be understood, I think, as Hamlet's recognition of the submergence of the moral self in a complex economy whose discursive currents may at any moment sweep it in any of several directions, making it lustful, vengeful, ambitious, or whatever.

In his scene with Ophelia, then, as elsewhere, Hamlet continues his habit of confronting other characters with a representation of what they are doing, but in this case the result is a complex and confusing map of the discursive economy which shapes and controls sexual desire, a map which may partly locate Ophelia for blame but mainly accuses the system of gender relations in which she is enmeshed, and which Hamlet urges her to escape. "To a nunnery, go—and quickly too" (3.1.141). When we last see her in the play she is, however, yet more completely a creature of erotic discourses, singing sexually suggestive songs and handing out flowers.

Most of Hamlet's representations are more in his control than this. The play within the play provides an obviously central case, which underscores the closeness of Hamlet's technique to that of a dramatist. But as my account of the nunnery scene suggests, Hamlet sees the world as full of such discursive portraiture, and it tells not only on others but on himself. Fortinbras's march through Denmark leads him to comment on how all occasions do inform against him, in the image of Laertes' grief he sees the portraiture of his own, and in the first player's emotion during the Pyrrhus speech he sees, again, a reproachful portrait of his own incapacity to force his soul to his conceit. This particular case deserves more detailed discussion.

> O what a rogue and peasant slave am I!
> Is it not monstrous that this player here,

But in a fiction, in a dream of passion,
Could force his soul so to his own conceit
That from her working all his visage wann'd,
Tears in his eyes, distraction in his aspect,
A broken voice, and his whole function suiting
With forms to his conceit? And all for nothing!
For Hecuba!
What's Hecuba to him, or he to her,
That he should weep for her? (2.2.544)

Hamlet admires the player for integration—for an ability to enter his role entirely, feel and project appropriate feelings, and move others to feel them. This is paradoxical, given Hamlet's earlier disavowal of "actions that a man might play," and it represents a discovery: that full theatricality, willing embracement of an external discursive script, may provide as complete a self as the full agency Hamlet has idealized in his god-like, violent, utterly sincere, and very imaginary father.

But in his soliloquy Hamlet himself seems capable neither of primitive agency nor of Stanislavskian identification with a role, as he experiments with several discursive identities which might express his predicament—first the coward whose bodily integrity is violated by everyone, then the ranting stage revenger, bent on violence. (Note how the distinction between mental interior and external world shows its artificiality as Hamlet plays with theatricality, but cannot find a particular expressive role.) He moves quickly from hypothesizing about his inner "self" to exploring its outer consequences (running through a discursive portrait of cowardice):

Am I a coward?
Who calls me villain, breaks my pate across,
Plucks off my beard and blows it in my face,
Tweaks me by the nose, gives me the lie i'th' throat
As deep as to the lungs—who does me this?
Ha!
'Swounds, I should take it: for it cannot be
But I am pigeon-liver'd and lack gall
To make oppression bitter, or ere this
I should ha' fatted all the region kites
With this slave's offal. (2.2.566)

He then attempts a dramatic reintegration of himself by adopting the discursive behavior of the revenger to which, however, he cannot "force his soul": "Bloody, bawdy villain! / Remorseless, treacherous, lecherous, kindless villain!" (2.2.576)

Finally, though, Hamlet recognizes that what has just happened to him—the momentary destabilization of his own personality in the face of the player's strong enactment of Pyrrhus, Priam, and Hecuba (which shames Hamlet because it is *interactive* for Hamlet in ways the player does not know)—can be arranged for others, and that instead of trying to pin himself to some simple essence of character, he should exploit the deconstructibility of the characters around him, their vulnerability to immediate discursive context, their insecure or shifting agency within the shared economies of moral discourse.

> —I have heard
> That guilty creatures sitting at a play
> Have, by the very cunning of the scene,
> Been struck so to the soul that presently
> They have proclaim'd their malefactions,
> For murder, though it have no tongue, will speak
> With most miraculous organ. I'll have these players
> Play something like the murder of my father
> Before mine uncle. (2.2.584)

In so doing Hamlet will tent to the quick not only his uncle but also his father's ghost, and the speech thus marks a large step toward casting off the paralysing sense of filial inadequacy and inferiority which has inhibited Hamlet up to this point. He underlines the philosophic complexity of the compromise between agency and discourse he has arrived at here by the wonderful pragmatic comment, "I'll have grounds / More relative than this" (2.2.600); that is, I will cease trying to anchor my behavior on either inner or outer certainties, and instead will seek to ground it on observation, probability, morality, desire, and so forth.[24] This is not the first striking anticipation of modern pragmatic and economic diction in the play, incidentally, merely a culminating example of it; Hamlet summed up his initial malaise by saying "How weary, stale, flat, and *unprofitable* / Seem to me all the *uses* of this world" (1.2.133, my emphases).

I am arguing, then, that Hamlet's peculiar mode of agency—one he gradually comes to accept in the course of the play—consists of the overt manipulation of discourses to produce interactive portraits which will, he hopes, reform the agency of others. He accepts that human beings have only a set of discursive shows to make for each other, some more effective, lasting, comprehensive, or morally desirable than others, and that therefore it is a mode of action (rather than evasion) to show others what they are doing and invite them to react. Even Hamlet's acts of improvisatory violence fall into this mode of agency, since each of them reflects an outrage back on its initiator, leaving him hoist with his own petard, or, more literally, hurt with his own sword, poisoned with his own poison.

I wrote above of the therapeutic interest of *Hamlet*'s exploration of sanity and interiority. I have attempted to show that the play strongly recontextualizes the inner-outer distinction, but the play also exemplifies, as Marjorie Garber has argued persuasively in *Shakespeare's Ghost Writers*, the connection between therapy and discursive reenactment or dramatization which is so important to psychoanalysis.[25] Over and over Hamlet, both for other characters and for himself, creates or sponsors an image of hidden or repressed horrors in order to exorcise, forgive, understand or change them. Thus it is appropriate, in connecting *Hamlet* and psychoanalysis, not only to set Hamlet on the couch but also to see in the play, as Garber does, a proleptic mimesis of the therapeutic situation and the peculiar discursive agency of the therapist. From this viewpoint it is interesting that Hamlet's mysterious change of feeling toward the end of the play is *like* the acceptance and loss of intensity felt at the end of successful therapy. Objective bad relations remain, so to speak, but their subjective intensity is lessened. Hamlet can speak of his dealings with Rosencrantz and Guildenstern in tones of calm self-justification as well as impatient contempt— "Why, man, they did make love to this employment. / They are not near my conscience" (5.2.57)—and can conclude his explanatory narrative to Horatio by speaking, coolly and externally, of his sanction and obligation to kill Claudius as a matter of the application of a moral discourse.

> Is't not perfect conscience
> To quit him with this arm? And is't not to be damn'd
> To let this canker of our nature come
> In further evil? (5.2.67)

These are questions, not assertions, but their status as confident and predictive self-justification is supported by the discursive situation in which they are uttered.

Hamlet values Horatio in explicitly discursive terms, as narratee and narrator: Horatio is both "as just a man / As e'er my conversation cop'd withal" (3.2.54) and the one who, if he loves Hamlet, will absent himself from felicity awhile "To tell my story" (5.2.354). Moreover, while Hamlet and Horatio enjoy relatively stable conversations which do not turn into interactive satires, Hamlet frequently expands or revises Horatio's picture of the economy in which these conversations function: "There are more things in heaven and earth, Horatio, / Than are dreamt of in your philosophy" (1.5.174). The same sort of expansion occurs in the graveyard scene, though in a less edifying direction:

> HAMLET: To what base uses we may return, Horatio! Why, may not imagination trace the noble dust of Alexander till a find it stopping a bung-hole?
> HORATIO: 'Twere to consider too curiously to consider so.
> HAMLET: No, faith, not a jot, but to follow him thither with modesty enough, and likelihood to lead it. (5.1.196)

Hamlet's dialogues with Horatio serve also to remind us that therapy consists as much in *challenge* to a complacent (or blocked) sense of self as in *acceptance* of limitation—as much in influence as in investigation.

In an aside while narrating his adventures aboard ship, Hamlet poses such a challenge by strikingly enlarging the role of the discursive economy in governing the meaning of an agent's acts.

> HAMLET: You do remember all the circumstance?
> HORATIO: Remember it, my lord!
> HAMLET: Sir, in my heart there was a kind of fighting
>   That would not let me sleep. Methought I lay
>   Worse than the mutines in the bilboes. Rashly—
>   And prais'd be rashness for it: let us know
>   Our indiscretion sometime serves us well
>   When our deep plots do pall; and that should learn us
>   There's a divinity that shapes our ends,
>   Rough-hew them how we will—
> HORATIO: That is most certain. (5.2.2)

The narrative settings here—the "kind of fighting" in Hamlet's heart of intuitive forces within him not fully visible for rational examination, and the prophetic comparison of himself to a bound mutineer being carried toward execution—prepare for the sense of liberation with which Hamlet gives up final responsibility for his actions and purposes, even as he is describing and taking credit for an energetic coup. Hamlet's providence is clearly one that cannot be fully known or predicted, one as likely to be at work in rash impulse as in deep plot ("a divinity that shapes our ends" sounds more like Socrates' daimon than Cromwell's God). Yet at the same time Hamlet is pointing to the hope (available to anyone trying to ride communally endorsed moral currents through a sea of troubles) that in the end he will have helped the community reform itself. In short, just as Hamlet's consistent philosophical and psychological interest in the limits of autonomy follows a pragmatic path, he also *moralizes* like a pragmatist here. Whatever serenity he has at the end of the play and whatever power he exerts on others come from his acceptance of dramatic pragmatism as a mode of action.[26]

In summary, then, *Hamlet*, classically defined as a play about action and individual sanity, maps Hamlet's discovery of the utility of agency through discursive representation. Hamlet mirrors or redoes what he finds in the world around him, but he mirrors *with a critical or moral difference* so that his representations of others amount to interpretive recontextualizations which demand reform. Hamlet thus eludes the scripted (and hence, to employ an opposition I am trying to show the falseness of, ultimately discourse-controlled rather than agent-originated) mode of violent activity which the Ghost enjoins and which Fortinbras and Laertes exemplify. Whatever "a divinity that shapes our ends" may be, it is not a script. Yet Hamlet also works through the discourses he inherits. Thus the play is not only about his development of a new mode of agency which acknowledges the controlling power of circumambient discourses, but also about his recovery of some comfort or poise (but not complacency) in his own agency: this, more than anything else, I suggest, explains the importance of *Hamlet* as an anticipatory text for Freud. The protagonist moves toward an acceptance of a mode of agency—something Freud considered mental health—even as the play moves him toward death. *Hamlet* points not, or not only, to an inescapable scripted condition of the textualized self per se, but to the modes of human agency which (anticipating Bakhtin) accept selfhood as a boundary condition and (unlike Foucault) make room for meaningful action amid constitutive discourses by finding "more relative grounds."

Hamlet illustrates the workings of a Bakhtinian discursive agent, and his method is a theatrically pragmatic one which involves continual performance with potentially therapeutic ends. The play thereby also enacts the disclosure of the only mode of agency we critics and theorists are likely to possess. No wonder we like it.

II

Transactions over Time

4

Money and Moral Luck in
The Merchant of Venice

The Merchant of Venice explores the intersection of four major value systems or vocabularies which interacted vigorously in Shakespeare's London and in his theater: religion, hereditary rank, capitalism, and love. In each system the play examines a structuring opposition: Christian/Jew, aristocrat/commoner, merchant/usurer, and homosocial/heterosexual, and in the play the overall pursuit of value brings all these systems into a visible market relation that provides a pragmatic account of what they mean in action. The play shows how blessings flow, and suggests that in order to be blessed in such a complex situation one must be able to use several vocabularies at once and play them off against each other. More overtly than any other, this play presents the world of human relations as a market of exchangeable values. At key moments, it also contextualizes apparent attempts to move moral discourse *out* of an economic frame, and I will suggest that it does so in such a way as to encourage skepticism of a pragmatic kind about invocations of a noncontingent morality.

"Those critics who idealize the Venetians," René Girard comments of *The Merchant of Venice*, "write as if the many textual clues that contradict their view were not planted by the author himself, as if their presence in the play were a purely fortuitous matter, like the arrival of a bill in the morning mail when one really expects a love letter."[1] Girard's simile is a brilliant one, and much of what follows unpacks it. As I discuss balances and movements of cash, credit, and obligation in this chapter, I shall suggest that in *The Merchant of Venice* bills and love letters are unusually difficult to distinguish—that the vocabularies of eros and of finance are superimposed here with extraordinary tightness.

The play offers a dense set of erotic, economic, and spiritual transactions. The erotic transactions, though unorthodox in ways I shall point out, link the play to Shakespearean comedy generally and are thus perhaps more ordinary than the rest, as women leave the control of their fathers and men loosen bonds to other men in order to marry.

The Merchant of Venice is, however, unusually explicit about the complexity of social love in that hardly any relation between two characters
is left in an emotional or erotic realm: all have some explicit economic
or legal analogue. "So is the will of a living daughter curb'd by the
will of a dead father" (1.2.24), complains Portia in act 1, punning on
emotional and legal senses of "will"; Bassanio has in the previous scene
told Antonio "To you . . . I owe the most in money and in love"
(1.1.130), declaring parallel, perhaps inseparable, financial and erotic
debts.[2] Money, of course, has a logic of its own, and the play presents
money relations in systematic detail.

To discuss the play's plot as a financial one, moreover, suggests
ways to criticise it historically. Since the credit market and the marriage market were, along with land sales, the main methods of raising
money available to the Elizabethen gentry and aristocracy, a play about
the recovery of an extravagant young aristocrat's decayed fortunes by
marriage to an heiress, and the rescue of his bondsman from a usurer's
grasp by an unexpected verdict in court, may be topical in a way that
will reward historical investigation.[3] The play's Venetian setting and
numerous fantastic elements do not prevent it from fitting patterns of
aristocratic indebtedness and cash-raising marriage that helped constitute the expectations of an Elizabethan audience about why and how
real young aristocrats married, and by reconstructing these expectations we can see how Shakespeare's characters—the openhanded merchant who despises interest and lends out of friendship; the beautiful,
loving, able, and forthcoming bride; the lord whose nobility and grace
protect him from his financial irresponsibility; the creditor whose
alienness and vengefulness allow debts to him to be miraculously dissolved—are likely to have been intensely wished-for or dreamed-about
figures.[4]

My primary claim in this chapter, therefore, is that financial transactions in the play reward a more detailed analysis than they have to my
knowledge received, and I shall survey the play with something of an
accountant's eye for cash flows, unpaid balances, and the like. Since,
as Bassanio and I have suggested, love and money reflect and express
each other in the play, such a literal-minded inquiry will draw up
perforce a second, vaguer balance sheet of erotic obligation. As I chart
these balances, I shall note points at which they suggest improvements
in readings of the play as a meditation on marriage and credit in an
emerging modern economy. The theological terms in which many economic issues—especially usury—appear, are also, I shall contend,
shown in the play to define a system of exchange or conversion which

works to the advantage of the "blessed": those who, by religion and social situation, are placed to take advantage of exchange patterns. *The Merchant of Venice* traces the ramifications of one complex circuit in a placeless market; it thus offers a concentrated example of the economic paradigm which this book finds at work everywhere in Shakespeare.

My discussion of the play's plot divides into four sections, one centering on Antonio and Bassanio, which asks why Antonio is sad at the opening of the play; one on Shylock's attempts to justify usury, which asks whether Shylock is Jacob, Laban, or Esau; one on Portia's handling of money; and one on luck and morality.

Antonio's Sadness

> Above all, money everywhere contrives to insert itself into all economic and social relationships. This makes it an excellent indicator: by observing how fast it circulates or when it runs out, how complicated its channels are or how scarce the supply, a fairly accurate assessment can be made of all human activity, even the most humble. (Fernand Braudel, *The Structures of Everyday Life*)

> In sooth I know not why I am so sad,
> It wearies me, you say it wearies you;
> But how I caught it, found it, or came by it,
> What stuff 'tis made of, whereof it is born,
> I am to learn . . . (Antonio in *The Merchant of Venice*)

It is worthwhile to speculate on what Antonio, in the opening lines of the play, says he does not know: why he is sad. Salerio and Solanio, the small fry of the Rialto with whom Antonio is glumly conversing, offer two explanations for his sadness: that Antonio is worried about his ships, which they rather inconsiderately imagine sunk in a variety of ways, and, barring that, that Antonio is in love. I shall argue that they are right on both counts. Antonio's reluctance to be sounded by them gives no more reliable clue to his state of mind than Hamlet's answers to the not-dissimilar queries of Rosencrantz and Guildenstern. To their first speculation, "I know Antonio / Is sad to think upon his merchandise," the merchant replies

> Believe me no, I thank my fortune for it—
> My ventures are not in one bottom trusted,
> Nor to one place; nor is my whole estate
> Upon the fortune of this present year:
> Therefore my merchandise makes me not sad. (1.1.41)

No merchant can admit to be at risk, of course: Chaucer writes of his Merchant that "Ther wiste no man that he was in debt," and limiting others' knowledge of one's finances is a professional necessity. But we know from what Antonio says later to Bassanio that he is misleading his less intimate friends here.

> Thou know'st that all my fortunes are at sea,
> Neither have I money, nor commodity
> To raise a present sum, therefore go forth
> Try what my credit can in Venice do . . . (1.1.177)

In other words, all Antonio's disposable estate *is* "upon the fortune of this present year," despite what he has said to Salerio and Solanio about it. He later writes in desperation to Bassanio in Belmont, "my ships have all miscarried, my creditors grow cruel, my estate is very low, my bond to the Jew is forfeit" (3.2.315). So Antonio's credit has already been heavily used, and the assets with which he secures loans do not cover his borrowings.

Antonio's credit, which he draws on in the absence of liquid assets, is protected by the sort of dissimulation we see him engaged in at the play's start; it is, however, threatened by his inability to look happy when his livelihood is at risk. His demeanor has come under scrutiny: "Believe me you are marvellously chang'd" (1.1.76), as Gratiano notes. There are rumors on the Rialto that, as Shylock later puts it, "his means are in supposition" (1.3.15), and the itemization Shylock gives— ships to Tripoli, the Indies, Mexico, and England, "with other ventures," as he says, "squand'red abroad," not only confirms the impression given by the obsequiousness of Salario and Solanio that Antonio is a big operator, but also suggests that he has become overextended. When noted at all, this is usually taken as a mere donnée of the plot, yet the play offers answers if we seek to know why Antonio should need or want to take risks.

There is manifold evidence, first of all, that Antonio is generous to the point of being unbusinesslike. "He lends out money gratis" (1.3.39), Shylock says bitterly, later adding, "He was wont to lend money for a Christian cur'sy" (3.1.43). Bassanio, probably with specific reference to the same habit from the viewpoint of a recipient rather than a competitor, calls him "the kindest man, / The best-condition'd and unwearied spirit / In doing courtesies" (3.2.291). This echoes Salerio's earlier comment that "a kinder gentleman treads not the earth" (2.8.35). Antonio himself says that he has formerly used his money to "oft deliver from [Shylock's] forfeitures / Many that have at times made moan to me" (3.3.22). Shylock obviously resents his personal losses from this ("He hath . . . hind'red me half a million" [3.1.48]), but he also seems to resent Antonio's persistent personalization of business relations, his interference with what would later be called the invisible hand of the marketplace. Shylock at one point calls him a "prodigal" (3.1.39), ignoring the term's New Testament valency; and if Antonio is lending money without interest to defaulters in order to prevent their forfeitures, he is indeed putting himself at financial risk.

Evidently, then, the liquid assets Antonio finds himself short of at the play's opening have ebbed away from him in this general way. We know, in addition, a good deal more exactly where some of Antonio's money has gone. The Venetian scenes of the first act are, after all, devoted to progressively more revealing discussions of Antonio's financial situation, from the evasions of his talk with Salerio and Solanio through his revealing private conversation with Bassanio to his uncomfortable arrangement to borrow three thousand ducats from Shylock. We must now examine the second and third of these.

When told by Solanio "Why then you are in love," Antonio only replies, "Fie, fie."[5] When he is alone with Bassanio, Antonio is free to proceed to what is evidently uppermost in his mind.

> Well, tell me now what lady is the same
> To whom you swore a secret pilgrimage—
> That you to-day promis'd to tell me of? (1.1.119)

Antonio has known, then, for an unspecified time, that Bassanio intends to woo a lady, and awaits details—indeed, from the line "you to-day promis'd to tell me of," he seems to have been pressing Bassanio for details and finally to be receiving them—except that he must wait some time to hear the answer to his question. Bassanio begins with apparent irrelevance:

> 'Tis not unknown to you Antonio
> How much I have disabled mine estate,
> By something showing a more swelling port
> Than my faint means would grant continuance:
> Nor do I now make moan to be abridg'd
> From such a noble rate, but my chief care
> Is to come fairly off from the great debts
> Wherein my time (something too prodigal)
> Hath left me gag'd: to you Antonio
> I owe the most in money and in love,
> And from your love I have a warranty
> To unburthen all my plots and purposes
> How to get clear of all the debts I owe. (1.1.122)

Bassanio, then, whom we have just seen cheerfully making dinner plans, is Antonio's debtor, evidently to a considerable extent. He will not apologize for this directly (he was living at "a noble rate," that is, one consonant with his rank, and his admissions of extravagance are qualified), but the speech is heavy with an uncomfortable sense of obligation. There is a particular discomfort—beyond that of a debtor speaking to a creditor—in the clause "To you / . . . I owe the most in money and in love." Taken literally, this means not only "you have given me money I have yet to return," but also "you have given me love I have yet to return"; it also, however, suggests that a return of love may partially compensate financial debt, or vice-versa. Certainly the debt to Antonio is not merely financial, but emotional as well; the bargains hitherto and henceforth between Antonio and Bassanio show Antonio's tendency to make financial arrangements personal ones, a tendency Shylock will later on parody with savage accuracy when he sets a pound of flesh as forfeit for a bargain.

If we consider the local impact of this speech, however, it emerges as a request for permission: it admits debts (as things, apparently, which might inhibit the disclosure Antonio has requested), and makes Antonio's love a "warrant" for Bassanio to unburden himself, even in embarrassment. This at any rate seems to be how Antonio understands the speech—as a request for reaffirmation. He delivers in sweeping terms:

> I pray you good Bassanio let me know it,
> And if it stand as you yourself still do,
> Within the eye of honour, be assur'd
> My purse, my person, my extremest means
> Lie all unlock'd to your occasions. (1.1.135)

He offers, then, not only his money but himself, and seems to be imagining, even desiring, an "occasion" for self-sacrifice. The wistful homoerotic suggestion (". . . my person . . . / Lie [s] all unlocked to your occasions"), since it is not taken up by Bassanio, perhaps explains the self-sacrificial impulse. He encourages Bassanio to ask him for money, but Bassanio apparently still cannot tell him what he needs it for:

> In my school-days, when I had lost one shaft,
> I shot his fellow of the self-same flight
> The self-same way, with more advised watch
> To find the other forth, and by adventuring both,
> I oft found both: I urge this childhood proof
> Because what follows is pure innocence.

> I owe you much, and (like a wilful youth)
> That which I owe is lost, but if you please
> To shoot another arrow that self way
> Which you did shoot the first, I do not doubt,
> (As I will watch the aim) or to find both,
> Or bring your latter hazard back again,
> And thankfully rest debtor for the first. (1.1.140)

By infantilizing himself here, Bassanio metaphorically shifts responsibility for the previous money lost to Antonio: it was after all Antonio who shot the first lost shaft, and who is being invited to shoot another whose flight this time Bassanio will watch. The relation between Antonio and Bassanio, then, seems to resemble that between Citibank and Zaire, whereby the creditor, by the magnitude of the investment, becomes the thrall of the debtor, who can cause ruin by defaulting on or repudiating the debt. Bassanio's promise that he will at worst return the second loan in good time is, as we shall see in following the flight of Antonio's cash, a questionable one. Antonio feels manipulated enough by Bassanio's evasive whimsy to object fairly strongly:

> You know me well, and herein spend but time
> To wind about my love with circumstance,
> And out of doubt you do me now more wrong
> In making question of my uttermost
> Than if you had made waste of all I have:
> Then do but say to me what I should do
> That in your knowledge may by me be done,
> And I am prest unto it: therefore speak. (1.1.153)

This is a complex piece of reproach; at the end of it, we may well wonder who is winding about whose love with circumstance. "I can deny you nothing; at any rate you should acknowledge that you are making emotional use of me, and not hide behind fictions of practicality which insult my intelligence and self-knowledge," might be a fair tendentious paraphrase in the Empsonian manner. We know from the sonnets that Shakespeare was interested in and had perhaps experienced such feelings: compare the opening of sonnet 57:

> Being your slave, what should I do but tend
> Upon the hours and times of your desire?
> I have no precious time at all to spend,
> Nor services to do till you require.

In any case, the financial upshot of Antonio's speech is clear. Everything he has is at Bassanio's disposal, and he is hurt that Bassanio hesitates to use it.

Bassanio at last, convinced no doubt that he hurts Antonio more by withholding details of his marriage plans than by revealing them, tells Antonio of Portia and, again without making a direct request, asks for money:

> . . . her sunny locks
> Hang on her temples like a golden fleece,
> Which makes her seat of Belmont Colchos' strond,
> And many Jasons come in quest of her.
> O my Antonio, had I but the means
> To hold a rival place with one of them,
> I have a mind presages me such thrift
> That I should questionless be fortunate. (1.1.169)

"Thrift," here, assimilates success in winning Portia to success in clearing his debt to Antonio; since "thrift" in its everyday dispositional sense is what Bassanio conspicuously lacks, he is imagining having his accounts redeemed in one great stroke—which will show him to have been "thrifty" in a grand way all along. Antonio immediately replies, in lines quoted above, that he has neither money nor goods to sell, which sounds like the beginning of a refusal. He continues, however:

> Therefore go forth
> Try what my credit can in Venice do,—
> That shall be rack'd even to the uttermost
> To furnish thee to Belmont to fair Portia.
> Go presently inquire (and so will I)
> Where money is, and I no question make
> To have it of my trust, or for my sake. (1.1.179)

Antonio again offers his "uttermost," and imagines his credit on the rack. It is interesting that they need to inquire "where money is," since the question suggests that all Venice may, like Antonio and Bassanio, have problems with liquidity. Antonio's final formulation—he will obtain cash "of my trust, or for my sake," glossed by a series of editors as "on my credit, or for friendship's sake"—suggests in turn that he hopes to find the sort of friendly creditor he himself is, but that he may have to borrow at interest, depending perhaps on "where money is."

At the end of the first scene, then, our balance sheet is already fairly detailed, though no precise sum has yet been mentioned. Bassanio is in debt to everyone, but especially to Antonio, and evidently can raise no money except from loving and forbearing friends; Antonio has ventured his clearly very considerable fortune at sea or generously given it away; Bassanio offers him a chance to recoup an otherwise irrecoverable debt by sponsoring his marital venture to Portia; Antonio does so, but insists that his gesture be read in emotional rather than financial terms (he never mentions Bassanio's debts to him, and it is Bassanio rather than he who represents the voyage to Belmont as a financial "plot and purpose").[6] Bassanio has been financially obliged, in effect, to ask Antonio's permission to woo—and this he has done reluctantly.

Thus far, the wooing of Portia can be seen as an instance of what Eve Kosofsky Sedgwick has defined as "male homosocial desire": "the whole spectrum of bonds between men, including friendship, mentorship, rivalry, institutional subordination, homosexual genitality, and economic exchange—within which the various forms of traffic in women take place."[7] Antonio, at least, has a stake in treating Bassanio's courtship of Portia as part of a complex economic and erotic transaction between two males. A comment of Sedgwick's suggests that she sees the difficulty of such subordinations as a Shakespearean theme: "as Shakespeare's Sonnets showed, the male path through heterosexuality to homosocial satisfaction is a slippery and threatened one—although for most men, in at least most cultures, compulsory."[8] I shall return to Sedgwick's illuminating arguments when I have finished tracing the economic patterns of the play—patterns, interestingly, which no male seems thoroughly to control.

Bassanio, seeking "where money is," finds Shylock, and we appear to encounter a recognizable business transaction at last. The scene, which culminates in the acceptance of the "merry bond," as unbusinesslike a proposition as one could find, starts with a discussion of terms.

SHYLOCK: Three thousand ducats, well.
BASSANIO: Aye sir, for three months.
SHYLOCK: For three months, well.
BASSANIO: For the which as I told you, Antonio shall be bound.
SHYLOCK: Antonio shall become bound, well. (1.3.1)

The focus seems to be on the bargain and its precise terms, not on the personal relations which lie behind it. It is worth noting that the loan will be to Bassanio, with Antonio "bound." This means, in our business language, that Antonio is a guarantor, but in Elizabethan terms it would suggest something yet more precise. Bassanio is a lord; Antonio is not. In England until the mid–seventeenth century a nobleman could not be arrested for debt. Lawrence Stone quotes a letter from Sir Robert Cecil to Alderman Rowe: " 'it may be you will be loth to deal with a baron of the realm without some collateral securities of meaner quality.'" Stone continues:

> It might indeed! Since the bodies of peers were immune and suits against them difficult, creditors often insisted that a nobleman's friends or his leading officers should join with him in a bond, recognizance, or statute. . . .
>
> Owing, perhaps, to a natural reluctance of friends to get too deeply involved, the commonest sureties used by peers were their own servants . . . Examples could be indefinitely extended, and there can be no doubt that this was normal practice. Satisfactory though this may have been to the creditors, the servants not infrequently found themselves less happily situated. In 1571 the servants of the Duke of Norfolk, in 1597, those of the Earl of Derby, in 1622 those of Bacon found themselves liable to arrest as sureties.[9]

There may, then, be a reminder in the initial terms of the arrangement, not merely that Antonio has credit and Bassanio has not, but that Bassanio is a noble and Antonio a merchant. This situates Antonio in class terms somewhere between Bassanio and Shylock, and that fact may help explain Antonio's extraordinary violence in repudiating Shylock's attempts to draw parallels between them later in the scene. (It is also a reminder that law of contracts is not blind to social difference, something which becomes vital in the trial scene.)

Shylock says, in an aside on Antonio's entry: "He hates our sacred nation, and he rails / (Even there where merchants most do congregate) / On me, my bargains, and my well-won thrift, / Which he calls interest" (1.3.43). And he clearly sees Antonio's temporary dependence on him as an opportunity to make some point about thrift and interest—one that he is not prone to make to Bassanio (whom Shylock seems to regard as of small consequence), but insists on putting to Antonio. Shylock's complaint about Antonio, partly practical ("he lends out money gratis, and brings down / The rate of usance here with us in Venice" [1.3.39–40]), is partly also a complaint about Antonio's categorization of his activities: "my well-won thrift, / Which he calls interest." Shylock continues his argument with another detail about Venetian finance:

> I am debating of my present store,
> And by the near guess of my memory
> I cannot instantly raise up the gross
> Of full three thousand ducats: what of that?
> Tubal (a wealthy Hebrew of my tribe)
> Will furnish me. (1.3.48)

Shylock, it would seem, makes a point here about circulation: Antonio, in tapping him for cash, has access not to an individual but to a system. Certainly Shakespeare is making such a point—already in two and a half scenes the search for venture capital has gone through two middlemen, has crossed boundaries of rank and religion, has brought friendship to the market to finance marriage (or marriage to repay friendship), and has offered a wide variety of definitions of "thrift."

If a discussion of interest is what Shylock wants, Antonio could hardly be more cooperative.

> Shylock, albeit I neither lend nor borrow
> By taking nor by giving of excess,
> Yet to supply the ripe wants of my friend,
> I'll break a custom. (1.3.56)

Shylock reverts to this, with a key emendation: "but hear you, / Me thoughts you said, you neither lend nor borrow / Upon advantage" (1.3.63–4). Antonio had used the word "excess," and we must remember here that Antonio lends out money "gratis," so that he treats any interest on a loan as "excess." It is perhaps relevant to note that the officially permitted annual rate of return in England after 1571 was ten percent, and moneylenders often got more.[10] Shylock turns Antonio's "excess" into the much more general "advantage," thus including the kinds of emotional return we have seen Antonio take from Bassanio earlier in the act.[11] Antonio, however, either does not notice the change, or will not split hairs: "I do never use it," he proudly replies. We can see this as an attempt by Antonio to imagine an economy in which self-interest is carefully bounded so as to make generosity, rather than profit, fundamental; Shylock's reformulations, and their resonances in the Antonio-Bassanio relationship, make this attempt seem hopelessly compromised from the start.

Jacob, Esau, or Laban?

Antonio's sadness, I have suggested, is a market-linked phenomenon. So is Shylock's apparently irrelevant and patently incomplete retelling of the Jacob story, which is so evidently meant to justify usury.

> When Jacob graz'd his uncle Laban's sheep,—
> This Jacob from our holy Abram was
> (As his wise mother wrought in his behalf)
> The third possessor: ay, he was the third.
> ANTONIO: And what of him? did he take interest?
> SHYLOCK: No, not take interest, not as you would say
>   Directly int'rest,—mark what Jacob did,— (1.3.66)

Shylock wishes to force Antonio to await his full exegesis of the biblical incident; Antonio, impatient, wishes to force him to the point.

The Jacob story itself is a multivalent subtext for Shylock to invoke here. Shylock claims to possess the patriarchs ("This Jacob from our holy Abram was"), and to interpret their example with authority. The lightly alluded-to story of Jacob's inheritance, however, is full of danger for him in an exegetical argument with a Christian in a Christian state. In general, as G. K. Hunter notes, Renaissance Christians held that "if Abraham and the other patriarchs of the Old Testament belong to the Christian tradition, they cannot belong to the Jewish one; and Jewish invocation of them is not simply alien but actually subversive."[12] Specifically, the Lord's words to Rebekah, when Esau and Jacob struggled together in her womb, were taken by Christians as the prefiguration of their own inheritance of the blessings of the Jews:

> And the Lord said unto her, two nations are in thy wombe, and two maner of people shalbe devided out of thy bowels, and the one people shalbe mightier than the other, and the elder shal serve ye yonger.[13]

St. Paul, in Romans 9:12–13, comments in "great heaviness and continual sorrow" for the Jews who have not accepted Christ:

> It was said unto her, The elder shall serve the yonger.
> As it is written, I have loved Jacob, and have hated Esau.

And Paul concludes:

> What shal we say then? That the Gentiles which folowed not righteousnes, have atteined unto righteousnes, even the righteousnes which is of faith. But Israel which folowed the Law of righteousnes, colde not atteine unto the Law of righteousnes. Wherefore? Because they soght it not by faith, but as it were by the workes of the Law . . . (Romans 9:30–32)

The Jacob story thus is full of danger for Shylock, first because, as part of the Hebrew Bible, the story has been converted and reappropriated for Christian purposes, and more specifically because it contains, from a Christian viewpoint, both a prophecy of Christian inheritance of blessings and a threat to those who trust in "the works of the law."[14]

Shylock seems unconcerned here with the story of how Jacob obtained his blessing: the deception of dim-eyed old Isaac, when Rebekah binds the kidskins on Jacob's hands and neck, is summed up neutrally by the phrase "as his wise mother wrought in his behalf." Shylock's concern is with how he used the blessing. This is the story he tells

Antonio, though he never completes or explains it. I quote at some length:

> ANTONIO: And what of him? did he take interest?
> SHYLOCK: No, not take interest, not as you would say
>   Directly int'rest,—mark what Jacob did,—
>   When Laban and himself were compromis'd
>   That all the eanlings which were streak'd and pied
>   Should fall as Jacob's hire, the ewes being rank
>   In end of autumn turned to the rams,
>   And when the work of generation was
>   Between these woolly breeders in the act,
>   The skilful shepherd pill'd me certain wands,
>   And in the doing of the deed of kind
>   He stuck them up before the fulsome ewes,
>   Who then conceiving, did in eaning time
>   Fall parti-colour'd lambs, and those were Jacob's.
>   This was a way to thrive, and he was blest:
>   And thrift is blessing if men steal it not.
> ANTONIO: This was a venture sir that Jacob serv'd for,
>   A thing not in his power to bring to pass,
>   But sway'd and fashion'd by the hand of heaven.
>   Was this inserted to make interest good?
>   Or is your gold and silver ewes and rams?
> SHYLOCK: I cannot tell, I make it breed as fast,—
>   But note me signior.
> ANTONIO: Mark you this Bassanio,
>   The devil can cite Scripture for his purpose,—
>   An evil soul producing holy witness
>   Is like a villain with a smiling cheek,
>   A goodly apple rotten at the heart.
>   O what a goodly outside falsehood hath!
> SHYLOCK: Three thousand ducats, 'tis a good round sum. (1.3.70–98)

What, we must ask, does Shylock want Antonio to "note," before he is thrown back on business by a series of insults in which his own behavior is taken as a text for moral commentary by Antonio to Bassanio? To learn we must go back to the Jacob story, this time to that part of it Shylock is citing in detail. Jacob served Laban, his uncle, for twenty years, while avoiding the wrath of Esau for the theft of Isaac's blessing. Laban tricks Jacob by substituting Leah for Rachel in the dark (there is a kind of rough justice in this, given what Jacob and Rebekah did to Isaac), and he keeps Jacob as a servant even after Jacob has married Rachel. The wand trick that Shylock likens to his own interest-taking occurs after the following exchange between Jacob and Laban:

> Iaakob said to Laban, Send me away that I may go unto my place and to my countrey . . . for thou knowest what service I have done thee. To whome Laban answered . . . tarie: I have perceived that the Lord hathe blessed me for thy sake. . . . Appoint unto me thy wages, and I wil give it thee. But he said unto him, Thou knowest, what service I have done thee . . . For the litle, that thou haddest before I came, is increased into a multitude: and the Lorde hath blessed thee by my comming. (Genesis 30:25–30)

Jacob then proposes the grazing arrangement Shylock describes, in which from the increase of Laban's flocks, Jacob comes to have wealth of his own.

Shylock's never-interpreted biblical parable, then, is an exceptionally rich one when applied to his situation as a Jewish money-lender in a cash-poor Christian state. He works for Antonio, supplying his needs and caring more providently for the money supply than the Christian merchants around him do, but because he is a Jew he is not allowed full participation in the economy, as Jacob is prevented by Laban from having flocks of his own. Yet Jacob, blessed by God and his own ingenuity, breeds his own streaked flock from Laban's smooth one, and is hated for it, as Shylock is hated for making money out of the money with which he supplies (or "blesses") the ventures of the Christians around him. Laban seeks to retain Jacob for the blessing Jacob brings—an economic one; yet he simultaneously denies Jacob rights to his gains, and indeed, as Jacob complains (Genesis 33:41)— and as the Jews of Europe had notorious right to complain—"thou hast changed my wages ten times." It is this relation between Jacob and Laban that Shylock is presumably attempting to adduce as an explanation of his own place in the Venetian economy, and more immediately, as a model for his relation to Antonio.

Shylock's claim goes unheard because Antonio so violently rejects any claim of kinship, even merely as a fellow human being, from Shylock, who is then driven to a much less sophisticated assertion of their relation: "What should I say to you? Should I not say / 'Hath a dog money? is it possible / A cur can lend three thousand ducats?' " (1.3.115). Shylock proposes the Jacob/Laban story as a model for the relation between usury and venture capitalism with the former "blessing" the latter, but he cannot be heard except as a "devil," and must go on to defend his mere humanity.

The entire incident offers rich territory for historically minded criticism to explore.[15] There is no doubt that loans at interest were essential, available, perilous, and feared in the last two decades of Elizabeth's reign, during which Stone estimates that "about two-thirds of the peerage seem to have been in growing financial difficulties."[16] R. H. Tawney calls usury "the mystery of iniquity in which a host of minor scandals were conveniently, if inaccurately, epitomized."[17] Walter Cohen, in an essay which seeks to read the play historically in both English and Italian terms, argues that Shylock, by contrast to Antonio, is "a figure from the past: marginal, diabolical, irrational, archaic, medieval."[18] But Shylock's abortive scriptural explanation of the usurer's relation to the capital needed by merchants is in fact an extraordinarily progressive one (rather like Bacon's in "Of Usury"); what the scene illustrates is the diabolism forced on Shylock by Antonio's near-hysterical resistance to any formal acceptance of the nature of the economic system he lives in. Cohen later comments that "if the play revealed that merchants were as exploitative as usurers, that they were in fact usurers [as was the case in England], then its entire thrust toward harmonious reconciliation could only be understood as a fiendishly oblique instance of ironic demystification."[19] Cohen represents this as an unacceptably complex intention, but the economic patterns I am concerned to trace here support such an understanding; with respect to Shylock, they enlarge the significance of his exclusion to encompass the exclusion of the demystifying self-defence he tries to offer. A Christian merchant, preserving homosocial connection to a Lord, cannot afford to understand the parable of economic relations offered by the Jew.

Shylock, however, cannot control the interpretation of the text he cites. He does not remain Jacob for long, and the Jacob story has an independent life in the play outside his speech. Lancelot Gobbo, Shylock's "unthrifty" servant, kneels backwards before his blind father, asks for a blessing, and gains it only after old Gobbo, feeling the back of his head exclaims "what a beard hast thou got" (2.2.89); the scene's parody of the deception of Isaac comes immediately prior to the entrance of Bassanio, who offers, as Christianity does to converts, "rare new liveries" (2.2.105). Lancelot begs employment, commenting that "The old proverb is very well parted between my master Shylock and you sir, you have 'the grace of God' sir, and he hath 'enough'" (2.2.140), suggesting that a blessing has passed to Bassanio. Jessica, fleeing Shylock's house to join Lorenzo, and taking with her a casket and bags of ducats, echoes Rachel, Laban's daughter, who steals his household gods when she flees in secret with Jacob. Shylock loses control of the Jacob story as soon as he introduces it: he becomes

Laban, his daughter and idols stolen, or Esau, bereft of blessing and compelled to witness a younger people thrive, rather than the Jacob he had been. Shylock plans to catch Antonio "on the hip," echoing a detail from Jacob's wrestling with the angel, but in the trial scene it is Gratiano who exclaims "Now infidel I have you on the hip" (4.1.330). And it is Portia who will not release Shylock until he has blessed her and hers.

Protecting the Endowment

Portia, "richly left" in Belmont and guarded by the casket test, is a source of all that is good in life for Bassanio if he can only find the proper intermediary. The caskets—gold, inscribed "who chooseth me, shall gain what many men desire"; silver, inscribed "who chooseth me, shall get as much as he deserves"; and lead, inscribed "who chooseth me, must give and hazard all he hath"—offer extraordinary opportunities for interpretation, which are complicated by Portia's telling Bassanio, "I stand for sacrifice," and ordering a song about how fancy is bred by visual appearances. The scene, in part, tests his willingness to take subtle direction from Portia. In a play about economic, erotic, social, and religious venturing, circulation, climbing, and conversion, however, finally only the lead casket, with its injunction to give and hazard, stands for, or enables, the variety of kinds of exchange that the play presents. In doing so it creates, though rather vaguely, an approximation of an Elizabethan marriage settlement with some advantage to the bride. "The father of the bride had to provide a substantial cash sum, known as a portion," says Lawrence Stone; "In return . . . the father of the groom had to undertake a far wider set of obligations. The most important was the provision of an annual allowance for support of the bride if and when she became a widow, and the ratio between this jointure, as it was called, and the cash portion was the main issue around which negotiations turned."[20] Portia's name is suggestive of the means to relieve debts (of various sorts) which she provides for Bassanio; choosing the lead casket, which promises no profit and exacts gifts and risks, shows that he on his side offers a "jointure" of sorts to balance the huge "portion" he hopes to receive. (What he hazards is Antonio's life.) It is worth noting here that the lead casket in Shakespeare's presumed source for this part of the play bears the legend, "Who chooseth me shall finde that God hath disposed for him," so that Shakespeare has chosen an economic moral to replace a providential one.[21]

In her speech ratifying Bassanio's successful casket choice, Portia blesses him with herself and her wealth in terms which echo the first-born's blessing that passed from Jews to Christians: "Myself, and what is mine, to you and yours / Is now converted" (3.2.166–7). Her control, as Shylock's was the bond, is the ring:

> This house, these servants, and this same myself
> Are yours,—my lord's!—I give them with this ring,
> Which when you part from, lose, or give away,
> Let it presage the ruin of your love
> And be my vantage to exclaim on you. (3.2.170)

Rings are signs of commitment and also tokens of wealth. Gratiano, who gets one from Nerissa, claims that his was of little cash value, as if that were relevant, when she condemns him for giving his away. Shylock lost two rings with Jessica, one a diamond that cost him two thousand ducats at Frankfurt, the other a turquoise Leah gave him when he was a bachelor, which Jessica, in an appalling parody of her mother's gesture, exchanges for a monkey. The dangers, then, involved in using something which has symbolic value for its exchange value is connected with rings in the play before the final scene. Like the circles they trace, rings are potential symbols of enclosure as well as of cycles of commitment and exchange.[22]

The instant Portia's house becomes Bassanio's, it begins to fill with guests: Gratiano will marry Nerissa and stay, Lorenzo and Jessica arrive hungry, having thrown away the money Jessica stole from her father's house ("you drop manna in way of starving people," Lorenzo says to Portia at the play's end), and Salerio brings a letter from Antonio. After welcoming them all in his new capacity as host, Bassanio is forced by the letter to explain in some embarrassment to Portia that, while he never pretended to be rich, "Rating myself at nothing, you shall see / How much I was a braggart" (3.2.256); his debts and Antonio's danger—evidently tactfully unmentioned before—are revealed, and we see Portia echoing his descriptions of Antonio as she learns the extent of this prior emotional and financial obligation.

BASSANIO: I have engag'd myself to a dear friend,
   Engag'd my friend to his mere enemy
   To feed my means.
          . . . But is it true Salerio?
JESSICA: . . . If law, authority and power deny not,
   It will go hard with poor Antonio.
PORTIA: Is it your dear friend that is thus in trouble?
BASSANIO: The dearest friend to me . . . (3.2.260)

She then asks the sum of the debt and delights all by saying, "What no more? / . . . / You shall have gold / To pay the petty debt ten times over. / When it is paid, bring your true friend along" (3.2.297, 305). Thus she reverses the current of cash that has flowed in her direction by sending Bassanio back to Venice on a tidal wave of ducats. Her speech, sometimes cited to show how far above financial concerns she is, concludes with a wonderful bow to the market—a line Pope thought unworthy of Shakespeare: "Since you are dear bought, I will love you dear" (3.2.312). She can securely outbid Venice for Bassanio and seems cheerful at the prospect of establishing credit in her own favor. Bassanio then reads out Antonio's letter:

> Sweet Bassanio, my ships have all miscarried, my creditors grow cruel, my estate is very low, my bond to the Jew is forfeit, and (since in paying it, it is impossible I should live), all debts are clear'd between you and I, if I might but see you at my death: notwithstanding, use your pleasure,—if your love do not persuade you to come, let not my letter. (3.2.314)

"O love!" Portia echoes in an immediate counter to this claim, and sends him off to the rescue: "Dispatch all business [their marriage] and be gone!" But she wisely chooses to follow to protect her investment.

What Portia also discovers here is, to return to the terms suggested by Sedgwick, the potentially homosocial aspect of her marriage to Bassanio. Describing the centrality of the homosocial relation of cuckoldry in Wycherley's *The Country Wife*, Sedgwick comments that in that play

> the triangular transaction between men of the possession of a woman—a transaction whose structuring presence in other texts sometimes requires some inferential work to detect—is simply the most patent subject. The status of women in this transaction is determiningly a problem in the play: not their status in the general political sense but their ambiguous status of being at the same time objects of symbolic exchange and also, at least potentially, users of symbols and subjects in themselves.[23]

Portia, discovering Bassanio's "engagement" to Antonio, turns immediately to money, to male disguise, and to the law to protect her status as a principal and to avoid becoming an object of homosocial exchange.

Seen in this light, the trial scene betrays an unexpected (and I believe hitherto unnoticed) but cogent financial logic. Bassanio, following Portia's initial suggestion, makes a series of offers to Shylock and to Antonio. We appear to be seeing the repayment of Venetian debts that Bassanio forecast when proposing his venture for the golden fleece of Belmont. Bassanio's offers are by no means confined to money:

> Antonio, I am married to a wife
> Which is as dear to me as life itself,
> But life itself, my wife, and all the world,
> Are not with me esteem'd above thy life.
> I would lose all, ay sacrifice them all
> Here to this devil, to deliver you. (4.1.278)

Bassanio, who hazarded all Antonio had for Portia and Belmont, now offers all Belmont, love and money together, to redeem Antonio.

What actually happens, however, is quite different. Portia leads Shylock to declare an intent to kill, by getting him to deny Antonio a surgeon's presence to staunch or cauterize the wound he will make in cutting the pound of flesh, and she catches him in ethnic and economic laws wider than those he has invoked.

> PORTIA: . . . if thou dost shed
>   One drop of Christian blood, thy lands and goods
>   Are (by the laws of Venice) confiscate
>   Unto the state of Venice.
>   . . .
> SHYLOCK: I take this offer then,—pay the bond thrice
>   And let the Christian go.
> BASSANIO: Here is the money.
> PORTIA: Soft!
>   The Jew shall have all justice,—soft no haste!
>   He shall have nothing but the penalty.
>   . . .
> SHYLOCK: Give me my principal, and let me go.
> BASSANIO: I have it ready for thee, here it is.
> PORTIA: He hath refus'd it in the open court,
>   He shall have merely justice . . . (4.1.306)

Portia seeks to protect her own money, which Bassanio seeks to give away. Shylock then attempts to end the trial:

> I'll stay no longer question.
> PORTIA: Tarry Jew,
>   The law hath yet another hold on you.
>   It is enacted in the laws of Venice,
>   If it be proved against an alien,
>   That by direct, or indirect attempts
>   He seek the life of any citizen,
>   The party 'gainst the which he doth contrive,
>   Shall seize one half his goods, the other half
>   Comes to the privy coffer of the state,
>   And the offender's life lies in the mercy
>   Of the Duke.
>   . . .

> DUKE: For half thy wealth, it is Antonio's,
>   The other half comes to the general state,
>   Which humbleness may drive into a fine.
> PORTIA: Ay for the state, not for Antonio. (4.1.342 . . . 369)

Each of these interventions protects Portia's endowment from threats; half Shylock's goods wipes out the debts Bassanio has to Antonio, and re-equips him as a merchant so that he will not turn into a dependent. Antonio then answers Portia's question "What mercy can you render him Antonio?" by endowing Lorenzo and Jessica, so that they will not be dependents of Portia and Bassanio (whose house they are looking after, not very thriftily, in Portia's absence). The forced conversion of Shylock completes the logic of his treatment in the play. His ducats, his servant, his daughter, his justifying biblical text have all been converted to serve Christians; now he himself must convert, a final victim of the cruelty of typology.

Even though Portia's portion survives the trial untouched, Bassanio continues to attempt to give it away. With the freed Antonio beside him, he says to the disguised Portia,

> BASSANIO: Most worthy gentleman, I and my friend
>   Have by your wisdom been this day acquitted
>   Of grievous penalties, in lieu whereof,
>   Three thousand ducats due unto the Jew
>   We freely cope your courteous pains withal.
> ANTONIO: And stand indebted over and above
>   In love and service to you evermore.
> PORTIA: He is well paid that is well satisfied. (4.1.404)

We may easily believe Portia's comment here. She not only has the delicious opportunity to refuse her own money, she has Antonio's precious testimony that the balance of erotic credit is now hers. She has, of course, ensured that the financial balance falls on her side (in fact, any of the original three thousand ducats not spent by Bassanio before he left Venice the first time count as profit to Portia). She pauses only to request the ring, which Bassanio first denies, then gives at a request from Antonio that Portia/Balthazar's "deservings and my love withal / Be weighed against your wife's commandement" (4.1.446). This produces material for Portia's final educative gesture. She has put Antonio in her debt, though he does not yet know this; with the ring she will teach Bassanio not to circulate her gifts, and turn Antonio from a rival into a surety for his love. She reproaches the ringless Bassanio on his return to Belmont, and he replies:

BASSANIO: Pardon this fault, and by my soul I swear
  I never more will break an oath with thee.
ANTONIO: I once did lend my body for his wealth,
  Which but for him that had your husband's ring
  Had quite miscarried. I dare be bound again,
  My soul upon the forfeit, that your lord
  Will never more break faith advisedly.
PORTIA: Then you shall be his surety: give him this,
  And bid him keep it better than the other.
ANTONIO: Here, Lord Bassanio, swear to keep this ring.
BASSANIO: By heaven it is the same I gave the doctor! (5.1.247)

Antonio, claiming a right from his near-sacrifice—a right both to exculpate Bassanio and to establish the supreme obligation all are under to the male "doctor"—becomes a guaranteeing middleman in the final transaction of the play, a transaction which binds both men in obligation to Portia.[24] Her triumphant manipulation of patterns of homosocial exchange—and her unusually successful defiance of their usual objectification of women—is now complete. She remarks presently: "I have not yet / Enter'd *my* house" (5.1.272, emphasis mine). She has, however, established her possession of it and of Bassanio, and she has established her mastery of the systems of exchange in the play which have routed all blessings, socioeconomic, erotic, and theological, toward Belmont.

If the pattern of credit and debit, payment and profit, is drawn in this play—as I have tried to show—with nearly the precision of an auditor's report, the character whose actions most shape and exploit this pattern is not Shylock or Antonio but Portia. She is both a better manipulator of exchange patterns and a more practical idealizer of them than her opponents Shylock and Antonio, who bless her with their thrift.

These claims leave, however, some vexing questions unanswered— for instance, whether the social values inscribed in *The Merchant of Venice* are historically conservative or progressive ones. On the one hand, Portia is, of course, a landed aristocrat, and the play shows, and apparently endorses, the fall of the goods of a progressive commercial exchange system into her lap. As in his story of Jacob and Laban, Shylock's "blessing" profits another—though in this case he must lose all that he values so that Portia may gain all she wants. From this viewpoint, the play offers reassurance (or warning) that, while the world may change, inherited privilege will be preserved. On the other hand, more than any other Shakespearean play, *The Merchant of Venice* shows a woman triumphing over men and male systems of exchange:

the male homosocial desire of Antonio is almost as thoroughly thwarted in the play as Shylock's vengefulness. In thus subverting some expectations while reinforcing others, the play is perhaps centrally concerned to show the wide availability of power through a placeless and various market which yet favors the flexible, the intelligent, and the already strong. I have suggested that the story of Jacob is a precisely inscribed subtext in *The Merchant of Venice*, but the Parable of the Talents also underlies its capitalist-spiritual logic, and the terrifying conclusion of that parable hangs over the end of the play: "unto every one that hath shall be given, and he shall have abundance: but from him that hath not, even that which he hath shall be taken away" (Matthew 25:29).

Moral Luck

In the introduction to this book I suggested that in some ways contemporary critiques of the certainty projects in modern philosophy give an unexpected currency to the way foundationalist ideas are investigated in contingent localized contexts in Shakespearean texts. In this chapter I have read *The Merchant of Venice* as a study in the complex circulation of financial and erotic obligation, and in doing so I have invoked this book's general description of pragmatism as an economic way of thinking. I want to close by turning to a specific philosophic debate, touched on in this play, about the relation between "pure" morality and circumstantial luck, and in so doing I take up the provocative argument of Bernard Williams's "Moral Luck."[25] Some readers may find it paradoxical for me to make this kind of use of one of the most trenchant philosophical critics of pragmatism. In "Moral Luck," however (as in "Persons, Character, and Morality," which precedes it in his book *Moral Luck*), Bernard Williams writes like a pragmatist, in that he denies the practical possibility of morality as a fixed system and suggests the substitution of a pragmatic economy for it.[26]

To cite the Parable of the Talents as I do above is to say that *The Merchant of Venice* demonstrates the centrality of what Bernard Williams calls, with deliberate paradoxicality, "constitutive moral luck." Commenting on the Kantian project to separate morality entirely from luck, he says of Kant's moral value that

> the capacity for moral agency is supposedly present to any rational agent whatsoever, to anyone for whom the question can even present itself. The successful moral life, removed from considerations of birth, lucky upbringing, or indeed of the incomprehensible Grace of a non-Pelagian God, is presented as a career open not merely to the talents, but to a talent which all rational beings necessarily possess in the same degree.

Such a conception has an ultimate form of justice at its heart, and that is its allure. Kantianism is only superficially repulsive—despite appearances, it offers an inducement, solace to a sense of the world's unfairness.[27]

Such a view of morality, Williams continues, will only offer solace if it engages central aspects of one's moral life (rather than being a last resort when one's luck is down, what Williams calls "the doss-house of the spirit"): "it must have a claim on one's most fundamental concerns as a rational agent, and in one's recognition of that one is supposed to grasp, not only morality's immunity to luck, but one's own partial immunity to luck through morality."[28]

Not only would such an immunity be a nice thing to have, something like it might have to be the case for a just world of the traditional liberal kind to exist. In any event, belief in such an immunity underpins long-held and widely shared beliefs about what would produce justice, whether it is to be had in this world or the next. It is invoked long before Kant, for example, in Christian moral thought about the next world; God's tribunal, as Claudius puts it in *Hamlet*, is a place distinguished from this world precisely because, while here luck can affect morality, there it cannot:

> In the corrupted currents of this world
> Offence's gilded hand may shove by justice,
> . . . 'tis not so above:
> There is no shuffling, there the action lies
> In his true nature. (3.3.57)

Claudius, in other words, sees heaven as the place where he cannot use social luck to buy off morality, but will face a judgment in which luck will have no part. This is something like a Kantian conviction (though one that has signally failed to make Claudius into a good person). It should be no great surprise to find such ideas articulated before Kant since, as Williams observes, "the Kantian conception embodies, in a very pure form, something which is basic to our ideas of morality."[29]

Nothing could be further from a morality immune to constitutive luck than *The Merchant of Venice* as I have presented it in this chapter. As my citation of the Parable of the Talents suggests, I think that the play emphasizes the role of constitutive luck in actual morality. The play illustrates something that Williams puts plainly:

> the aim of making morality immune to luck is bound to be disappointed. The form of this point which is most familiar, from discussions of free-will, is that the dispositions of morality, however far back they are

placed in the direction of motive and intention, are as 'conditioned' as anything else.[30]

And he goes on to call this "the bitter truth (I take it to be both) that morality is subject, after all, to constitutive luck."[31] It is constitutive luck that makes it possible not only for Portia and Bassanio to be happy, but to be morally exemplary in their happiness; that is, they can uphold the Christian aristocratic virtues—generosity, hospitality, and harmonious well-being—because they are entitled to these by birth and so inclined by temperament. While my account of the play has insisted on the precisely delineated extent to which Portia's generosity is self-serving and Bassanio's feckless, they also possess the luck (particularly Portia) to have special moral opportunities, and they take up these opportunities with gusto, thus making themselves popular with audiences both inside the play and outside it.[32]

If it were only constitutive moral luck that were in question, however, the topic might not be worth raising, since it merely allows me to restate in a different vocabulary something already sufficiently explained. In fact, however, both Portia and Shylock raise moral issues in the trial scene in ways that invoke a more complex conflict between moral contingency and moral autonomy of the kind Kant systematizes. Moreover, Williams's full argument in "Moral Luck" clarifies the retrospective effects of the trial scene on the moral quality of Bassanio's courtship of Portia, so that the plot of *The Merchant of Venice* as a whole anticipates some aspects of a contemporary discussion of contingent luck and moral autonomy.

In the trial scene, as already noted, Bassanio seeks to buy off Shylock's revenge:

BASSANIO: For thy three thousand ducats here is six!
SHYLOCK: If every ducat in six thousand ducats
   Were in six parts, and every part a ducat,
   I would not draw them, I would have my bond!
DUKE: How shalt thou hope for mercy rend'ring none?
SHYLOCK: What judgement shall I dread doing no wrong? (4.1.84)

In two ways, materially and morally, Shylock is told that he would profit by forgiving Antonio. This juxtaposition of Bassanio's cash offer and the Duke's advocacy of the "golden rule" of reciprocity underlines the extent to which the Duke offers an argument for charity no less economic than Bassanio's bag of gold. But Shylock claims in reply that the righteous are given a kind of autonomy; doing no wrong, they can be in or out of a network of exchanges at will, and need not fear judgment; thus Shylock approaches the Kantian claims to moral immunity from luck discussed above.

But Shylock continues:

> What judgment shall I dread doing no wrong?
> You have among you many a purchas'd slave,
> Which (like your asses, and your dogs and mules)
> You use in abject and in slavish parts,
> Because you bought them,—shall I say to you,
> Let them be free, marry them to your heirs?
> Why sweat they under burthens? let their beds
> Be made as soft as yours, and let their palates
> Be season'd with such viands? you will answer
> "The slaves are ours,"—so do I answer you:
> The pound of flesh which I demand of him
> Is dearly bought, 'tis mine and I will have it:
> If you deny me, fie upon your law! (4.1.89)

This outburst is both puzzling and powerful, even though the purpose it purports to justify—cutting Antonio—is monstrous. Walter Cohen comments that

> although the Christian characters in the play are better than Shylock, the Christian characters not in the play are not. In his famous "Jew" speech and in his declamation on slavery, Shylock adopts the strategy of equating Christian with Jew to justify his own murderous intentions. . . . But by the end of act 4 his analogies are strictly irrelevant to most of the Christian characters in the play. The Christians either have given up the practices that Shylock attributes to them or have never been guilty of them at all: certainly no Christian slaveholders appear in *The Merchant of Venice*.[33]

Cohen is surely generally right about the greater moral attractiveness—or what could more neutrally be described as moral advantages—of the Christians in this play, but he may be rash in his final assertion. Jessica tells Lorenzo, left in charge of Belmont, that Launcelot Gobbo has been reproving him for raising the price of pork by converting Jews to Christianity. He replies to Launcelot: "I shall answer that better to the commonwealth than you can the getting up of the negro's belly: the Moor is with child by you Launcelot!" (3.5.34). Black servants in aristocratic Christian households in the Renaissance were often slaves; Fernand Braudel comments of fifteenth-century Portugal, "as for the black slaves who ended up on the Portuguese market, they provided the households of the rich with the inevitable black servant."[34] One of the points of the suggestive exchange between Lorenzo and Launcelot may be to prepare us for the lack of any rebuttal to Shylock's comments about slavery in the next scene (though there is no way we could decide for certain whether or not this particular black servant was bought or inherited, rather than simply employed, by Portia).

Whether we are meant to think of Portia as a slave-holder or not, Shylock's speech forces attention to questions about the moral rights ·of persons and how such rights interact with property rights and with luck in birth. Immediately after invoking the moral autonomy of a virtuous rational agent who does no wrong, Shylock points out one of the social consequences of consistent acceptance of this autonomy: the inappropriateness of using human beings as means, and the unacceptability of slavery. Moreover, the sequence of his questions to the Christians (why not free them, marry them to your heirs, lift their burdens, soften their beds, and season their palates with your fine foods) moves from general liberation to the particular modes of conditioning in taste which contribute to the enhanced selfhood of an elite subject, a self whose realm of choice expansively includes both pursuit of dynastic ambitions and personal aesthetic cultivation. Shylock's example makes it very clear that this elite self-fashioning, the Renaissance selfhood celebrated by Burckhardt, is based on property rights, not on a universal access of rational subjects to the moral realm, not even on the right later identified by Hobbes as possessing one's body (which slavery as an institution tramples on). "You will answer, / 'The slaves are ours.'" If the Christians make this answer, Shylock implies, then they are in no position to argue that Antonio should be exempt from his contractually forfeited pound of flesh; one appalling social practice here underwrites another.

Shylock's appeal to the fearlessness of the righteous, then, suggests that one can to some extent insulate oneself from untoward circumstances (or bad luck) by obeying the laws of the community; if the law of Venice cannot be assimilated to a moral law which would guarantee moral autonomy to subjects, then it cannot (and should not be asked to) guarantee Antonio's safety from Shylock's knife.

The idea of moral autonomy flashes out, as it were, in Shylock's speech, and then is immediately shaded in such a way that Shylock's claim to autonomy links him to a privileged place in an exploitative slave-holding economy. But Shylock also speaks here as a Jew, and "the law" for him has at least two meanings: the Jewish law which he follows, thereby satisfying moral demands specific to him, as well as the Venetian law of contracts which gives him his vengeful hold on Antonio. The power of Shylock's position comes from the conflation of these claims to law, and the way they combine (with other factors in his character) to suggest a personality inimical to luck and bent on thriving without reference to it.

Shylock's double invocation of law recalls Rorty's suggestion that we think of civil society as a Kuwaiti bazaar surrounded by a set of clubs consisting of people who share and mutually reinforce core values, the bazaar being the multicultural economy in which each person attempts to interact profitably across differences. Antonio characterizes Venice in exactly these terms:

> The duke cannot deny the course of law:
> For the commodity that strangers have
> With us in Venice, if it be denied,
> Will much impeach the justice of the state,
> Since that the trade and profit of the city
> Consisteth of all nations. (3.3.26)

In glossing this passage John Russell Brown quotes a sixteenth-century *History of Italy* which says that "strangers . . . haue so muche libertee there, that though they speake verie il by the Venetians, so they attempte nothyng in effecte against theyr astate, no man shall controll them for it. . . . If thou be a Jewe, a Turke, or beleeuest in the diuell (so thou spreade not thyne opinions abroade) thou arte free from all controllement."[35] Venice functioned, or was perceived in England to function, very much like Rorty's market surrounded by clubs, the market where "many of the people . . . prefer to die rather than share the beliefs of many of those with whom they are haggling, yet . . . haggl [e] profitably away nevertheless."[36] Another point being made in the trial scene, then, and being underlined by Shylock in his discussion of slavery, is that one's private moral virtue, one's club identity, does not protect one in the marketplace, where one must take one's luck under whatever slight protection the civic law provides.

I have discussed Portia's protection of her endowment in the trial scene already, but her most famous speech there, like Shylock's invocation of the law, suggests the possibility of moral agency independent of moral luck. I quote at some length.

> PORTIA: Do you confess the bond?
> ANTONIO: I do.
> PORTIA: Then must the Jew be merciful.
> SHYLOCK: On what compulsion must I? tell me that.
> PORTIA: The quality of mercy is not strain'd,
>   It droppeth as the gentle rain from heaven
>   Upon the place beneath: it is twice blest,

It blesseth him that gives, and him that takes,
'Tis mightiest in the mightiest, it becomes
The throned monarch better than his crown.
His sceptre shows the force of temporal power,
The attribute to awe and majesty,
Wherein doth sit the dread and fear of kings:
But mercy is above this sceptred sway,
It is enthroned in the hearts of kings,
It is an attribute to God himself;
And earthly power doth then show likest God's
When mercy seasons justice: therefore Jew,
Though justice be thy plea, consider this,
That in the course of justice, none of us
Should see salvation: we do pray for mercy,
And that same prayer, doth teach us all to render
The deeds of mercy. I have spoke thus much
To mitigate the justice of thy plea,
Which if thou follow, this strict court of Venice
Must needs give sentence 'gainst the merchant there.
SHYLOCK: My deeds upon my head! I crave the law. (4.1.177)

Portia enjoins mercy precisely on the ground that merciful action springs from free agency, that it is not constrained and seeks no immediate profit. In this it imitates the agency of the socially powerful whose actions are not at the command of others, and Shylock, of course, has already linked this special agency of the powerful to the slavery of others. But Portia, by implying at least the possibility of a community reconstituted by commitment to mercy (a standard Christian hope), suggests that a form of wide-spread (if not unconditioned) moral advantage might be possible in a community composed of those who have been blest by the mercy of others and themselves bless others with mercy. But she endorses morally unconditioned action by citing the example of those loaded with constitutive moral luck.

In summary, the trial scene offers several perspectives on the possibility of moral action unqualified by circumstantial luck. Shylock has both suggested that by following the law one can avoid blame, and demonstrated that the law of this particular community has no categorical respect for the moral autonomy of persons. Portia, on the other hand, has recommended gratuitous generosity on the specific grounds that it is unconditional, that it occurs under no "compulsion," as Shylock puts it.

But while these positions are offered in dialogue with each other, they neither answer nor refute each other. Instead they point to the problem that moral action like other action is multiply conditioned and yet the notions of unconditionality and freedom of choice cling to those of morality and responsibility. Thomas Nagel, another antipragmatist, writing in response to Williams's argument, puts it in this way,

> The area of genuine agency, and therefore of legitimate moral judgment, seems to shrink under this scrutiny to an extensionless point. Everything seems to result from the combined influence of factors, antecedent and posterior to action, that are not within the agent's control. Since he cannot be responsible for them, he cannot be responsible for their results—though it may remain possible to take up the aesthetic or other evaluative analogues of the moral attitudes that are thus displaced.[37]

These aesthetic attitudes—and Portia's appeal to the opportunity that mercy gives to behave becomingly like a monarch is an aesthetic, indeed a snobbish, appeal as well as a moral one—put one back in an economy of social behaviors from which moral reflection is meant to release us.

Let me close this chapter by briefly extending this argument to make a final point about the retrospective effect of the trial scene on our appreciation of Portia and Bassanio. Williams's essay chiefly concerns not the constitutive moral luck which precedes, and thus conditions, a moment of moral choice, but rather moral luck with respect to outcomes, the contingencies of consequence which retrospectively determine the moral meaning of action. Gauguin deserts his family to go to Tahiti and paint; if he fails as an artist, or dies on the voyage, his act is morally different from what it turned out to be. More generally, if an act I undertake has a bad consequence I should have anticipated—a contingent consequence that might not have happened but did happen—then I will feel not merely "agent-regret" but will be judged culpable and will feel moral responsibility.[38] Nagel gives a cogent example of this kind of contingency: "If one negligently leaves the bath running with the baby in it, one will realize, as one bounds up the stairs toward the bathroom, that if the baby has drowned one has done something awful, whereas if it has not one has merely been careless."[39] From this point of view, one of the things the trial determines is whether Bassanio will turn out to have been morally culpable in allowing his friend to mortgage his body or not. Bassanio, it will be remembered, courted Portia with borrowed money on the supposition that his success in wooing could redeem past extravagance and repay his creditors. But through the unforeseen but foreseeable consequences of the merry bond, it turns out that Bassanio's otherwise successful suit may now cause the death of his benefactor. Antonio gives Bassanio the means to retrospectively moralize past fecklessness, and Portia in the trial supplies him with the moral luck of not having to blame himself for Antonio's death. Portia, then, does not merely tidy an economic balance sheet and put the balance of erotic obligation in her own column, she also ensures Bassanio's relative moral blamelessness. Loving Bassanio in this play means supplying him with moral luck; the morally attractive are blessed not only by privileges which they exploit but by others who wish them to remain lucky.

Who Pays in the *Henriad*?

PRINCE: Why, what a pox have I to do with my hostess of the tavern?

FALSTAFF: Well, thou hast called her to a reckoning many a time and oft.

PRINCE: Did I ever call for thee to pay thy part?

FALSTAFF: No, I'll give thee thy due, thou hast paid all there.

PRINCE: Yea, and elsewhere, so far as my coin would stretch, and where it would not I have used my credit.

FALSTAFF: Yea, and so used it that were it not here apparent that thou art heir apparent—But I prithee sweet wag, shall there be gallows standing in England when thou art king?

1 Henry IV

Like *The Merchant of Venice*, probably composed the year before *1 Henry IV*, the Henry plays turn on relations of debt, homosocial affection and rivalry, and the troubled inheritance of blessings.[1] Many of the patterns discussed in the previous chapter on *The Merchant of Venice*, where I argued that erotic and economic blessings all run toward Portia and the sophisticated Christian commercial aristocracy she represents, also shape the *Henriad*. In the tetralogy, however, Shakespeare shows the placeless market at work by auditing a messy process of intergenerational royal legitimation rather than a marriage venture. Without quite the same precision, and on a larger scale modifying materials less at his own disposal, Shakespeare charts a flow of money, affection, obligation, legitimacy, and authority from many springs into the royal lap of Henry V. Hal has no hesitation, as does Hotspur reorganizing the map of Britain, to "have the current in this place damm'd up, / And here . . . run / In a new channel fair and evenly" (*1H4* 3.1.97).[2]

Hal retrenches at the expense and pain of friends and family as well as enemies, and at most points, I will argue, he understands what he does in economic terms, as a transaction which yields him either a profit or a debt that in turn places him under an obligation he must erase. Injuries to Hotspur, to Henry IV, to Poins, to Falstaff, and to the French are not only turned to Hal's advantage, but figure in the play as debts repaid or liabilities eliminated; any remaining liabilities are potential lingering obligations which might hamper Henry as king. Before Agincourt he bargains with God, asking that future gestures pay off any remaining obligation he owes to Richard II's memory.

Ultimately, this chapter argues that Shakespeare presents royal legitimacy in pragmatic terms, as a node of advantageous purposeful exchanges in an economy of credit and negotiation. Thus the Henry plays "de-divinize" kingship in roughly the way the sonnets go about explaining their own survival or *The Merchant of Venice* supplies an unromantic context for various loving gestures. Richard Rorty comments on the de-divinizing perspective of Harold Bloom on poetry, Nietzsche on truth, and Freud on conscience:

> The strategy is the same in all these cases: It is to substitute a tissue of contingent relations, a web which stretches backward and forward through past and future time, for a formed, unified, present, self-contained substance, something capable of being seen steadily and whole.[3]

I have named this "tissue" an "economy" throughout this study, not only because the terms in which it is figured by Shakespeare are very often economic ones, but because these "contingent relations" generally operate as and through transactions between competing individuals, groups, and discourses. Unlike tissues, moreover, economies cause pain. Economic terms and transactions are particularly striking in the *Henriad*.

It is not unusual to argue that the *Henriad* provides the materials for a demystification of royal power and of state power.[4] I believe, however, that here, as in *The Merchant of Venice*, the dramatic organization is more tightly woven with economic metaphors and responds more completely to a pragmatic analysis than has yet been been shown— partly, no doubt, because in current criticism socioeconomic speculators tend to privilege ideological fissures and to assume that the recognition of unified dramatic effect must serve mystified social idealization rather than demystified social understanding. I do not agree. Throughout this book, and especially in this chapter, I read plays or sequences of plays as reacting to the exchange patterns in Shakespeare's culture by trying to incorporate the density and variety of one or more phases in an exchange cycle—showing how gain and loss are distributed, how widely varied institutions are involved, how a placeless market can bind disparate events into something like a dramatic structure. By testifying to the dense pattern of transactional analysis in these plays— and by noting how fully these transactions are worked out inside them—I hope to show, as in the previous chapter, how detailed an account Shakespeare has drawn up.

As my epigraph suggests, perhaps the most elaborate and most interesting set of erotic, financial, and historical obligations lies between

Hal and Falstaff. The activities of Falstaff promote our sense of the economy of this play as an "affluent" one (to return to terms I developed in chapter 2). Hal is himself wise to the ways of accumulating wealth and opportunity, but Falstaff (unhampered by assets as he is) is dedicated to promoting circulation, to fertilizing the market, and thus becomes not only an important instructor in market behavior for Hal, but also an important counter to him: where Hal resists outflow, Falstaff encourages it. The difference between Hal and Falstaff is something that critics have made much of—too much, as I will argue— yet there is a difference; when Falstaff is excluded, the economy of these plays is impoverished.

I begin, however, with Henry IV's problems with the Percies and the relatively clear-cut relation between Hal and Hotspur, then turn to the more complex and ambiguous relation between Hal and his father, before coming at last to Hal's relations with Falstaff. Falstaff is, I will argue, more closely bound by the economic logic that serves Hal in his quest for legitimation than is usually thought; the carnivalesque repudiations of obligation that Falstaff frequently offers are part of his consistent economic strategy.

č

Even before Hal comes forward as a contender for royal legitimacy, Henry IV repudiates obligation incurred before his reign, in particular the support he received from the Percies in his contest with Richard II. A king under obligation is in danger himself and dangerous to others. As Worcester says of Henry IV to Northumberland and Hotspur early in *1 Henry IV*:

> . . . bear ourselves as even as we can,
> The King will always think him in our debt,
> And think we think ourselves unsatisfy'd,
> Till he hath found a time to pay us home:
> And see already how he doth begin
> To make us strangers to his looks of love. (1.3.279)

Erotic and political obligations, and the dangerous need of kings to feel free of them, are identified here, and we are reminded of the homosocial coin in which Henry Bolingbroke self-consciously rewarded the Percies in *Richard II*:

> I count myself in nothing else so happy
> As in a soul rememb'ring my good friends,
> And as my fortune ripens with thy love,
> It shall be still thy true love's recompense. (2.3.46)[5]

Hotspur's anger at the king in *1 Henry IV* is thus fuelled by a sense of political and erotic betrayal (see 1.3.246–251). He does not, however, feel that the royal love denied to his family has been redirected toward Hal, though he has thought of the possibility and made contingency plans: "but that I think his father loves him not, . . . I would have him poison'd with a pot of ale" (1.3.228). (Henry IV says he wishes it could be proved that some fairy switched the two boys in their cradles [1.1.85], so Hotspur probably has good warrant for the erroneous belief that the king does not love his son.)

Hal, in turn, mocks Hotspur's martial energy with manic playfulness after he and Poins have robbed Falstaff at Gad's Hill:

> PRINCE: What's o'clock, Francis?
>
> FRANCIS: Anon, anon, sir.
>
> PRINCE: That ever this fellow should have fewer words than a parrot, and yet the son of a woman! His industry is up-stairs and downstairs, his eloquence the parcel of a reckoning. I am not yet of Percy's mind, the Hotspur of the north, he that kills me some six or seven dozen of Scots at a breakfast, washes his hands, and says to his wife, "Fie upon this quiet life, I want work". "O my sweet Harry", says she, "how many hast thou killed today?" "Give my roan horse a drench", says he, and answers, "Some fourteen", an hour after; "a trifle, a trifle". I prithee call in Falstaff; I'll play Percy, and that damned brawn shall play Dame Mortimer his wife. (2.4.94)

The transition from Francis the drawer to Hotspur occurs with mysterious abruptness. Perhaps Hal mocks Hotspur's monomania in contrast to his own propensity to be "of all humours" (2.4.90), as A. R. Humphreys suggests in a note, but the odd shift to Hotspur occurs on the word "reckoning"—bill to be paid—and Hal says that he is "not *yet* of Percy's mind," suggesting that he will assume that mind to pay a reckoning at some point.

As it turns out, Hal thinks of Hotspur very much as an instrument of credit.[6] He says to his father in the first forgiveness-of-prodigality scene:

> I will redeem all this on Percy's head,
>
> . . . .
>
> . . . For the time will come
> That I shall make this northern youth exchange
> His glorious deeds for my indignities.
> Percy is but my factor, good my lord,
> To engross up glorious deeds on my behalf,
> And I will call him to so strict account

That he shall render every glory up,
Yea, even the slightest worship of his time,
Or I will tear the reckoning from his heart. (3.2.132, 144)

Hal, who at the opening of the play has called Mistress Quickly to the
reckoning many a time and oft but never (yet) called on Falstaff to pay
his part, vows to exact a strict payment from Hotspur, who has been
acting as his agent. Hotspur, had he not been in rebellion (and so far
he has won no military kudos as a rebel; rather he has excelled in
English border wars against the Scots), would indeed have properly
been a factor engrossing glorious deeds, but for Hal's royal father
rather than Hal. "Is not this an honorable spoil? / A gallant prize?"
(1.1.74), says Henry IV at the opening of *1 Henry IV* in delight at
Hotspur's victory over the Douglas. The claim that Hotspur is engrossing greatness for *Hal* bears an ominous hint that Hal plans to
succeed his father quickly, as well as showing that Hal intends to win
instantly in one violent encounter the honor and reputation which
Hotspur has accumulated in years of bloody effort. In either case Hotspur's honor is a credit for the Plantagenets to use rather than to repay;
Henry IV's anger at Hotspur at the outset of *1 Henry IV* derives from
Hotspur's apparent desire to keep prisoners for himself rather than
deliver them to Henry for royal profit.

Honor here is itself an exchangeable commodity which, like money,
can move all at once from one person's possession to another's—hence
Hal's use of a vocabulary of mercantile transaction on the battlefield.
To the Douglas he says, claiming to have enlarged his strength with
the spirit-hoards of men Douglas has killed:

The spirits
Of valiant Shirley, Stafford, Blunt are in my arms.
It is the Prince of Wales that threatens thee,
Who never promiseth but he means to pay. (5.4.39)

Hal pays out in effort, but he also means to profit by the exchanges
he enters into, as he makes clear to Hotspur when they finally meet:

HOTSPUR: . . . would to God
    Thy name in arms were now as great as mine!
PRINCE: I'll make it greater ere I part from thee,
    And all the budding honours on thy crest
    I'll crop to make a garland for my head. (5.4.68)

When he has killed Hotspur, Hal's battlefield mourning for him (which
many actors turn into purely generous pathos) is partly a meditation

on how much Hotspur has diminished and thus potentially on how much Hal has expanded:

> Fare thee well, great heart!
> Ill-weav'd ambition, how much art thou shrunk!
> When that this body did contain a spirit,
> A kingdom for it was too small a bound;
> But now two paces of the vilest earth
> Is room enough. This earth that bears thee dead
> Bears not alive so stout a gentleman.
> If thou wert sensible of courtesy
> I should not make so dear a show of zeal;
> But let my favours hide thy mangled face,
> And even in thy behalf I'll thank myself
> For doing these fair rites of tenderness. (5.4.86)

Though he sees his "spirit" as in some way smaller or less "stout" than Percy's—either naturally so, or because it has not yet broken free from the confinements which hem it in—Hal thanks himself as if he had indeed engrossed Hotspur's identity with his honors.

Thus far all of Hal's comments on Hotspur are of a piece, and while his attitude toward taking over the mana of enemies may remind one disconcertingly of rumors that Idi Amin kept the hearts of erstwhile political rivals in the refrigerator, his plan has nothing overtly unrealistic about it given that he himself can command the valor and skill to kill Hotspur, as he does. Hal has "redeemed time" vis-à-vis Hotspur by forcibly, yet "honorably," appropriating Hotspur's treasury of honor. Moreover, Hal both understands and represents this as a profitable transaction which comes at the end of a speculative venture in which Hotspur has been his unwitting agent.

One of the curiosities of the Henry plays, however, is that this very feasible plan of Hal's does not appear to work. He does not seem to gain all Hotspur's honors by slaying him; he remains in disrepute with his father and the court in *2 Henry IV* and with the French aristocrats in *Henry V*. It is, in fact, at Agincourt, and not until then, that Hal assumes Hotspur's mantle. There are several possible reasons for this.

Hotspur dies in part for his father's and uncle's sins; at any rate his greatness in death is accentuated by comparison with their ignoble behavior. Northumberland fails to arrive for the battle and Worcester fails honestly to deliver Henry IV's terms to Hotspur. Worcester's reasons are interesting; he believes that Henry's pardon for Hotspur might turn out to be sincere, but not Henry's pardon for himself or his brother.

> My nephew's trespass may be well forgot . . .
> All his offences live upon my head
> And on his father's. We did train him on,
> And, his corruption being ta'en from us,
> We as the spring of all shall pay for all. (5.2.16)

Hal, laying his scarf over Hotspur's mangled face, expects this separation of paternal guilt and filial glory to be accomplished:

> Adieu, and take thy praise with thee to heaven!
> Thy ignominy sleep with thee in the grave,
> But not remember'd in thy epitaph! (5.4.98)

But Hal has not separated himself from *his* father in the course of the battle; indeed, as his claim to the Douglas about the spirits of Blunt, Shirley, and Stafford suggests, he too fights inevitably as one of Henry IV's simulacra, however much he may individuate himself both by valor and by proleptic hints of his own future sovereignty. When they finally meet, he says to Hotspur:

> Two stars keep not their motion in one sphere,
> Nor can one England brook a double reign
> Of Harry Percy and the Prince of Wales. (5.4.64)

Thus Hotspur is an obstacle to Hal's "reign," but the chief such obstacle is of course Hal's own father, whom he has just rescued from the Douglas. Hal is placed in the paradoxical situation of having to accrue honor by taking it from Hotspur, yet also to preserve credit by yielding honor accrued to Henry IV.

It is not only, then, the resurrected Falstaff's attempt to steal credit for slaying Hotspur which prevents Shrewsbury from serving as Hal's full redemption of time. Hal aims, I believe, not simply, perhaps not at all, at reconciliation with his father, but at a particular kind of legitimized inheritance from him, and thus the Hotspur transaction does not pay off for Hal as fully or immediately as it might have. "I could have better spared a better man" (5.4.103), says Hal over what he thinks is Falstaff's corpse immediately after killing Hotspur, and there may be glancing reference to his father here, conflicted and contradictory in that Hal has "spared" his father in rescuing him from the Douglas, but could also happily "spare" him in the sense of "doing without him" which he applies to the dead Falstaff.

ё

Hal's relation to his father is more difficult to describe than his relation to Hotspur. Hal himself seems much less certain of its substance. Though at the beginning of *1 Henry IV* Hal seems cynical about politics under Falstaff's tutelage, we know from his early soliloquy (1.2.190) that he in fact has serious plans to emerge as the sun from behind a cloud—which in the metaphorics of the history plays implies that he looks forward to kingship. Without exactly saying so, Hal seems preoccupied with the problem of legitimate inheritance, which is to say with the questionable legitimacy of his father's rule and the danger that the same questions will trouble his own. The cause cited in the chronicles for father-son distrust—that Henry IV believed his son to be planning usurpation[7]—is never mentioned by Shakespeare. And, though Hal impersonates his father in Eastcheap and allows Falstaff to do so, Hal is uncommunicative about his father outside his father's presence.[8] It seems plausible, then, to posit a Hal who in this one area is puzzling his way among imperatives he cannot articulate or perhaps even comprehend, his own fluent rationalizations of his course notwithstanding.

One of these imperatives is the tavern-haunting which maintains his distance from his father; aside from attraction to Falstaff, Hal appears to have no clear diagnosis of his own ambivalence about the court. Moreover, while the parable of the prodigal son obviously governs his father's understanding of his various returns (and covertly authorizes the occasional hints that Falstaff, that "roasted Manningtree ox with the pudding in his belly" [*1H4* 2.4.446], who "run and roared, as ever [Hal] heard bull-calf" at Gad's Hill [2.4.256], is fated to be a mature version of the fatted calf whose sacrifice should celebrate that event), clearly something about Hal's heroic return in *1 Henry IV* remains incomplete, since both the distance and the reformation have to be reenacted in *2 Henry IV*.[9] I have already suggested that the Shrewsbury enactment of the prodigal's return was incomplete because Hal's full redemption involves coming into his inheritance. Henry IV does not die tidily at Shrewsbury and allow his heroic son to become a better reincarnation of him. King Henry survives, and the reformed, returned son cannot simply replace his father, but instead must enact a provisional reconciliation with him. Genuine or lasting reconciliation has not been achieved, for reasons about which the play does not speak directly. They become somewhat clearer when the cycle must be gone through again in *2 Henry IV*, yet more harrowingly, with clearer accusations by Henry IV of parricide (after Hal has apparently stolen the crown) and with the father's actual death, the brutal casting off of a father-surrogate in Falstaff, and the adoption of a pure state superego as father in the person of the Lord Chief Justice.

Hal's alienation, like the Percy rebellion and his father's sickness, grows partly, of course, from an oedipal reenactment, but it also grows out of the mythic guilt of Henry IV: from the fact that, as a half-willing regicide, Henry IV is a national parricide whose paternity to the state must therefore always be in question and whose bequest to his son must necessarily be troubled.[10] As Hotspur puts it before Shrewsbury, Henry IV's hostility led the Percies "to pry / Into his title, the which we find / Too indirect for long continuance" (*1H4* 4.3.103). Hal's future is part of this "continuance," and so Hal must manage not to inherit Henry IV's guilt while, to paraphrase Claudius in *Hamlet*, "retaining the offence" in the form of the crown. To avoid reenacting his father's crime he must *not* be parricidal (and thus he rescues his father from death), and yet to avoid being a simple "continuance" he must at the same time punish his father, cause his death, and take kingship from him rather than receiving it (and the guilt of its usurpation) passively from Henry's bloody hands. For that reason Hal's oddly mute and joyless "prodigality"—the distance from his father which does not appear to arise from any actual taste for dissolute behavior on Hal's part—exists (especially in *2 Henry IV*) precisely as pure resistance and distance, which must, however, at key moments eloquently protest against being interpreted as parricidal aggression or even filial hardheartedness. To put it more sweepingly, Hal can only come close to his father when his father may be about to die, but his father must only be allowed to die while acknowledging that his son would protect him from death if he could.

Shakespeare thus takes the plot of the prodigal's return and makes it into something more delicate and sinister, a systematic taking of advantage that Hal himself seems to pursue consistently but not to understand. Certainly he understands it less well than he does his relationships to Hotspur and Falstaff. While Hal can cheerfully express his intentions toward Hotspur as a mercantile venture, his intentions toward his father remain veiled even from him. His Machiavellian soliloquy in *1 Henry IV*, which expresses his intentions toward Falstaff, begins with Hal's claim "I know you all, and will awhile uphold / The unyok'd humour of your idleness" (1.2.190) and ends with Hal's pledge that he will "so offend, to make offence a skill, / Redeeming time when men think least I will" (1.2.211), makes full sense in *2 Henry IV* only when the king too is one of those whom Hal "knows" and at whose expense he will eventually shine, but we have no evidence that Hal recognizes this. A logic of state beyond his control (a discourse of legitimation which is not governed by the will of any particular subject) seems to be at work like an invisible hand here. An objective correlative—or at any rate a satisfactory explanation—is, nonetheless, not lacking for Hal's repeated departures and returns.

"I'll so offend to make offense a skill, / Redeeming time when men least think I will" suggests a repetitive and punitive strategy, which, without being aware of its true object, Hal pursues purposefully. Such unconscious intentions, and the sense of the uncanny they bring to apparently fully explained action, are present from the beginnings of drama. Jean-Pierre Vernant, describing complexities of motive in Greek tragedy, writes of

> this duality, or rather tension, in the psychology of the protagonists. All that the hero feels, says, and does springs from his character, his *ethos*, which the poets analyze just as subtly and interpret just as positively as might, for example, the orators or a historian such as Thucydides. But at the same time these feelings, pronouncements, and actions also appear as the expression of a religious power, a *daimon* operating through them.[11]

In this instance, however, we can find a less mystical explanation for Hal's unconscious intentions. The daimon haunting him, despite his own suggestion that it is "a devil . . . in the likeness of an old fat man" (*1HIV* 2.4.441), is his own, and England's, need that he become a legitimate monarch. The prodigality which is the daimon's work is largely confined to acts of displaced aggression against father figures followed by denials of parricidal intent and attempts at reparation. The mythic blow to the Lord Chief Justice followed by the even more vaguely presented punishment of alienation from his father's council serves as a pattern for Hal's actions while his father remains alive. His final rejection of Falstaff is only the last in a series of humiliations and disempowerments he makes Falstaff suffer, and he constantly and increasingly separates himself from Falstaff throughout both parts of *Henry IV*. He is, however, simultaneously doing the same thing to his own father, so that he is left in *2 Henry IV* complaining insultingly to Poins of how completely he has been thrown into low company (2.2.9).

Hal's promise "to pay the debt I never promised"—reversed on the battlefield when he announces himself as one "who never promises but he means to pay"—is much emphasized both by those who see Hal fashioning himself coldly for successful monarchy and by those who see him casting off evil and delighting his family in the manner of the prodigal son. But if we think of Hal as a scourge to his father— something he evidently is but denies with passionate sincerity at every opportunity—then the declaration can be seen to mean more than Hal intends. However illegitimate the Percies' claim in their rebellion to be merely heeding the outcry of Richard's spilt blood, Henry IV's usurpation and the murder of Richard have created a debt which Hal can only pay by denying his father the consolation of untroubled succession. So Hal alienates himself from his father while saving his father's physical life. In rejecting Falstaff he underlines his refusal to gratify the affections and designs of any father except the state in person of the Lord Chief Justice. This is the kind of reckoning up of accounts, and use of defeated or dead enemies to clear balance sheets, which we see everywhere in the history plays. Henry IV is made to pay for Richard, and Falstaff for Henry IV, in a succession of sacrificial reckonings which Hal cannot be said to control, however thoroughgoing his performance of them may be. When finally he announces to his brothers and the Lord Chief Justice, "My father is gone wild into his grave, / For in his tomb lie my affections" (5.2.123), he half-acknowledges that his own ambivalence pursued his father fury-like to the grave.

The economic analysis of dynastic processes must be a grim one. Our sense of its grimness, however, comes partly from an anti-economic prejudice: a sense that what is most noble, or most intimate, must be imagined in terms insulated from the marketplace. But the plays also suggest (and this is the strength of the school of providential readers against whom most recent critics of the play have reacted) that a proper inheritance of blessings may be of immense common profit. A reservoir of public love, trust, and need waits to make itself available to a legitimate sovereign, a kind of mother-love which rewards the victor in the male agon of succession on which the plays concentrate. Richard Wheeler, citing Gaunt on England as "this teeming womb" (*R2* 2.1.51) and Henry IV on civil war as England "daub[ing] her lips with her own children's blood" (*1H4* 1.1.6), comments that "an England infused with the symbolic attributes of a mother offers, in the midst of factionalized encounters, not a further source of conflict, but an absolutely undivided loyalty for Hal, which he serves even when he seems to flaunt his father."[12] Hal gains this love fully at Agincourt. Phyllis Rackin, in her persuasive recent account of the history plays as enacting in themselves a kind of contest between providential and Machiavellian modes of historical explanation, comments that Hal "uses Agincourt as an enormous trial by combat to establish the legitimacy of his rule and earn his place in providential history."[13]

The national mother-love that allegedly greets Henry (whether at his coronation or after his victories at the end of *Henry V*) functions as a last-minute heart transplant for the *Henriad*. To the extent that one can locate a "heart" in the sequence as a whole, critics have traditionally looked, and still look, to Falstaff.[14] Hal is often opposed to Falstaff as coldness to warmth, calculation to improvisation, work to play, reason of state to anarchic eros, social order to chaos.[15] But Falstaff cannot be opposed to Hal in terms of a transcendence of an economic understanding of his situation. Falstaff is at least as prone to think in these terms as Hal.

⛎

Falstaff operates within a vast network of transactions of which he is thoroughly aware: he plays them off against each other, systematically exploiting the variety and convertability of social goods to defer all final payments. In one sense the prince is Falstaff's great investment— the Portia to his Bassanio—whose coronation will redeem all his past extravagance, but in another Falstaff understands the system of exchanges to be a boundless pattern which permits endless ingenious substitutions and redescriptions, and thus he does not seriously entertain the idea of a final payoff. No one knows where to have him, but this does not mean that he does not know where he is.

Humanist critics of the *Henriad* have, at least since Samuel Johnson and Maurice Morgann, stressed Falstaff's magnificent freedom, his comic overthrow of convention and obligation. A. C. Bradley's comment that "the law, and the categorical imperative, and our station and its duties, and conscience, and reputation, and other people's opinions . . . are to him absurd; and to reduce a thing *ad absurdum* is to reduce it to nothing and to walk about free and rejoicing,"[16] or W. H. Auden's that the essential Falstaff is "the Falstaff of . . . Verdi's opera . . . the unkillable self-sufficient immortal whose verdict on existence is *Tutto nel mondo è burla*,"[17] may be taken as typical. Both of these critics go on to note the extent to which Falstaff turns out to be vulnerable to Hal and to the political necessities Hal serves. Auden compares Falstaff to a mermaid who falls in love with a mortal prince: "the price she pays for her infatuation is the loss of her immortality without the compensation of temporal happiness."[18] We hear from these critics a story of the joyous autonomy of the human spirit, a spirit contained and wounded, cribbed, cabin'd, and confined by the social and political conditions of human life, yet heroically laughing at them—a comic version of what William Empson, thinking of Falstaff and Hal as well as of the sonnets, calls "the feeling that life is essentially inadequate to the human spirit, and yet that a good life must avoid saying so."[19] That spirit is more concentrated or more vivid (to risk the circularity involved in most praises of life) in Falstaff than in Hal, and Bradley at the end of his essay does not hesitate to identify it with what he values in Shakespeare's genius:

> To show that Falstaff's freedom of soul was in part illusory, and that the realities of life refused to be conjured away by his humour—this was what we might expect from Shakespeare's unfailing sanity, but it was surely no achievement beyond the power of lesser men. The achievement was Falstaff himself, and the conception of that freedom of soul, a freedom illusory only in part, and attainable only by a mind which had received from Shakespeare's own the inexplicable touch of infinity which he bestowed on Hamlet and Macbeth and Cleopatra, but denied to Henry the Fifth.[20]

The opposition between Falstaffian freedom and love and Henrician coldness and manipulation that Bradley, Empson, and Auden all emphasize remains an important part of Stephen Greenblatt's influential recent discussion of the Henry plays. Thus Greenblatt notes (shortly before quoting Empson) that Falstaff's claim to be "genuinely [Hal's] adoring friend and not merely a parasite" is part of "the fantasy of identity that Falstaff holds out to Hal and that Hal empties out," and goes on to say that Falstaff is not exhausted by Hal's treatment of him: "the dreams of plenitude are not abandoned altogether—Falstaff in particular has an imaginative life that overflows the confines of the play itself."[21] Greenblatt also retains and indeed takes as central Bradley's sense that the play compels us to admire Henry for his very success in doing those things for which we dislike him. In an utterly characteristic vein, much mocked by later critical generations, Bradley tells us what Hal should have done with Falstaff:

> He ought in honour long ago to have given Sir John clearly to understand that they must say good-bye on the day of his accession. And, having neglected to do this, he ought not to have lectured him as his misleader. It was not only ungenerous, it was dishonest. It looks disagreeably like an attempt to buy the praise of the respectable at the cost of honour and truth. And it succeeded. Henry *always* succeeded.[22]

Compare Greenblatt, here discussing the ways the rejection of Falstaff is remembered in *Henry V*:

> Hal's symbolic killing of Falstaff—which might have been recorded as a bitter charge against him—is advanced by Fluellen as the climactic manifestation of his virtues. . . . The betrayal of friends does not subvert but rather sustains the moral authority and the compelling glamour of power. That authority, as the play defines it, is precisely the ability to betray one's friends without stain.[23]

There is a yet more important continuity than a shared attitude toward Henry V between Bradley's idealist humanism and Greenblatt's skeptical historicism.

After an acute demonstration that the rejection of Falstaff was entirely in character for Hal, who exhibits from the first "that readiness to use other people as means to his own ends which is a conspicuous feature in his father," Bradley reaches what he feels is a puzzle:

> The natural conclusion is that Shakespeare *intended* us to feel resentment against Henry. And yet that cannot be, for it implies that he meant the play to end disagreeably; and no one who understands Shakespeare at all will consider that supposition for a moment credible. . . . Thus our pain and resentment, if we feel them, are wrong, in the sense that they do not answer to the dramatist's intention. But it does not follow that they are wrong in a further sense. They may be right, because the dramatist has missed what he aimed at. . . . We wish Henry a glorious reign and much joy of his crew of hypocritical politicians, lay and clerical; but our hearts go with Falstaff to the Fleet, or, if necessary, to Arthur's bosom or wheresomever he is.[24]

Bradley is on shaky ground, of course, when he says that Shakespeare cannot have wanted the play to end unpleasantly, as if some law of genre or principle of Shakespearean composition guarantees unequivocal endings (consider, for example, the ends of *Richard II* and *Troilus and Cressida*). Question-begging phrases like "no one who understands Shakespeare at all will consider . . ." are, indeed, unusual in Bradley, who, like Greenblatt, ordinarily persuades us calmly and without bullying, and this one may be taken to signal that Bradley is bluffing his way over an ideological crevasse, in this case one having to do with nationalism. What Bradley means, presumably, is that Shakespeare, in the course of depicting the evolution of the English hero-king, cannot mean us to harbor cynical reservations about his character at the same time that we are celebrating his coronation; he may also mean that Shakespeare as craftsman must have intended us to have tidy feelings at the end of his play. That is, both patriotism and commitments to aesthetic wholeness seem endangered by Bradley's resentment of the rejection of Falstaff: therefore Shakespeare must not have intended Bradley to feel it.[25] As seen above, Bradley neatly transcends the problem by implying that the political cannot fully contain the human, and that Shakespeare is the greater for not squeezing Falstaff into a rejectable package.

Bradley's picture of Henry's crafted, efficient, and inexorable rise as the container, and Falstaff as the spontaneous, desirable, and partly uncontainable contained, invites comparison with Greenblatt's brilliant exploration of the collaboration between social containment and social subversion, where subversion is the retrospective object of contemporary, possibly sentimental, social eros. After quoting Maynard Mack on Hal as "an ideal image of the potentialities of the English character" (a remark Mack may derive from Bradley),[26] Greenblatt observes that "such an ideal image involves as its positive condition the constant production of its own radical subversion and the powerful containment of that subversion."[27] I do not cite humanist readings of the Falstaff-Hal relation in order to turn on them categorically in the manner to which readers of contemporary Shakespeare criticism have become accustomed. Nor do I assimilate them to Greenblatt in order to indict or question him for resuscitating or adapting humanist aesthetic categories in his social ones.[28] Rather, my concern is to point out that the kind of economic pragmatism I see at work in the *Henriad* supplies a framework for characterizing not only Hal's commitment to power but also Falstaff's commitment to freedom.

We have more detailed financial information about Falstaff than we do about any other character in Shakespeare, not excluding Timon or the characters in *The Merchant of Venice*, whose debts and credits I discussed in the previous chapter. Falstaff lives in a perpetual flow of petty credits and debits, often the results of tricks or illicit transactions; and all of them have a way of suddenly and (were Falstaff not Falstaff) embarrassingly becoming explicit. Falstaff also embodies and promotes carnival and festivity with magnificent self-consciousness: he knows who pays for carnival and makes sure that it is not himself. Whether we take our ideas of carnival from Barber or from Bakhtin, this strategic festivity on Falstaff's part involves some adjustment of received notions of what carnival is all about.

Bakhtin is fascinated by what he calls the language of the marketplace, but one reads him in vain for attention to the fact that the oaths and invitations and parodies and obscenities which characterize "the language of the people" on this site are lubricated by a continuous flow of money and goods in exchange. Bakhtin's lack of distinction between carnivals (where festive purposes dominate and lubricate exchange) and fairs (where economic purposes dominate and lubricate festivity) is an index of this inattention on his part to the importance of the economic function of markets and fairs. He does not see the possible relation between the demystifying language of the marketplace he celebrates and the de-idealizing regulation of value by demand and supply (to the extent that they were allowed to dominate) in the early modern markets and fairs. Carnival per se—that is, actual carnivals like the one Rabelais wrote an account of[29]—might, on the one hand, be on particular occasions of state celebration a gift from the ruling classes or the church to the people; the festive grotesquerie of markets and fairs, on the other hand, arises from the recognition that underlying the idealized ceremonies of the rich were exchange-systems and money circulation which made the state into a grotesque body whose blood and excrement were goods and money.

Though the Henry plays are not much concerned with marketplaces per se, they elaborately document, in both festive and official settings, the particulars of supply and demand, of indebtedness or wealth. When a feast is toward, it is normally clear who is paying for it, and this is especially the case when Falstaff is involved, since he is often sponsoring but never paying. We see this in the epigraph quoted from the opening of *1 Henry IV*, where Hal points out that he has never called for Falstaff to pay his part, and also near the end of *2 Henry IV*, where Falstaff patronizes Shallow and prepares to fleece him.

The accounts picked from Falstaff's pockets by Hal after Gad's Hill reappear when a desperate Mistress Quickly has Falstaff attached for nonpayment of debt before he marches to confront the rebels in Gaultree Forest. Many debts in the play, and all of Falstaff's, have an erotic aspect:

> FALSTAFF: What is the gross sum that I owe thee?
> MISTRESS QUICKLY: Marry, if thou wert an honest man, thyself and the money too. Thou didst swear to me upon a parcel-gilt goblet, sitting in my Dolphin chamber, at the round table, by a sea-coal fire, upon Wednesday in Wheeson week, when the Prince broke thy head for liking his father to a singing man of Windsor—thou didst swear to me then, as I was washing thy wound, to marry me, and make me my lady thy wife. (2.1.82)

It is probably significant that Falstaff should make such a promise at a moment when he was at odds with Prince Hal (apparently for likening his father to an impersonator of Richard II—i.e., pointing out the illegitimacy of his rule),[30] since he has little time for women when he and Hal are on good terms. The erotic and economic links are sometimes underlined:

> PRINCE: Sirrah, do I owe you a thousand pound?
> FALSTAFF: A thousand pound, Hal? A million, thy love is worth a million, thou owest me thy love. (*1H4* 3.3.134)

But Hal from the opening of *1 Henry IV* characteristically turns aside such claims of obligation:

> FALSTAFF: . . . banish plump Jack, and banish all the world!
> PRINCE: I do, I will. (2.4.473)

Because Hal and Falstaff both display acute awareness of the manipulability of love and holiday, any categorical opposition between Henry's antifestive legitimization procedures and Falstaff's carnival is too stark;[31] it fails, moreover, to distinguish between carnival's officially encouraged uses and excessive or indecorous ones, the sort which excite official repression. Bakhtin, of course, sees the *spirit* of carnival as rejecting just this sort of distinction or limitation. But the *Henriad* is full of precise intelligence about where in social usage such lines are drawn, and Falstaff himself is an expert in manipulating the human tendency to forget particular obligations in the spirit of generous neglect of rule sponsored by carnival. Thus a carnival site like the Eastcheap tavern is not immune to cash reckonings even by people who are festive agents, such as Mistress Quickly. Indeed, it is built on such reckonings—at considerable human cost, which Hal explores in interrogating Francis the drawer. One mode of containment suggested by Greenblatt's account of the play is the accepted rhythm by which carnival festivity gives way to solemn festivity or crisis—periods of public solidification or reckoning—so that the socially mandated periods of carnival can recur. Hal, the master of transformations, is particularly alert to decorum in such matters, as is shown by his insistence that celebration of the victory at Agincourt not precede or contaminate the Te Deum at the battle's end.

To describe the relationship between Hal and Falstaff in the pragmatic terms that the play encourages, Hal is always aware that no carnival suspends settlement of outstanding debts indefinitely, and Falstaff lives by such suspensions. Yet the inscription of cultural conflict occurs not only between the court and the tavern, but within the economy of each, and Falstaff is a figure not only of excess but of manipulation of the carnivalesque.

Thus, as far as the rejection of Falstaff is concerned, it matters that Hal—or rather Henry V—rejects him when engaged in a royal coronation procession, a piece of public ceremony but one inconsistent with carnival, though directly prior to a period of mandated public celebration. (There is only one genuine public festival in the Henry plays—that following Hal's coronation—and Falstaff evidently spends it in the Fleet.) Much of the problem with Falstaff's behavior is that he does not observe the solemnities which are meant to bound carnival, at least in the early modern calendar: he fails to suspend parody and irreverence for battle and public crisis or for public ceremony. He has no other mode. Even the Lord Chief Justice, who presumably disapproves of carnival behavior at any time, reproaches Falstaff with a failure to observe decorum, to know when to do what: "Doth this become your place, your time, and business?" (*2H4*, 2.1.64). Perhaps

the spirit of carnival, as in Sir Toby Belch, defies time, especially
closing time, yet the medieval church calendar which allotted carnival
frequent and lengthy time periods made clear when it was meant to
happen and when not—not *during* coronations or battles or religious
services, for instance, though *after* any one of them.[32] (The eventual
imposition of central control on English public houses took the form
of strictly regulating their hours.)

One feature of taverns of which the plays make much is the possibility of running up large unpayable debts by customarily buying current
consideration with promises of future payment. Since this, notoriously, is what Hal does with audiences in his first soliloquy and with
his father in their first interview, there seems a further hidden parallel
between Falstaff's promissory behavior (much of it contingent on Hal's
accession to the throne) and Hal's own promissory behavior. At the
rejection, Hal is repudiating old debts, and making it difficult for Falstaff to pay both old and new ones, a point underscored by Falstaff's
reaction to his rejection:

> KING: . . . I banish thee, on pain of death,
>   As I have done the rest of my misleaders,
>   Not to come near our person by ten mile.
>   For competence of life I will allow you,
>   That lack of means enforce you not to evils;
>   And as we hear you do reform yourselves,
>   We will, according to your strengths and qualities,
>   Give you advancement. [*To the Lord Chief Justice*]
>   Be it your charge, my lord,
>   To see performed the tenor of my word.
>   Set on. *Exit King* [*with his train*].
> FALSTAFF: Master Shallow, I owe you a thousand pound.
>
>   (*2H4*, 5.5.63)

Despite such similarities, however, Falstaff and Hal have clearly
opposed views of the point or proper use of the availability of credit
and the rapid circulation of value. Hal seeks accumulation and defends
his ever-larger sum of grace and power against outflow; though Falstaff
also likes to avoid repayment, he does not seek accumulated wealth—
Falstaff rejoices in circulation for its own sake. The reassurance Henry
V offers his nervous brothers immediately after his father's death
makes this contrast between prodigal circulation and royal accumulation explicit and offers a regal naturalization of it, one which may look
back to John of Gaunt's comparison of England to a jewel set in the sea:

> The tide of blood in me
> Hath proudly flow'd in vanity till now.

Now doth it turn, and ebb back to the sea,
Where it shall mingle with the state of floods,
And flow thenceforth in formal majesty. (5.2.129)

Henceforth Hal will be the inevitable reservoir into which his kingdom's value flows, and should his blood rise in the future his whole nation's will rise with it.

Falstaff expresses his attitude to circulation of value most clearly when he parts from Prince John after the non-battle at Gaultree Forest.

> Good faith, this same young sober-blooded boy doth not love me, nor a man cannot make him laugh; but that's no marvel, he drinks no wine. . . . A good sherris-sack hath a twofold operation in it. It ascends me into the brain, dries me there all the foolish and dull and crudy vapours which environ it, makes it apprehensive, quick, forgetive, full of nimble, fiery, and delectable shapes, which delivered o'er to the voice, the tongue, which is the birth, becomes excellent wit. The second property of your excellent sherris is the warming of the blood, which before, cold and settled, left the liver white and pale, which is the badge of pusillanimity and cowardice; but the sherris warms it, and makes it course from the inwards to the parts' extremes. It illumineth the face, which, as a beacon, gives warning to all the rest of this little kingdom, man, to arm; and then the vital commoners, and inland petty spirits, muster me all to their captain, the heart; who, great and puffed up with this retinue, doth any deed of courage; and this valour comes of sherris. So that skill in the weapon is nothing without sack, for that sets it a-work, and learning a mere hoard of gold kept by a devil, till sack commences it and sets it in act and use. (4.3.85)

Allusions to Falstaff as "Sir John Sack and Sugar" (*1H4*, 1.2.110) or "that huge bombard of sack" (*1H4*, 2.4.445) make clear that he intends some self-reference here, but it is particularly telling that he thinks of sack as that which activates the hoarded gold of learning and sets it in social motion. Like Falstaff, sack lubricates processes of exchange, and these are the processes of life. He thus takes credit for the newfound excellence of Prince Hal:

> Hereof comes it that Prince Harry is valiant; for the cold blood he did naturally inherit of his father he hath like lean, sterile, and bare land manured, husbanded, and tilled, with excellent endeavour of drinking good and good store of fertile sherris, that he is become very hot and valiant. If I had a thousand sons, the first human principle I would teach them should be to forswear thin potations, and to addict themselves to sack. (4.3.115)

So Falstaff on his cultural fatherhood of Hal, and on the general fertilizing function of his commitment to intake, expenditure, and circulation—a function which even his grotesquerie furthers: at Gad's Hill the fleeing Falstaff "sweats to death, / And lards the lean earth as he walks along" (2.2.103). Vicissitudes of value attendant on irregular circulation do not bother Falstaff as they do others above and below him. Pained by his great toe, he plans to "turn diseases to commodity," implicitly including therein even the "consumption of the purse" of which he also complains (*2H4* 1.2.250, 1.2.237).

Falstaff is contrasted at the bottom of the social scale to Robin Ostler, who "never joyed since the price of oats rose, it was the death of him" (*1H4* 2.1.11), and at the top to both Henry IV and Henry V, who suffer from insomnia due to the cares of kingship, which Henry V describes in terms of the unstable value of ceremony: "What are thy rents? what are thy comings-in? / O ceremony, show me but thy worth!" (*H5* 4.1.249). Because Falstaff battens on the instability not only of exchange relations and evaluation but also of human feeling— he continually converts the feelings of others from anger or disgust to laughter and affection—he is a figure not so much of freedom from value systems as of joyous participation in their inevitably contingent and manipulable operation. He inhabits and bridges many contexts and profits from his mobility like a merchant: "I will devise matter enough out of this Shallow to keep Prince Harry in continual laughter the wearing out of six fashions" (*2H4* 5.1.75), he says overoptimistically in Gloucestershire. He can only be defeated when, as in the rejection scene, he is refused the opportunity to recontextualize: "I know thee not, old man. . . . Reply not to me with a fool-born jest" (*2H4* 5.5.46).

☙

"The same arts that did gain / A power, must it maintain," Marvell advises Cromwell in the "Horatian Ode."[33] But for Henry V the insta-bility and rapidity and reversability of evaluation processes represented by Falstaff—which as prince he has employed to his own advantage toward Hotspur and his father, and to his own delight in conversation with Falstaff, and which have taught him much about how to handle contingency—cease to be welcome. Having gained a power by rapid transitions of role, he will maintain it by insistence on the stability, and continuous accumulation, of royal value, and in this Falstaff would not only be an embarrassment but also a formidable intellectual antag-onist.

Although in *Henry V* the disguised king enters into heated argument about royal value with the commoner Williams, ending in an exchange of gages, Henry resolves the dispute by sending out Fluellen as his surrogate bearing Williams's glove and then, having enjoyed Fluellen's anger when Williams strikes him, buying Williams's loyalty with a glove full of crowns. The glove itself circulates and returns bearing a profit, but the king buys his own immunity therewith. Thus is "a little touch of Harry in the night" ultimately mediated: someone else takes the return blow, and Harry "touches" at the last with a glove stuffed with money. It is a lesson in his royal resolve to insulate himself from the dangers and vicissitudes of exchange. (The nobler side of this resolve is seen in Henry V's repeated convincing denials that he would let himself be ransomed if defeated by the French.) The play ends with Henry's final expression of accumulative eros:

> Je quand sur le possession de France, et quand vous avez le possession de moi—let me see, what then? Saint Denis be my speed!—donc votre est France, et vous êtes mienne. (5.2.187)

The *Henriad*, then, shows how royal power is pragmatically produced in, and to some extent by, an economy of credit and negotiation, and the plays offer an extremely circumstantial account of a set of transactions which, expertly manipulated by Hal (who nonetheless is not always conscious of what he does), yields, in Henry V, the kind of hero-king who can serve plausibly as a national fount of honor and appear to be above such economies. His words to Katherine, however, like his relationship to Falstaff, attest that he can never entirely rise above such economies any more than Falstaff can sink below them.

Hal is as aware as Falstaff of the convertibility of transactions and the fluidity of social meanings, but, once past the obstacle posed by his patrimony, he becomes committed to that stability and authority of which legitimate kings are meant to be not only a symbol but a source. What Falstaff continually mocks is just this idea of a final vocabulary, of an authority which cannot be endlessly and comically redescribed, of a debt which cannot be converted into jest and thus deferred, denied, or denatured. Hal pays or repudiates debts in order to remove himself from circulation. This impulse of his is prefigured at the very beginning of *1 Henry IV*, in the passage I used as an epigraph:

> PRINCE: Why, what a pox have I to do with my hostess of the tavern?
> FALSTAFF: Well, thou hast called her to a reckoning many a time and oft.
> PRINCE: Did I ever call for thee to pay thy part?
> FALSTAFF: No, I'll give thee thy due, thou hast paid all there. (1.2.46)

Falstaff cites the economic "reckoning" between Hal and Mistress Quickly as a relationship; Hal, repudiating the relation by asserting that it is fully paid, casts a premonitory doubt over whether his relation with Falstaff will be sustained by any credit on Falstaff's side. Hal's "reckonings" look toward finality.

This does not make him a figure for reality as opposed to Falstaff as imagination, or for work as opposed to Falstaff as play, or even for power as opposed to Falstaff as freedom: rather, Hal becomes someone who has found what is, for him, a final vocabulary and who does not need or wish to be reminded of its provisionality any longer. History is on Falstaff's side; death on Hal's.

6

Pragmatism and Influence in
A Midsummer Night's Dream

❧

"Shakespeare," writes Harold Bloom in *The Anxiety of Influence*, "is the largest instance in the language of a phenomenon that stands outside the concern of this book: the absolute absorption of the precursor."[1] The precursor Bloom has in mind is Marlowe, but his comment could stand as a gloss on the whole gigantic enterprise of Shakespearean influence- and source-studies. Shakespeare's reading, considerable as it has long been known to be, does not in the collective commentary serve as a shaping or deforming force in the development of his drama. Shakespeare is said to *use* sources, not struggle with them, and he is not generally represented as having been pushed by what he learned from them in directions commentators can map exactly. "Some can absorb knowledge, the more tardy must sweat for it. Shakespeare acquired more essential history from Plutarch than most men could from the whole British Museum," writes T.S. Eliot in "Tradition and the Individual Talent,"[2] possibly providing a hint for Bloom's "absolute absorption." Such a comment does not so much embed Shakespeare in an intellectual matrix as leave him gliding mysteriously above it, free of the questions other authors must abide.

Great changes in his dramaturgy, if not self-made by his own quickening power, tend in our current commentary to be attributed to Shakespeare's professional responsiveness to changes in political atmosphere, to popular taste, or to alterations in the company or stage for which he wrote. Thus Shakespeare might take part in a vogue for Roman plays or romances, in conjunction with his contemporaries, and at times lead or follow them (leading Marlowe in developing the chronicle play, following Fletcher in developing romance on Italian tragicomic models). But whatever struggles Shakespeare undertook, they are thought to differ from the interpersonal *agon* which has been identified in many poets and some dramatists (Wordsworth vs. Milton, Euripides vs. Aeschylus) and which brings the objects of academic writing into the same hot arena of rivalry as academic males themselves (Bloom vs. Eliot or, more locally, Bloom vs. W.K. Wimsatt, to whom *The Anxiety of Influence* is, with some irony, dedicated). Nor are Shakespeare's struggles found to be those of the intellectual author with an important set of ideas he can neither entirely make his own nor entirely discard (Shaw and Nietzsche, Chaucer and Boethius).[3]

Contemporary historicist or cultural materialist accounts of influence tend to deemphasize the kind of intracanonical relations over long time periods that I will discuss in this chapter and the next; they concentrate, admirably I think, on the density of a particular historical moment, the complex interaction of different struggles taking place at any time in the cultural or ideological field, and the probability that authors orient their work primarily toward their living contemporaries and thus to their own intervention in contemporary experience. Critics of this bent are skeptical about the personal relations Bloom asserts between great poets across gaps of time and cultural change. They are also skeptical, however, about Shakespearean immunity from or superiority to influence in general. They wish to anchor Shakespeare more firmly, rather than letting him glide free, and they feel that his genius has probably been sufficiently celebrated—and appropriated for elitist, nationalist, sexist, or imperialist projects—while his particular evolution has been insufficiently linked to precise and demystified accounts of the culture he worked in.[4] But this skepticism about Shakespeare's independence calls also, I believe, for more discussion of the literary influence of predecessors who were canonized in his own time.

A minor thesis of this book resurfaces here: Shakespeare's pragmatism as it lurks in the shadows of his authorial persona—his negative capability, absence of an identifiable set of structuring metaphysical assumptions, and reticence—derives partly from the complexity of his acknowledgement of the varieties of social value and of the various social behaviors and vocabularies that grow up around them. From whom can artists learn this acknowledgement? From other artists, surely, as well as from their social and institutional experiences. But they will not learn this through a Bloomian *agon*, because an artist given to this complexity and variety does not stake particular claims to surpass other artists any more than to a quasi-metaphysical poetic authority; like pragmatists de-divinizing philosophy, such artists will not tend to exaggerate the social power of what they do. Bloom himself now argues, qualifying former claims, that Shakespeare derives vital aspects of his art from Chaucer, but does not claim that this happens according to the agonistic mechanisms of influence with which Bloom has been so thoroughly associated: "Chaucer, rather than Marlowe or even the English Bible, was Shakespeare's central precursor in having given the dramatist the crucial hint that led to the greatest of his originalities: the representation of change by showing people pondering their own speeches and being altered through that consideration."[5] "Precursor" is used here in a much less agonistic sense than in Bloom's previous works: Chaucer gave Shakespeare "the crucial hint" by treating character more as a dynamic economy and less as a fixed essence.[6]

The texts of widely recognized authors like Chaucer were active in varying ways in Elizabethan and Jacobean culture. But Bloomian accounts of influence have tended to overleap the complex mediations necessary to an exact account of that activity. They instead stage imaginary first-hand encounters between poets who appear cheek by jowl only on syllabi and reading lists, which omit noncanonical authors and nonpoetic materials. My own account of this influence attempts to mediate between Shakespeare and Chaucer through a consideration of Chaucer's reception in Shakespeare's time. I agree with an admiring tradition that Shakespeare was not daunted by Chaucer, but I also agree with most of my contemporaries that Shakespeare's work is subdued to what it works in: I present a Shakespeare who explores his debts to the past by examining in what ways his precursors are of present use to him. This chapter, then, points toward a general pragmatic account of influence in Shakespeare and suggests finally that he reflected on influence in a pragmatic way.

Such a general account of Shakespeare's response to influence—one which neither glamorizes him as a phoenix-like exception nor programmatically minimizes his ability to take plots from one place but make meanings somewhere else—will have to do several things. It must take into account the way canonized literary artists of the past were mediated by Shakespeare's culture. Second—and my primary goal in this chapter—it must compile instances of acknowledgment in Shakespeare of Chaucer and take note of what he does at moments when Chaucer seems to have been in his mind. The self-conscious registration of Chaucer, upon which a Bloomian might build a case for an agonistic reading, appears to me not as anxiety, but as something more relaxed, as an acknowledgment in the form largely of Chaucerian jokes. Lest these seem my jokes, I lay out the evidence for them minutely before I offer an argument about them. *A Midsummer Night's Dream* contains a registration of debts to Chaucer's accomplishments as an author of integrative fictions, and specifically to the relation between the "Knight's Tale" and the "Miller's Tale" at the opening of the *Canterbury Tales*. This claim in particular calls for fairly elaborate argument, if only because the "Miller's Tale" is not acknowledged by scholars as a source in discussions of *A Midsummer Night's Dream*. Chaucer is also,

of course, an important general influence on Shakespeare, and I will
address this general influence as well.

ॐ

A number of innovative features of *A Midsummer Night's Dream* spring
into focus when set against Chaucer and the reception of Chaucer in the
1590s. Some of these are large—the advance in integration of diverse
materials which the play has long been alleged to signal—and some
are very particular, having to do with the obscenity and censorship
with which Chaucer was associated. In the 1590s, Chaucer had come
to stand for the successful and acceptable integration specifically of
bawdy materials into larger literary wholes, and Shakespeare, by in-
serting carefully mediated bits of bawdry into *A Midsummer Night's
Dream*, was testing both the limits of Chaucerian integration and those
of Elizabethan censorship.

Like many others, I take *A Midsummer Night's Dream* to mark a step
forward in Shakespearean dramaturgy, demonstrating a new capacity
on his part to integrate astonishingly daring and diverse materials and
to make them comment on one another.[7] He not only handles multiple
plots fluently, but switches among different worlds, each having a
distinct ethos, with extraordinary assurance. I also take it as established
that at about the time of *A Midsummer Night's Dream* Shakespeare was
reading Chaucer, not only from the use of the "Knight's Tale," the
"Merchant's Tale," "The Legend of Good Women," and probably the
"Tale of Sir Thopas" in *A Midsummer Night's Dream*, but also from
the use of *Troilus and Criseyde* and other poems in *Romeo and Juliet*.[8]
Reminiscences of Chaucer are frequent from this point on in Shakespeare's career: Ann Thompson argues that he seems more familiar
with and interested in Chaucer than was any other Elizabethan or
Jacobean dramatist.[9] But while it is also an accepted belief in Shakespearean source studies that Shakespeare was *not* influenced by "The
Miller's Tale,"[10] I shall argue below that this is probably wrong. Much
of the sophistication in bringing together different materials within one
work evidenced by *A Midsummer Night's Dream* could be learned by
reading the "Knight's Tale" and the "Miller's Tale" in sequence, and
Shakespeare encodes an acknowledgment of his debt to Chaucer's
fabliau at various points in *A Midsummer Night's Dream*.

When we attempt to mediate Shakespeare's encounter with Chaucerian comedy through the Elizabethan reception of Chaucer, who had
already reached his status as a well-spring of English poetry and as
the "English Homer," we do not find a precise commentary which
anticipates the twentieth-century recognition of Chaucer's endless so-

phistication. But we do find a useful (and hitherto underemphasized) account of what Chaucer might mean to comic writers on the English stage.[11] It comes in Francis Beaumont's epistle, dated 1597, included in the forematter to Thomas Speght's 1598 edition of Chaucer's *Works*.[12] Francis Beaumont, misidentified by Caroline Spurgeon as the father of the Jacobean dramatist of the same name, is now taken to be the Beaumont, educated along with Speght at Peterhouse, who became Master of Charterhouse and lived to 1620.[13] He contributed a letter, dated "Leicestershire, 1597," to Speght's *Chaucer*. In it he reminds Speght of their years together in college, and of "those ancient learned Men of our time in *Cambridge*, whose diligence, in reading of [Chaucer's] Works themselves, and commending them to others of the younger sort, did first bring you and me in love with him: and one of them at that time, and all his Life after, was (as you know) one of the rarest men for Learning in the whole World."[14] This comment conveys the tone of scholarly invocation of authority that prevails throughout the letter.

Beaumont's defense of Chaucer is learned and fascinating. He first notes that Chaucer, like Horace, understands that speech changes, and that the speech of any given time may be divided into a stable learned speech and an ever-evolving vulgate. He quotes *Troilus and Criseyde* 2:22 (a line sufficiently different from that in modern editions to indicate how incomplete Speght's reform of previous editions actually was), "I know that in fourme of speech is chaunge / Within a hundreth yeere,"[15] and compares the changes that have sundered Chaucer from Elizabethan readers to those in ancient times: "this hath happened amongst the Latin Writers themselves, when theirs was a spoken Tongue, as ours now . . . yet . . . divers of [the words of] *Cecilius*, *Statius*, *Ennius* and *Plautus*, were by latter Latinists rejected; and now again many of them, by the last Writers of all (though before, as it were by Proclamation, put down for baseness) are upon a new touch warranted for good, and pass abroad as Sterling."[16] Thus he indicates his hopes that Speght's edition will inaugurate a revival in which Chaucer's language, at least, will prove a model for contemporary speech.

He then goes on, in a passage of interest in connection with the indications from other authors that Chaucer was used to justify ribald publications in the 1590s, to defend Chaucer against the charge of "incivility," that is, ribaldry or obscenity: "Touching the Incivility *Chaucer* is charged withal; what *Roman* Poet hath less offended this way than he?" He cites Virgil's *Priapus*, Ovid's *De Arte Amandi*, "*Horace* in many Places as deep as the rest," and closes with the most notorious: "*Catullus* and *Tibullus*, in unclean Wantonness, beyond measure pass

them all."[17] Having established that there is a great tradition of wantonness among canonical poets, he links Chaucer—in a move of some
critical originality—to the Latin comic playwrights:[18] "Neither is *Plautus* nor *Terence* free in this behalf: But these two last are excused above
the rest, for their due Observation of *Decorum*. . . . And may not the
same be said for *Chaucer?* How much had he swarved from *Decorum*,
if he had made his Merchant, his Miller, his Cook, his Carpenter, tell
such honest and civil Tales, as were told of his Knight, his Squire, his
Lawyer and his Scholar?"[19] He quotes, then, the Reeve's reproof to
the Miller and two pleas by the narrator of the *Canterbury Tales* not to
be tarred by the obscenity of either the Miller or the Reeve on the
ground of objective reportage: "I mote rehearce / Her tales all, been
they better or werce . . . "

Finally, Beaumont argues that Chaucer is in effect the father of
English comic drama, or at any rate a better model than the Latin
playwrights, because he is more inclusive and his plots are more original. The claim about Chaucer as an inventor of a new kind of comedy
is entirely Beaumont's own:

> For no man can imagine in his so large compass, purposing to describe
> al *English mens* Humours living in those days, how it had been possible
> for him to have left untouch'd their filthy Delights; or in discovering
> their desires, how to have express'd them without some of their Words.
>   And now to compare him with other Poets: His *Canterbury* Tales
> contain in them almost the same Argument that is handled in Comedies:
> His Stile therein for the most part is low and open, and like unto theirs:
> but herein they differ; The Comedy-Writers do all follow and borrow
> one from another. . . . The Ring they beat is this, and out of the same
> Track they go not; To shew the Looseness of many Young-men; the
> Lewdness of some Young-women; the crafty School Points of old Bawds;
> the little regard of honest disposed Serving-men; the miserable Wretch-
> edness of divers old Fathers, and their Folly in countenancing and com-
> mitting their Sons to the Charge and Government of most impudent
> and flattering Parasites. . . . *Chaucer's* Device of his *Canterbury* Pilgrimage
> is merely his own: His Drift is to touch all sorts of men, and to discover
> all Vices of that Age; which he doth so feelingly, and with so true an
> Aim, as he never fails to hit whatsoever mark he levels at.[20]

For Francis Beaumont, then, Chaucer represents an alternative to the
limited comic plotting of Roman New Comedy (which, without the
benefit of Northrop Frye's transfiguring redescription,[21] does indeed
sound low) and provides a model of an ampler and more socially various English comedy.

Chaucer's poetry was widely available in the sixteenth century in complete folio editions—more than complete, indeed, since they included more and more non-Chaucerian material as the century went on. The first edition that concerns us here is John Stowe's 1561 reissue of William Thynne's 1532 text, printed by John Kingston, which, as Charles Muscatine points out in his bibliographic survey, "is doubtless the *Chaucer* that was studied by Sir Philip Sidney and Edmund Spenser and at least leafed through by the young Shakespeare."[22] The second is Thomas Speght's edition of 1598, reissued with new front matter and little textual change in 1602 and reprinted in 1678, which despite new readings in the General Prologue, is "otherwise . . . a close reprinting of the 1561 edition (the issue without woodcuts), following it page for page."[23]

In both the 1561 and 1598 editions, the text of Chaucer's complete works begins as it does in modern editions with the opening of the *Canterbury Tales* rather than some earlier work: the "General Prologue" (then entitled "The Prologues of the *Canterbury* Tales"), followed by the "Knight's Tale," the "Miller's Tale," and the "Reeve's Tale." Sixteenth-century commentary tended to emphasize Chaucer's learning and eloquence and to stress putative connections to Wycliff in order to establish him as a proto-Protestant. This is Spenser's Chaucer—the Spenser who could take the dream of the elf-queen from the "Tale of Sir Thopas" and give it to Arthur in book 1 of the *Faerie Queene* with no apparent sense of incongruity. As one approaches the end of the century, however, one begins to read, in the available collections of allusion and critical commentary, about Chaucer's racier accomplishments as well.

In 1590, for instance, an anonymous author (probably Robert Greene) produced *The Cobler of Canterbury*, containing "tales . . . told in the Barge between Billingsgate and Grauesend: imitating herein *old father Chaucer*." In another pamphlet entitled *Greene's Vision*, which supposedly contains Robert Greene's deathbed penitence, "Greene" calls this, in a speech of self-exculpation addressed to Chaucer himself, "a merrie work . . . a little tainted with scurrilitie, such reverend *Chaucer* as your selfe set foorth in your iourney to *Canterbury*." Chaucer answers Greene's worries about his own ribaldry: "If thou doubtest blame for thy wantonnes, let my selfe suffice for an instance, whose Canterburie tales are broad enough before." This use of Chaucer as a defense of wantonness is echoed by Sir John Harington, who comments as follows in the "Apology" preceding his translation of *Orlando Furioso:*

> me thinkes I can smile at the finesse of some that will condemn him [i.e.
> Ariosto], & yet not onely allow, but admire our Chawcer, who both in

words & sence, incurreth far more the reprehension of flat scurrilitie, as I could recite many places, not onely in his millers tale, but in the good wife of Bathes tale, & many more, in which onely the decorum he keepes, is that that excuseth it, and maketh it more tolerable.[24]

Harington's comment is especially telling, since it suggests that then (as now) the "Miller's Tale" was well-known for ribaldry. Certainly this citation together with those from *The Cobler of Canterbury* and *Greene's Vision* establish what would seem highly probable in any case: that Chaucer's prestige was used to justify fictions which verged on obscenity and represented common life with comic realism. Several references to Chaucer in the years 1596 and 1597 suggest that the phrase "a Chaucer's jest" had a slang meaning for literati at that time, almost certainly an obscene one. These references include: "A pleasant wench of the country (who beside *Chaucers* iest, had a great felicitie in iesting)" [Sir John Harington]; "For Venus was a toy, and onely feigned fable / And *Cressed* but a *Chawcers* ieast, and Helen but a bable" [Nicholas Breton].[25]

Derek Brewer and Caroline Spurgeon both quote a passage from George Whetstone's *Promos and Cassandra* (1578) which allows a bit more specificity, especially when the speech is quoted in full. The play is a source for *Measure for Measure*, and like its Shakespearean successor has a low-life subplot concerning prostitution. Lamia, the madam of a brothel and a prostitute herself, laments the severe new regulations (instituted by Promos, the Angelo figure) that attempt to shut down her trade:

> Of force nowe Lamia, must be chaste, to shun a more mishap.
> And, wanton girle, how wilt thou shift, for garments fine and gay?
> For dainty fare, can crust content? who shal thy houserent pay?
> And that delights thee most of all, thou must thy daliaunce leave;
> And can then the force of lawe, or death, thy minde of love bereave?
> In good faith, no: that wight that once, hath tast the fruits of love,
> Untill hir dying daye will long, Sir *Chaucers* iests to prove.[26]

Here "Chaucer's jest" appears to mean "sexual intercourse," or possibly "bawdry," in the sense of "verbal descriptions of sexual activity" which can be "proved" by actual intercourse. A passage from a 1585 medical dictionary suggests, according to Brewer, that Chaucer, the only English author quoted in 600 pages, was "as it were, the D. H. Lawrence of the time":

> Natura, *Plin.* muliebra, *Eid.* cunnus, *Horat.* [. . .] Le con. A woman's privy member called of Chaucer a quaint.[27]

This is evidence not only about Chaucer's reputation for obscenity, but about the reputations of the two particular tales mentioned by Harington above, since the noun "queynte," meaning "cunt" (though not in philological opinion a variant spelling of the same word),[28] appears once very graphically in the "Miller's Tale" ("And privily he caughte hire by the queint"), twice in the "Wife of Bath's Prologue," and nowhere else in Chaucer.[29]

None of this evidence of Chaucer's association—or the association of the "Miller's Tale"—with bawdry establishes, of course, that Shakespeare read on after finishing the "Knight's Tale," but it does show that he would have had ample occasion to do so. (The notion purveyed from some contemporary university lecterns, that the "Miller's Tale" is a student's reward for finishing the "Knight's Tale," does not seem to have had currency in the 1590s). This contemporary warrant encourages us to ask what might have happened if, as he was writing *The Taming of the Shrew* or *Two Gentlemen of Verona*, he read the "Knight's Tale" and the "Miller's Tale" in sequence. Chaucerians might be tempted to describe the encounter in grandiose terms, as Shakespeare's first encounter with an English comic sensibility and fictive design from which even he could learn.[30] I have already suggested that I consider Chaucer unusually like Shakespeare in his recognition of social life as a dissonance of competing vocabularies, in his reluctance to countenance any one final vocabulary, and in his recognition that literature can show how fixed systems may be redescribed as, or within, dynamic vocabularies—in short, his pragmatism. The *Canterbury Tales* itself, by its structure of juxtaposition and the perpectivism enforced by the association of tale with teller, puts particular tales into a transactive relation with others near them, and the first example of how powerful this dynamic can be comes in the relation between the "Miller's Tale" and the "Knight's Tale". Chaucer was clearly seen by Beaumont as having lessons in comic technique to teach dramatists, and as an alternative source to the Latin comedians for varied plots containing a range of social types.

If, about 1594, Shakespeare had read not merely the "Knight's Tale" but the "Miller's Tale" as well, he would thus have learned much about plot. The plot of the "Miller's Tale" parodies in a number of ways the main plot of the "Knight's Tale," but at a different social level and with a genially reductive attitude, typical of fabliau, which makes the romantic chivalry of Palamon and Arcite seem absurd, while at the same time showing (in the person of the quasi-chivalric Absolon) how elite ideas echo and parody themselves in the activities of commoners. The two tales together might seem to point to a Lylyan comedy of compartmentalized social groups, except that the connections between the "Miller's Tale" and the "Knight's Tale" are much more significant and artful than in Lyly.[31]

The plot of the "Miller's Tale" is itself multiple and interwoven; it suggests a number of innovative features of *A Midsummer Night's Dream*. The fantastically elaborated scheme of Nicholas to sleep with Alison, his old landlord John's young wife, by convincing John that Noah's flood is about to be reenacted, runs in parallel to Absolon's unsuccessful courtship of Alison, yet the two plots do not touch until the superbly prepared climax. John falls asleep in his suspended kneading trough, ready to float out under the eave when the waters rise; Nicholas and Alison sneak down in the dark night to the ground-floor bedroom for sex; the dainty Absolon, "somwhat squaimus / Of farting,"[32] his mouth sweetened, comes courting, and calls at the window for his beloved: "What doe you honycombe, sweet Alisoun? / My faire bird, and my sweet sinnamon: / Awake lemman mine." Alison's response is famous now, may well have been famous in Shakespeare's time, and deserves extended quotation if only to show how entirely readable the Elizabethan Chaucer was:

> The window she undoth, and that in hast
> Have do (qd. she) come off and speed thee fast,
> Least that our neighbours thee espie.
>   This Absolon gan wipe his mouth full drie.
> Darke was the night as any pitch or cole,
> And at the window she put out her ers hole,
> And Absolon sped neither bet ne wers,
> But with his mouth he kist her bare ers
> Full sauorly: and as he was ware of this,
>   Abacke he stert, and thought it was amis,
> For well he wist a woman had no berde
> He felt a thing all rowe, and long herde,
> And said: fie, alas what have I do?
> Te he (qd. she) and clapt the window to.[33]

Absolon rushes off, his warm desire quenched, borrows a piece of hot iron from an early-rising blacksmith, returns to the window, and asks for another kiss. Nicholas, "risen for to pisse," presents, farts, is duly scalded, and screams "Helpe, water, water, for Gods hert!"

> This carpenter out of his slumber stert,
> And heard one crie water, as he were wood,
> And thought, alas now commeth Noes flood,
> And set him up withouten words mo,
> And with an axe, he smote the corde atwo:
> And down goeth all . . . [34]

John's awakening occurs at a moment when the enraptured listeners or readers have entirely forgotten him. It is the marvelous double valency of Nicholas's cry for water which crosses the two stories. "O, 'tis most sweet, / When in one line two crafts directly meet";[35] this superb plot effect in Chaucer's tale is recreated in *A Midsummer Night's Dream*.

A Midsummer Night's Dream uses unexpected awakenings as a means of crossing plots and is the first of Shakespeare's plays (aside from the Induction to *The Taming of the Shrew*) to do so. Characters fall asleep in one plot and wake in another, frequently in a manner to accentuate audience pleasure at the coming together of disparate events and separate social strata. Helena wakes both Lysander, who announces an herb-induced intention to "run through fire . . . for thy sweet sake" (2.2.102), and the hitherto unresponsive Demetrius, who, in what becomes a permanently altered state, addresses her as "goddess, nymph, perfect, divine" (3.2.137). Oberon wakes Titania after brushing her with an antidote, and shows her Bottom asleep beside her, to her amazement and disgust. Hermia wakes after her serpent-dream to find Lysander gone, much as Bottom wakes from his "most rare vision" to find his fellow actors "Stolen hence" (4.1.202). Theseus has huntsmen sound horns to wake the piled-up sleeping lovers, who are amazed at the coming together of the marriage-plot that sent them into the wood and the fairy-plot that rearranged them there. Having found this device for cutting between different states of mind or compartments of experience, Shakespeare uses it in *A Midsummer Night's Dream* to an unparalleled extent. The perfect Chaucerian instance of the unexpected awakening, which crosses over socially constructed borderlines, occurs when Bottom, newly translated, attempts to keep up his courage by singing:

> BOTTOM: I see their knavery: this is to make an ass of me, to fright me if they could. But I will not stir from this place, do what they can; I will walk up and down here, and I will sing, that they shall hear I am not afraid.
> [*Sings.*] The ousel cock, so black of hue,
>   With orange-tawny bill,
>   The throstle, with his note so true,
>   The wren with little quill—
>   [*The singing awakens Titania*]
> TITANIA: What angel wakes me from my flowery bed? (3.1.115)[36]

Further signs that Shakespeare might have read and appreciated the "Miller's Tale" manifest themselves in the play's special relation to obscenity. *A Midsummer Night's Dream* has an odd and comical relation to ribaldry and a strong interest in censorship. The movement of the mechanicals outside the walls of Athens for their rehearsal is an analogue to the movement of the adult companies to theaters in the liberties of the London suburbs, and Bottom's comment that "there we may rehearse most obscenely and courageously," which is usually taken simply as an amusing malapropism, doubtless refers also to the frequent complaint in the City that plays were obscene, playhouses sinks of sin, and so on.[38] Outside the walls it takes less courage to be obscene. "Pyramus and Thisbe," like all English plays after 1581, has to be passed in advance of first production by the Master of the Revels, in this case Philostrate, whom Theseus calls "our usual manager of mirth" (5.1.35). The commission of the Master of the Revels was far-reaching: he was empowered by the Privy Council in 1581 to hear plays in advance of public performance and "to order and reforme, auctorise and put downe, as shalbe thought meete or unmeete unto himself or his said deputy."[38] His power included the suppression of ribaldry wherever it occurred, as a letter from the Privy Council to the Lord Mayor written a few months later makes clear by excluding from a request for permission to play within the city those "comodies and enterludes . . . which do containe mater that may bread corruption of maners and conversacion among the people."[39] Critics have paid less attention to this criterion, however, than to more overtly political reasons for censorship. The licensing activities of Edmund Tilney and his successors are well-known (though we know little about Tilney's own level of moral irritability), and they included suppressing or ordering alterations in plays thought obscene. Thus Gerald Bentley quotes from the better-documented Sir Henry Herbert: "The comedy called *The Young Admiral*, being free from oaths, profaneness, or obsceneness, hath given me much delight and satisfaction in the reading, and may serve for a pattern."[40]

"Pyramus and Thisbe" as abortively rehearsed in the wood seems textually quite distinct from the play Theseus and Hippolyta watch, yet some variant of it has been read over and passed for performance by Philostrate. This is what Bottom means when he says, with characteristic optimism and inaccuracy, "our play is preferred" (4.2.36). The actual decision to perform it is left to Theseus's judgment, and he has to insist, since Philostrate recommends against it. Indeed, Philostrate's attitude might be summarized by the narrator's comment in the *Canterbury Tales* as he introduces the "Miller's Tale": "Blame not me, if that ye chuse amis."[41]

At the same time, despite Bottom's malapropism and the scorn evinced by both fairies and Athenian aristocrats for the mechanicals'

cultural attainments and dramatic capacity, they do not appear to in-
tend ribaldry. Indeed, they are self-censoring:

> QUINCE: Yea and [Bottom has] the best person too; and he is a very
> paramour for a sweet voice.
> FLUTE: You must say paragon. A paramour is, God bless us, a thing of
> naught. (4.2.11)

In fact, their innocence (and the prudishness of critics) is such that the
palpable obscenities of "Pyramus and Thisbe" go generally unre-
marked, though they often arouse giggles in performance. Thus Flute's
lips, too pure to pronounce "paramour" without embarrassment, proclaim on the Athenian stage their habit of kissing Snout the Joiner's
testicles:

> O wall, full often hast thou heard my moans,
> For parting my fair Pyramus and me!
> My cherry lips have often kiss'd thy stones,
> Thy stones with lime and hair knit up in thee. (5.1.186)[42]

Wall, who will not leave the stage until he has "my part discharged"
(5.1.202), has, after introducing himself as Snout, informed the audience that he is "such a wall as I would have you think / That had in
it a crannied hole, or chink."[43] He is courted by Pyramus for this
attractive feature: "Thou wall, O wall, O sweet and lovely wall, /
Show me thy chink, to blink through with mine eyne" (5.1.174). The
standard stage direction, "Wall stretches out his fingers," is editorial;
Wall's other possible chinks could not with decorum be shown.

   This incidental Chaucerian ribaldry, which marks *A Midsummer
Night's Dream*'s coded acknowledgment of its debt to the "Miller's
Tale," culminates in a restaging of the tale's most famous moment:

> PYRAMUS: O kiss me through the hole of this vile wall.
> THISBE: I kiss the wall's hole, not your lips at all. (5.1.198–199)

In this moment the crossed loving and misdirected kissing that have
occurred throughout the play—a physical expression of Chaucerian
multilevel plotting, notably in the two acts Titania spends kissing Bottom's hairy ass-head[44]—are recapitulated as a ribald conjunction of
body parts, which has no real point except to allude to the hilarious
climax of Chaucer's fabliau.

   Issues of censorship are developed still further in the play, in ways
related to the covert obscenity of "Pyramus and Thisbe." Theseus's
court censors "Pyramus and Thisbe" in a variety of ways: not only by
prior reading for the master of the revels, but also through Theseus's
commitment to "take what they mistake" (5.1.90) and to interpret or

filter the mechanicals' performance as the product of "Love . . . and tongue-tied simplicity" (5.1.104), *whatever* they do. Shakespeare shows how obscenity is judged and regulated, but also ignored, permitted, and simply not heard, partly because of a theory of general social decorum that interposed itself as a filter between different social strata. Decorum permitted, indeed encouraged, commoners to be gross (much as Beaumont justified Chaucer's bawdry as appropriate to the persons who utter it), and dramatic entertainment formed a vehicle for the transgression of social borders within the context of a social form which had some acknowledged cultural value (which is more or less how Greene justified his own bawdry as modeled on Chaucer's). From this point of view, *A Midsummer Night's Dream* offers a detailed pragmatic account of how Chaucerian bawdry worked covertly in Shakespeare's culture.

Current historicist scholarship usually sets contemporary sources or analogues alongside a play's text in order to present a clash or agon of discourses. Current influence-studies usually register precursors in order to chart an author's struggle to cast off a father. But Shakespeare's precursors were neither too oppressive (as in a Bloomian analysis) nor too dissolved in the contemporary perspective (as in a New Historicist one) for him to use in a practical, conscious, and above all reflective way.

Shakespeare could have learned from Chaucer some of the distinctive qualities—social inclusiveness, irony about the impact of situation on attitude, alertness to a variety of evaluative responses—of a pragmatic take on social norms and rules. Obscenity, unacceptably transgressive writing or performance, is a limit case which both defines and tests social norms; the uncertainty or historical variability of the obscene, and the way certain presentations of the obscene allow it legitimacy, demonstrate the constructed and therefore alterable and contingent nature of the socially acceptable. Shakespeare may well have seen in Chaucer an example of how to treat explosive social materials without being held responsible for them, especially since Chaucer seems to have been invoked by Shakespeare's contemporaries in order to justify potentially obscene writing. Certainly the comically accidental-looking obscenity of *A Midsummer Night's Dream*, which generations of critics have filtered out of their descriptions of the play, picks up a pragmatic Chaucerian interest in juxtaposing different social types and playing their vocabularies against one another in a comedy of social groups. Seen in this Chaucerian light, *A Midsummer Night's Dream* says as much about how a Renaissance elite would have heard, not heard, and thus (in a Foucauldian vein) regulated sexual discourses as it says about how an imagined group of low-life comics would have naively emulated such discourses. Asymmetrical social groups are mutually parodic in this play, and the play enacts not class conflict, but a distorted mirroring of self-definitions (again Chaucerian), which serves to remind us that social relations of domination and exclusion (such as might be categorically thought to exist between the Knight and the Miller, or between Theseus and Bottom) are rarely seen by those within them as absolutes, and are more violent and overt at some times than at others.

III

Pragmatism and Perspectival Politics

Always Already in the Market:
The Politics of Evaluation in
Troilus and Cressida

The line of attitudes this book explores can be variously described. Philosophically, the attitudes spread across a spectrum which includes in one direction logocentric or metaphysical systems of explanation and in the other antifoundationalist or sceptical ones. Anthropologically, this spectrum may be redescribed as a range of exchange systems ordered according to the ever-incomplete transition between gift exchange and market exchange; politically, it demarcates an array of social systems ordered according to an even less sharply marked transition between aristocratic empire and bourgeois protocapitalism. All of these explanatory spectra are usually, and perhaps inevitably, invoked in a historicized form, so that to situate oneself on any of them is to hypothesize a past when evaluations were made on a different basis from that dominant in the present, and yet to recognize that some remnant of that past system is residual in the present, even as some next stage may be emergent. The density and interest of any particular present consists in part in the confusion of these distinctions, in the difficulty of deciding which spectrum one is on and where one is on it, in the swirl and clash of unharmonized evaluative modes. To register this density, urgency, and dynamism by making an economy rather than a structure the paradigm for explanation, as I suggest Shakespeare does, goes some way, but perhaps not all the way, toward meeting the complexity of the situation.

The Renaissance had a very different set of attitudes toward the past, especially the classical past, from ours, but it shared with us (and with most known societies) the availability of a nostalgic contrast between the bad, complex, unstable present and the good, simple, orderly past. Such contrasts were often drawn by Shakespeare's contemporaries and were particularly acute at the end of the sixteenth century.[1] Current commentary treats late-Elizabethan nostalgia with varying degrees of specificity as epiphenomena of the failure of Essex, the aging of Elizabeth, the bifold religious authority of the Reformation, and the large historicized transition from feudalism to capitalism.

At any historical moment we know of—perhaps because of the inter-personal dynamics of human generations—an explanatory contrast be-tween unity and division or faith and doubt or stability and chaos seems to be available, and usually (except in the immediate aftermath of wars and revolutions) it seems to simplify the past and complicate the present.

It is the more startling, then, to find in *Troilus and Cressida*— Shakespeare's "earliest" play in terms of the putative date of its events—a rabid allegiance to market forces and an unrelieved econo-mism with almost no residue of inherited absolutist conviction to work upon. Shakespeare has chosen to begin the Western tradition on noth-ing but appetite and ambition; the play not only puts philosophic de-bate in an attenuated atmosphere without established positions but also—unusually for Shakespeare—ignores the plenitude of human do-ing which in other plays (*1 and 2 Henry IV* provide strong examples) surrounds and contextualizes individual actions. *Troilus and Cressida* is a thought-experiment which takes up the problem of generating value without large systems of belief or intricate patterns of productive activ-ity in which to float it. Two preeminent activities of the male aristocrat, love and war, empty out through deflation and reveal themselves as non-self-sustaining. This process is inseparable from, but also arguably prior to and more pervasive than, the semantic instability which has made *Troilus and Cressida* a favorite play of deconstructors.[2]

Jonathan Dollimore, in a trenchant brief discussion of the play, argues that its anti-essentialism "foregrounds social process."[3] He sug-gests that both nature and time at moments hold the rhetorical place of the absolute to which recourse is made in the play, but that both are undermined. About nature he is entirely right, though I would put this somewhat differently. The play postulates a strong chaotic tendency in nature, and the speeches in which nature is invoked are themselves determined by local and immediate political aims—in other words, the play's culture does not sustain a consistent enough view of nature to make it available for individual stabilization.[4] About time, however, which according to Dollimore "functions as a surrogate uni-versal" in order to "legitimate fatalism,"[5] there is more to be said. It is true that all the characters recognize what Ulysses suggests so memora-bly to Achilles: that unless they manage the present with extraordinary success, future time will erode them into oblivion: "O let not virtue seek / Remuneration for the thing it was" (3.3.169).[6] The fact that Ulysses' comments have a locally contingent purpose involving his own political aims does not undercut this particular assertion of fatalism.

But as in the sonnets, the *longue durée* in *Troilus and Cressida* is presented as a kind of market, rather than a surrogate universal, and the play's insistence on market terms suggests that, like merchants, its characters approach instability of value in time and place as a risky opportunity for accumulation. Since, as prototypical aristocrats, they are committed to maintaining the solidity of their own value over time, this makes them merchants whose stakes are their own primary identities. In addition, the play reworks classic texts by Chaucer and Homer, that is, texts whose accumulated canonical value would have made them for Shakespeare exemplary of the endurance value of literary texts; *Troilus and Cressida* works extensively with the awareness that its audience not only already knows, but already highly values, its characters and the story in which they are enmeshed.

Inhabiting a play-world as free of foundational absolutes as *The Importance of Being Ernest* or *Endgame*, all characters in *Troilus and Cressida* seem to know that they have lengthy prospects of renown or infamy, so that time appears as an opportunity for ultimate retrospectively fixed value as well as immediate value oscillation or uncertainty; as C. C. Barfoot puts it, "the major figures in *Troilus and Cressida* are inclined to regard themselves and others as live advertisements for the advantages of appearing in a primary epic."[7] Linda Charnes goes further than Barfoot to argue that in *Troilus and Cressida* male characters know what they are supposed to be (i.e., they have somehow read the Western tradition, or at least Homer and Chaucer) and persistently experience a sense of dislocation from the legendary identities they are meant to fulfill. They are advertisements for the psychological *disadvantages* of living in a primary epic, yet their discomfort is only an exacerbated version of the paradigmatic Lacanian awareness of lack, and they have pinned their efforts at self-stabilization on mutual honorific recognition—the support of a male, martial, homosocial community: "The male fantasy in this play is to move freely between the symbolic (the realm of honor, renown, reputation) and the imaginary (the realm of the confirming, immediate gaze) without any of the threats posed by the 'intrusion' of women."[8]

Charnes, following Eve Sedgwick, sees this fantasy as a doomed one, but particularly doomed in this play because heroes so persistently fail to look heroic to each other. As Charnes points out, Aeneas's failure to recognize Agamemnon is only the most obvious of many indications that the physical presence of a hero in *Troilus and Cressida* has no Homeric semidivine glow about it. As is characteristic of pragmatism's general interest in the ways human agency actually operates in a world without essential props for it, I want to suggest that the near-impossibility of satisfactory self-stabilization in *Troilus and Cressida* reflects the peculiarly limited kind of value market portrayed in it.

By recognizing that we are watching the operations of a market world which can elsewhere be more generous, we can avoid the temptation to see the play as presenting the idea that self-stabilization is in itself necessarily an *ignis fatuus*. In its insistence that all its characters be part of the same deflationary market, the play illustrates the instability of value markets in a world where there is neither private life (that is, a distinct, to some extent idiosyncratic, market of value that each character partially insulates from public scrutiny) nor common life (that is, a massive inertial set of more-or-less valued practices which seem to go on without saying, and would supply a thick liquid in which successful actions or individuals could make waves). The private life of Troilus and Cressida is conceived of by both of them in market terms, and their love affair no sooner gets going than it is subordinated to a public exchange of prisoners. The private life of Helen and Paris is the center of the war and thus the oft-reviled rationale for all public life we see. The private lives of Achilles with Patroclus and Achilles with Polyxena are revealed to us as pieces of information being used in political manipulation—thus again as commodities in a public market.

In *Troilus and Cressida* an ancient code of values is radically demystified by being viewed through the lens of a market economy. Thersites describes the matter of Troy in terms of a narrowing market-view of sex—a view of sex as either bought or stolen: "All the argument is a whore and a cuckold: a good quarrel to draw emulous factions, and bleed to death upon" (2.3.74). To retell the story of Troy as that of "a whore and a cuckold" is to foreground anxieties not only of male homosocial rivalry and mutual humiliation, but also of possession and circulation, the penetration of love and war by the market. Chaucer's *Troilus and Criseyde* and Chapman's *Iliad*, the main source texts, emphasize aristocratic preoccupation with fixed value and archaic self-sufficiency (the "standing out" from social markets represented by Achilles in his tent or his rage) and with the cultivation of self relatively uncluttered by anxieties of social class or the need to appear successful to the public (Troilus's love). Each subtext already inscribes some of the problems found in *Troilus and Cressida*, but neither focuses single-mindedly on exchange patterns in the way Shakespeare's play does.

Women, words, tokens, and blows are exchanged in the play. All are slippery and many are false, not what they were meant to be, nor what received tradition leads us to remember and thus to expect. Helen has passed from the Greeks to the Trojans in revenge or delayed profitable exchange for Hector's aunt Hesione: "for an old aunt whom the Greeks held captive, / [Paris] brought a Grecian queen" (2.2.79). Cressida passes from the Trojans to the Greeks in exchange for the captured Antenor. Both women are objects of considerable evaluative discussion, which might lead us to an analysis of objectification and degradation of women by men, a major feature of the play.[9] But the evaluation crises do not focus exclusively or even primarily on gender; they turn reflexively on themselves and become debates over the nature of the activity of valuing. This brings on an anxiety about assessment amounting almost to vertigo.

How may value in men or women be assessed? How may it be maintained or fixed? What causes it to fluctuate? In one form or another these questions are asked and given hypothetical answers over and over in the course of the play. The first two scenes, which convey Troilus's love and then Cressida's, bring up such issues insistently, above all through the activity of Pandarus as middleman. Pandarus whets Troilus's love for his niece: "And her hair were not somewhat darker than Helen's—well, go to, there were no more comparison between the women," and he adds, "I would somebody had heard [Cressida] talk yesterday . . . I will not dispraise your sister Cassandra's wit, but—" (1.1.41). Pandarus attempts to establish Cressida's value by comparing her to publically accepted exemplars (in Helen's case a standard) of beauty and intelligence. Of course these comparisons are of little use if Pandarus can cite only his own opinion; thus he searches for any objective or quasi-objective measures of value he can find. Cressida is *almost* as fair as Helen, for instance. Or, as he says to Cressida in the next scene, Troilus "is very young; and yet will he within three pound lift as much as his brother Hector" (1.2.117). When, in the pageant of Trojan heroes returning from battle, Hector appears, Pandarus points out his battered helm to Cressida with the enthusiastic remark, "there be hacks!" (1.2.210). When, at last, Troilus appears on the street in their view (seen first by the cunning Cressida, who asks "what sneaking fellow comes yonder?"), Pandarus replies (after initial misidentification), "'Tis Troilus! There's a man, niece! . . . Look you how his sword is blodied, and his helm more hacked than Hector's . . . O admirable man! Paris? Paris is dirt to him, and I warrant Helen, to change, would give an eye to boot" (1.2.230).[10]

In his attempts to talk up value, Pandarus only draws attention to the relativity and changefulness of values (especially values conferred by erotic attraction). This energetic comparison quite explicitly makes of Troilus's excellence a good for exchange or consumption. At the same time, however, Pandarus tries to stabilize his evaluations by

drawing on Helen and Paris, the centers of public regard in the state—
René Girard calls them Troy's "beautiful people"[11]—both positively
and negatively in his attempt to sell Troilus and Cressida to one another. "You are a bawd," Cressida says to Pandarus as he leaves her,
recognizing the extent to which he converts both of them into exchange
items; we can see this as an aspect of Pandarus's market-view of the
world (as protopander), which colors his expressions even when he is
not directly pursuing the social aggrandisement of his relative or the
erotic satisfaction of his friend. When he visits Helen and Paris, for
instance, he says to her, "my niece is horribly in love with a thing you
have, sweet queen" (3.1.94), and when Pandarus makes clear it is not
Paris, the "thing" in question which Helen has and Cressida wants
appears to be the commodified penis of a son of Priam and what the
use of it signifies.

Pandarus's erotic mercantilism, however, is also an aspect of the
world he views. Troilus and Cressida both end their first scenes with
short soliloquies; each reflects on what Pandarus is trying to do, and
both see the enterprise as one concerning the acquisition of an object of
value or the maintainence of one's own value. Troilus, after Pandarus's
departure, hears the alarm bell:

> Peace, rude sounds!
> Fools on both sides, Helen must needs be fair
> When with your blood you daily paint her thus.
>
> . . . .
>
> Tell me, Apollo, for thy Daphne's love,
> What Cressid is, what Pandar, and what we.
> Her bed is India; there she lies, a pearl.
> Between our Ilium and where she resides,
> Let it be call'd the wild and wand'ring flood,
> Ourself the merchant, and this sailing Pandar
> Our doubtful hope, our convoy and our bark. (1.1.89)

In a speech which begins with a brilliant sketch of the peculiar tribute
to Helen's beauty that the slaughter around Troy offers (like Marlowe's
"Is this the face that launched a thousand ships," which Troilus virtually quotes later),[12] Troilus goes on to imagine himself as a merchant
seeking Cressida's bed as a distant market and herself as a supremely
valuable good.[13] It is unclear how far this comparison could extend;
since Troilus wants Cressida desperately, he does not seek her in order
to exchange her later for something else as a true merchant would, and
it is one of the play's telling ironies that this is what happens to her.
(Critics blame Troilus for passivity vis-à-vis the prisoner exchange,[14]

but he has to a very large extent committed himself in advance to its logic.) Troilus does recognize that the attempt to obtain an extraordinarily valuable and distant commodity makes him like an exchanger or venturer. He uses the royal "we" here (as rarely elsewhere in the play), as if to prevent this mercantilism from contaminating his nobility.

Cressida, in her turn, having wittily resisted Pandarus's attempts to sell her on Troilus, soliloquizes:

> Words, vows, gifts, tears, and love's full sacrifice
> He offers in another's enterprise;
> But more in Troilus thousand-fold I see
> Than in the glass of Pandar's praise may be;
> Yet hold I off. Women are angels, wooing:
> Things won are done; joy's soul lies in the doing.
> That she belov'd knows naught that knows not this:
> Men prize the thing ungain'd more than it is.
> That she was never yet that ever knew
> Love got so sweet as when desire did sue.
> Therefore this maxim out of love I teach:
> 'Achievement is command; ungain'd, beseech.'
> Then though my heart's content firm love doth bear,
> Nothing of that shall from mine eyes appear. (1.2.287)

This is a more complex statement than Troilus's, less direct too in its invocation of an ethic of exchange. But Cressida recognizes Troilus's attempt on her as an "enterprise" and sees her own task as the maintenance of her own value, which will tumble when she yields to Troilus, since "men prize the thing ungain'd more than it is."[15] Her commitment to a chaste withholding of herself is a commitment to a process of deferral and bargaining, during which she will be wooed and highly valued; this process will give way to a state of being a possession or an achievement when she and Troilus make love: "Things won are done." That consummated love may itself be a dynamic process (as, say, in *Antony and Cleopatra*), rather than a deadly state, is suggested in *Troilus and Cressida* only by Helen and Paris, whose love, painted with Greek and Trojan blood, is maintained by their grisly centrality. They are in no danger of losing predominance over others by loving, since for Troy and the Greeks their love does not end, but rather makes possible and continues the "doing" in which (Cressida suggests) "joy's soul lies"—it is itself the pearl over which opposing armies clash. Cressida, unlike the princely Troilus, is in the highest degree concerned to maintain or increase her own value, and her derogations of him in conversation with Pandarus serve this end. Since Cressida loves Troilus, this strategy cannot provide her with everything she wants: a characteristic problem of economic strategies that involve withholding oneself from a market full of goods one desires.[16]

Ulysses, as suggested above, thinks of these evaluative problems in the longer term, though his presentations of them tend also to have short-term goals in mind. The debate in the Greek camp, which closes with Ulysses' famous speech on degree, shows an interesting consonance with the logic of value in the love plot and an even more interesting historicizing reflection on that logic.

Ulysses' first major speech, following complaints of disorder and demoralization in the ranks from Agamemnon and Nestor, contrasts two modes of being, each simultaneously natural and cultural. The first is an ordered hierarchy, in which the specialty of rule is not neglected; the general (here Agamemnon, who unlike Paris is no one's "honey-sweet lord") is the hive to whom all foragers repair to seek and make honey; and the harmony of the enterprise resembles the order of the planets as they cooperate happily with the sun in the midst. The second mode of being is an anarchy, in which "each thing meets in mere oppugnancy" and envy:

> Force should be right—or rather right and wrong,
> Between whose endless jar justice resides,
> Should lose their names, and so should justice too.
> Then everything includes itself in power,
> Power into will, will into appetite,
> And appetite, an universal wolf,
> So doubly seconded with will and power,
> Must make perforce an universal prey,
> And last eat up himself. (1.3.116)

In the absence of secure positive absolutes, architects of social control set up a threat of engulfing negativity. Usually they invoke both ends of an order-anarchy spectrum, as Ulysses has here. His negative vision, in context at any rate, borders on the comic. There's more than a hint here of Dickens's Sir Leicester Dedlock, who believed (when he learned that his housekeeper's son had helped defeat the Tories in an election) that "the floodgates of society are burst open, and the waters have—a—obliterated the landmarks of the framework of the cohesion by which things are held together!"[17] Ulysses is of course formidably more intelligent than poor Sir Leicester, and his apocalypse is rhetorically more impressive. Like Sir Leicester, though, Ulysses treats the *use* of social hierarchies as markets of opportunity for personal advancement as if this meant the *destruction* of all meaningful and socially received ranks and degrees, leaving an anarchy in which our own drives, the sole directive forces, find no stable external objects or expressions and thus "eat up themselves."[18]

That Ulysses is really talking about social mobility, not anarchism, is clear from his application of this terrifying picture:

> . . . this neglection of degree it is
> That by a pace goes backward, with a purpose
> It hath to climb. The general's disdain'd
> By him one step below, he by the next,
> That next by him beneath: so every step,
> Exampled by the first pace that is sick
> Of his superior, grows to an envious fever
> Of pale and bloodless emulation. (1.3.127)

In short, an ethic of competition and emulation has replaced one of rank and loyalty: men who do not challenge the *principle* of hierarchy (though Ulysses also attempts to associate them with such a challenge) seek, nonetheless, to use hierarchies precisely as "the ladder of all high designs"—here not communal designs but individual ones.

This is, of course, a literary allegory of the passage from idealized feudalism to early modern capitalism. Social degrees do not change, but the ethos in which they are sought and defended does, and social life shifts toward being seen as a market of opportunity and away from being seen as a hierarchy of relations of gift exchange in which vassals pledge fealty to lords for material protection and metaphysical security. At each step in the gradual historical process (as the quotation from *Bleak House* suggests), such apocalyptic metaphysical defenses of conservatism can be and invariably are offered.

Shakespeare as usual ignores the superbly archaic aristocratic justifications that Achilles invokes in Chapman for his anger against Agamemnon—an anger based precisely on the conservative rights of lords to claim parity with their prince Agamemnon, and to set the terms by which their excellence is appreciated. There were, that is, available sixteenth-century and indeed Shakespearean terms in which Achilles might have been represented that would line up well with the Homeric Achilles transmitted by Chapman: as an overmighty subject, a noble resistant to royalty and centralization, on the one hand, and to market evaluation, on the other. (Coriolanus, a noble who helped expel the royal Tarquins and resists sharing power with the citizens of Rome, occupies just this position, which can also be historically allegorized as feudalism's doomed resistance, on one hand, to the absolutist state and, on the other, to the rise of the bourgeoisie.) But the Achilles in *Troilus and Cressida* is curiously like a new man, even a self-made man, and his anxiety about his future value can therefore easily be aroused. The primordial aristocrats, models for the rest, here are full of commercial anxiety.[19]

Ulysses' "degree" speech combines with an elaborately staged admonition to Achilles; after his fable of natural stability in hierarchies of value comes his artificial pageant of instability in martial evaluation. Ulysses directs a promenade of the general staff before Achilles' tent, one lord after the next feigning elaborate inattention, and, himself the last in line, lingers to explain to the vexed Myrmidon a theory of human value which contradicts his "degree" speech by making individual worth entirely dependent on continual cultivation of fickle public demand. A man, says Ulysses, "cannot make boast to have that which he hath / Nor feels not what he owes but by reflection" (3.3.98); that is, we know and measure ourselves in others' responses. This, he continues, obliges us to participate in a notably theatrical market of public evaluation:

> . . . no man is the lord of anything . . .
> Till he communicate his parts to others;
> Nor doth he of himself know them for aught,
> Till he behold them form'd in the applause
> Where th'are extended. (3.3.115)

Charnes comments of these passages:

> the aim of the "speculation," the hazarding all upon the market value of Helen, is to become visible, present to oneself, to experience as viable subjectivity an identity that has been emptied by its own intertextual redundancy. But according to Ulysses, Achilles' mirroring is not enough [quotes 3.3.112–20]. For Ulysses, ever concerned with "authorship," seeing and being seen is merely prologue. Until one is "communicate[d]," turned into reproducible matter, one doesn't know oneself "for aught." Shot through with imaginary representations, the play nevertheless reveals these figures' relationships to their "real conditions of existence"—or, to put it more plainly, although they feel as if they're in a play, they are anyway.[20]

Though Ulysses is, as Charnes points out, holding a book at this point, his comments to Achilles do not insist that the hero seek *textuality* (with the eventual aura-losses of mechanical reproduction which Charnes may have in mind) rather than that he aggressively circulate himself in a theaterlike market, where his "parts" can be both extended and applauded. These possibilities do not exclude each other, nor would I wish to deny the level of textual self-consciousness Charnes persuasively demonstrates in the play. To a deconstructionist, who accepts that *il n'y a rien de hors-texte*, the economic consciousness I argue for throughout this book is, of course, a kind of textuality. But I am inclined to see things the other way around: that it is the subject's involvement in a bottomless flux of evaluations, rather than a centerless web of textuality, which is the foremost antifoundational intuition for Shakespeare.

The written text that Ulysses holds is, at any rate, a theater prop in a staged drama of evaluation.[21] Achilles, as intended, worries that he has suddenly encountered oblivion in terms which suggest both erasure and devaluation: "What," he asks, "are my deeds forgot?" The famous reply echoes (as many critics have noted) Cressida's fears about gratifying Troilus's desire:

> Time hath, my lord, a wallet at his back
> Wherein he puts alms for oblivion . . .
> Those scraps are good deeds past, which are devour'd
> As fast as they are made, forgot as soon
> As done.
>   . . . Emulation hath a thousand sons . . .
>   O let not virtue seek
> Remuneration for the thing it was;
> For beauty, wit,
> High birth, vigour of bone, desert in service,
> Love, friendship, charity, are subjects all
> To envious and calumniating Time.
> One touch of nature makes the whole world kin—
> That all with one consent praise new-born gauds. (3.3.145)

The pun on "gauds" and "Gods" hints that newborn Gods will indeed succeed those who might be expected to support Achilles' claims to permanance. Virtue *does* seek "remuneration" but must do so for current publicly appreciated actions, not for its inherent excellence. There are no "lords and owners of their faces" here who "do not do the thing they most do show" and thereby "inherit heaven's graces" while withholding themselves from the market of public regard;[22] according to Ulysses, such self-appraising virtue hangs "quite out of fashion, like a rusty mail. (3.3.152)"

Ulysses' two presentations, the "degree speech," which purports to enjoin on us the value confidence conferred by a secure place in a great chain of being, and the "time" speech, which suggests that we must continually act in order not to lose our audience's attention and thus lose value entirely, amount to the opposition of a feudal ethic and a market ethic. But, for market reasons, Ulysses characteristically espouses different sides of the argument in different places for clear rhetorical ends. He takes, in effect, both sides in the same debate that energizes the Trojans in their discussion of Helen: How is her worth to be determined? Are there categories of worth which are not dependent on public demand?

In the Trojan debate Troilus believes that, as an aristocrat, his evaluations of things should set their value and that this set value should thenceforth remain safe from time. He approves Paris, who "would have the soil of [Helen's] fair rape / Wip'd off in honorable keeping her" (2.2.149). This is superficially similar to Ulysses' market-oriented claim that "Perseverance, dear my lord, / Keeps honour bright" (3.3.150), but here it involves persevering in a wrong to demonstrate that it is right: Troilus is obsessed with the redemption of *single* actions or particular commitments in order to keep them "bright," while Ulysses recommends a lifetime of continual action, continual participation in the market, to prevent greatness from being forgotten. So the two positions are actually opposed, and Troilus is obsessed not with the erosion of reputation but rather with the susceptibility of present judgments, feelings, evaluations, or deeds to future reinterpretation and alteration. He wants the present to be guaranteed consistency, and this desire is connected with his view of himself as an aristocrat. "Can it be," he asks those who would return Helen, "That so degenerate a strain as this / Should once get footing in your generous bosoms?" (2.2.153). What is honorable should remain so, and aristocrats are committed to this conservative activity, which is opposed to the acceptance of value fluctuation in marketplaces. Troilus's choice amounts to the risky overinvestment in a *particular* object, characteristic of lovers, in contrast to the commitment to exchange objects for profit, characteristic of merchants.

The Trojan debate deserves systematic discussion. Hector proposes to return Helen and end the war:

> Let Helen go.
> Since the first sword was drawn about this question
> Every tithe soul 'mongst many thousand dismes
> Hath been as dear as Helen—I mean, of ours.
> If we have lost so many tenths of ours
> To guard a thing not ours nor worth to us
> (Had it our name) the value of one ten,
> What merit's in that reason which denies
> The yielding of her up? (2.2.17)

The arithmetic is difficult but the meaning is clear: people's lives are at some level equal in worth, though in war we reckon our own people as more valuable than others; Helen, who is not our own, has cost many lives already. This is market-reasoning of a sort. Troilus counters with another assessment, continuing the butcher's-scale imagery:

> Fie, fie, my brother:
> Weigh you the worth and honour of a king
> As great as our dread father's in a scale
> Of common ounces? Will you with counters sum
> The past-proportion of his infinite? (2.2.25)

Troilus uses mercantile language both to protest against mercantile thought (summing with counters) and to suggest that other forms of value, other markets of demand, are in question.

The key exchange follows:

HECTOR: Brother,
    She is not worth what she doth cost the keeping.
TROILUS: What's aught but as 'tis valued?
HECTOR: But value dwells not in particular will:
    It holds his estimate and dignity
    As well wherein 'tis precious of itself
    As in the prizer. 'Tis mad idolatry
    To make the service greater than the god. (2.2.51)

Thus Hector stands for a reasonable judgment of the return on a commitment or investment, and he comes near a distinction between use-value and exchange-value, proposing an economy in which both general utility and particular opinion confer value. We do not set in our own minds the value of others, rather we consult their use and their general reception. That this issue is bound up in whether or not we think like merchants is shown by Troilus's counterargument:

> We turn not back the silks upon the merchant
> When we have soil'd them, nor the remainder viands
> We do not throw in unrespective sieve
> Because we now are full. . . .
> For an old aunt whom the Greeks held captive,
> [Paris] brought a Grecian queen, whose youth and freshness
> Wrinkles Apollo's, and makes stale the morning.
> Why keep we her?—The Grecians keep our aunt.
> Is she worth keeping?—Why, she is a pearl
> Whose price hath launch'd above a thousand ships,
> And turn'd crown'd kings to merchants. (2.2.70)

From this it is clear both that the debate pivots on the conflict between mercantile and noble motive, and that Troilus, knowing this, resorts to mercantile language once again even as he asserts noble motive. Nonetheless, he defends nobility (as Achilles, by contrast, does not) by believing it noble to persevere in a value estimate whatever the consequences of that perseverance. This view of nobility and value is given a terrible test at the play's end, as many have noted.[23]

The relation of value to market also informs the politics of sex:

> TROILUS: This is the monstruosity in love, lady: that the will is infinite, and the execution confined: that the desire is boundless, and the act a slave to limit.
>
> CRESSIDA: They say all lovers swear more performance than they are able, and yet reserve an ability that they never perform: vowing more than the perfection of ten, and discharging less than the tenth part of one. They that have the voice of lions and the act of hares, are they not monsters?
>
> TROILUS: Are there such? Such are not we. Praise us as we are tasted, allow us as we prove. Our head shall go bare till merit cover it: no perfection in reversion shall have a praise in present. We will not name desert before his birth . . . Troilus shall be such to Cressid as what envy can say worst shall be a mock for his truth, and what truth can speak truest, not truer than Troilus. (3.2.79)

I quote at length because the passage illustrates a key evolution in Troilus's thinking, an evolution from anxiety to principle: the implicitly invoked guarantor of his own faithfulness here is his royalty, that which allows him to say of himself "our head shall go bare till merit crown it" while crowning himself, once again, by his choice of possessive pronoun.

Sexual as well as philosophic anxiety is expressed in this speech, obviously, and for such worries the "we" provides a different sort of context. Sexual experience tests neither partner individually so much as it does both together: "allow us as we prove" is only sensible advice, especially when no sexual vaunting precedes the encounter. This is one of the moments when the play hints at the possible relief from public markets available in local private ones. But in the present case the invocation of a potentially shared, mutually guaranteeing, private sphere is presented in language which riddlingly mixes reference to sexual performance with fears about fidelity and which is clearly skeptical about the possibility of sustained privacy: to promise eternal love is to "swear more performance than they are able." Even Troilus's comment that "the desire is boundless and the act a slave to limit" can refer not only to the sexual act but also to the duration of companionship (even if life-long) between lovers. Love seems to offer transcendence, but also reminds us of radical contingency, and this is as true of its durability as it is of its most intense expression. So Troilus turns to the same reasoning he used in the Trojan debate, the idea that the commitments of the honorable (and especially of the royal) are guaranteed through time by their position at the center of the identity of the commitment-maker. The individual shows his social strength by personally guaranteeing the stability of a particular evaluation. Troilus claims a kind of autonomy. But the particular evaluation he cares most about is a relational one, and values that reside in his relation to Cressida are obviously vulnerable to changes not only in her thinking but also in their circumstances.

The play continually shows, often in incidental comic ways, how conversational relations do not necessarily promote convergent meanings or evaluations. Pandarus, for instance, has a tendency to foreground the extent to which speech depends for its meaning or value on context by breaking off statements with an exclamation—"well, go to!"—and thus requiring his hearer to fill out his meaning. This reliance on context depends in turn on friendliness or cooperation and fails in its absence, as is seen in the exchange between Pandarus and Paris's servant:

> PANDARUS: Friend, you, pray you, a word: do you not follow the young
>   Lord Paris?
> SERVANT: Ay sir, when he goes before me.
> PANDARUS: You depend upon him, I mean.
> SERVANT: Sir, I do depend upon the Lord.
> PANDARUS: You depend upon a notable gentleman, I must needs praise
>   him.
> SERVANT: The Lord be praised! (3.1.1.)

In this conversation, Pandarus assumes the desire to cooperate in his interlocutor, and he gets a lesson in linguistic equivocation of a characteristic sort: compare Feste and Viola in *Twelfth Night*, the Fool and Lear, the gravedigger and Hamlet, or Falstaff and the Lord Chief Justice. With varying degrees of playfulness, all these dialogues emphasize the necessity of intentional interpretive mutuality to carry conversation forward and demonstrate that logical connection is insufficient to guarantee communication. *Troilus and Cressida* revises its source texts in rather the way the servant twists Pandarus's questions. The play thus establishes that, to retain meaning, heroic reputations or classic narratives depend similarly on friendly interpretation and recontextualization. The play is full of local joking about the distorting reception of words and the deflating reception of values, and it itself is a larger instance of this.

> PANDARUS: What music is this?
> SERVANT: I do but partly know, sir: it is music in parts.
> PANDARUS: Know you the musicians?
> SERVANT: Wholly, sir.
> PANDARUS: Who play they to?

SERVANT: To the hearers, sir.
PANDARUS: At whose pleasure, friend?
SERVANT: At mine, sir, and theirs that love music.
PANDARUS: Command, I mean, friend.
SERVANT: Who shall I command, sir? (3.1.16)

By reiterating "friend" here, Pandarus tries to remind the servant of the Gricean principles of conversational cooperation which should prevent this kind of breakdown from happening: "Make your conversational contribution such as is required, at the stage at which it occurs, by the accepted purpose or direction of the talk exchange in which your are engaged. One might label this the COOPERATIVE PRINCIPLE."[24] We can presume, I think, an accent difference in performance to signal the class tensions that might explain the servant's noncooperation. In any case everyone finds Pandarus suitable to be jested with and made use of. But it is important to see how Pandarus flounders in this relatively benign conversational market. The exchange offers a particularly clear justification of Barbara Herrnstein Smith's claim that communication should be modeled as *differentially consequential interaction:* that is, an interaction in which each party acts in relation to the other differently—in different, asymmetric ways and in accord with different specific motives—and also with different consequences for each. . . . *Caveat emptor, caveat vendor.*"[25]

Cressida's first encounter with the Greeks, when she is passed from man to man and kissed by many before she says a word, is a fiercer instance of Herrnstein Smith's differentially consequential interaction. She is caught in an economy of giving and withholding, one she embraced earlier with Troilus, that now confines her to an unappealing choice between being promiscuously used or accepting the protection of a predatory male. Moreover, Ulysses, having with the others encouraged her flirtatiousness, then condemns her for it. She is one those "encounterers" who "wide unclasp the tables of their thoughts / To every ticklish reader," and (here showing an interest in how written histories will record the subjugation of women to the markets in which they are exchanged) he enjoins all male inscribers to

> set them down
> For sluttish spoils of opportunity
> And daughters of the game. (4.5.58)

When she finds an opportunity to speak (following the example of Patroclus, she makes fun of the cuckold Menelaus and denies him a kiss), she merely tries to exercise some control over the game of homosocial rivalry by showing that she can play it—as she has in the flirtation with Troilus and subsequently with Diomedes. What other game is there? Cressida's isolation, and the absence of private life in the play generally, are further suggested by the unusual fact that she does not speak to (or in the presence of) another woman of the course of the play, and virtually every man she speaks to has some homosocial plan of which she is a part.[26]

As I suggested above, Troilus's idea that one can sustain value by noble will is given a terrible test at the play's end, where he must view the chief object of his valuation, Cressida, giving his token to Diomed. He attempts to maintain her value as a sign, but can do so only by detaching sign from referent—"No, This is Diomed's Cressida" (5.2.136), "This is, and is not Cressid" (5.2.145). Finally he makes a martial bargain which will render his humiliation endurable: "as much as I do Cressid love, / So much by weight hate I her Diomed" (5.2.166). Troilus is forced into the exchange of equivalent values in another bow to the market. The transmutation of love into violence here is cognate with the lesson Achilles has learned from Ulysses: that public success is so necessary to value over time that Achilles should assure himself permanent glory by having his followers assassinate a disarmed Hector.

The test of Troilus poses a parallel challenge to the audience, since the audience's evaluation of the matter of Troy—the noble stories of Homer and Chaucer—can be supposed to approach in intensity Troilus's commitment to the permanent value of Cressida. This is and is not the *Iliad*; this is and is not *Troilus and Criseyde*. For many years literary critics responded more or less as Troilus does—as much as I the *Iliad* and *Troilus and Criseyde* love, so much by weight I hate Shakespeare's degraded version of them. But we need to respect a play which can so deftly make our canonical aesthetic evaluations seem as prone to shocking reversal as individual erotic ones.

In terms of the broader spectra of description with which I opened this chapter, I have tried to show how extreme *Troilus and Cressida* is in pushing a story we expect to be on the side of gift exchange on the anthropological spectrum, transcendent support for human excellence on the philosophic spectrum, and solid aristocratic authority on the political spectrum firmly toward market exchange, demythologization, and social mobility. The ugliness many find in the play arises from the intensity with which it forces all its characters to partake of the same demystifying economy, and from the corresponding absence of a dense matrix of habitual productive activity with relatively stable value which in actual societies usually surrounds the intense competition for reputation within elites. Shakespeare reworks the same issues in a more expansively realized social milieu in *Coriolanus*.

8

Nobility, the Market, and the Moral Economy of the Roman Crowd in *Coriolanus*

❦

Throughout this book I have presented Shakespeare as a pragmatist who redescribes the structures of his culture as dynamic economies, recognizing the instability and mutability this description involves. To some extent previous chapters have shown how social transformations take place onstage. Hamlet's change in attitude as he accepts dramatic pragmatism or the change in methods and concepts of royal rule from Richard II to Henry IV to Henry V might count as such transformations. But in other cases treated in this study, Shakespeare takes a genre like the Petrarchan sonnet sequence or a narrative source like the matter of Troy and refashions its structuring assumptions in economic terms. *Coriolanus* offers an unusual, perhaps unique, opportunity to watch the imposition of a marketlike political economy on an aristocrat formed by and personally committed to republican virtue of an old-fashioned anti-economic kind. The play both demonstrates that the Roman state always was a more dynamic and mutable economy than some of its outstanding members thought it was or should be, and shows that state acquiring institutions that will further this transformation. The individual tragedy of Coriolanus is part of a social transformation toward an idea of a commonwealth as a market economy of competing interests, and away from an ancient idea of a polis as a people united by loved things held in common.[1]

Seen abstractly, the plot of *Coriolanus* is entirely economic. Food, voices, and service in war circulate in exchange, none of them smoothly. At the play's beginning, the people have refused war service in the recent past. The senate has refused to make grain available to them. The people then offer violence. The senate awards them representation (and, presumably, food, though this goes unstated). The patricians and plebeians then fight side by side, as officers and men in war, and Rome seems to be close to harmony after a victory. But Coriolanus objects to the power of the people's voices. The people refuse their constitutionally necessary voices to him. He offers violence; they offer violence. He is banished, thereby refusing war service, and when this strike does not produce results, he offers violence from the outside by joining the Volsces. Morally, however, he cannot carry through on this offer even when it is militarily within his grasp. In fact none of the many offers of violence in the play is carried through to the finish, but each is at least somewhat successful in reminding the city of the value of the group or person who proffers it. Seen in this very abstract way, the play is a parable of political economy, illustrating how threats of civil violence and acts of withheld service ultimately underwrite the power of aggrieved groups in a city, and how self-destructive it would be to carry out such threats fully if one had the power to do so.

The reason that the Roman political economy cannot function without overt conflict in the play is that its participating groups have incompatible ideas about it. Those incompatible economic ideas both constitute and, in the end, destroy the play's hero, Coriolanus.

One could go several ways from this claim. One way, not taken here, would be toward an exact account of how *Coriolanus* mediates between classical republicanism, with its ideas about civic economy, and the different political thought of the Renaissance. Another, which I do take, is to see the play as a comparative study of aristocratic and market moral economies and the constraints they place on an exceptional subject, one who undertakes a self-conscious defence of nobility as he understands it. A third path, which I will follow, though not far, reads the Roman politics of *Coriolanus* as, in part, a topical comment on the politics of England at the time of its composition.

Coriolanus exemplifies how a social crisis can be based on a clash between different ideas about economy, and how the emergence of a new idea can devalue someone who has tied himself to an old one. In the broad sense of pragmatic economy which I am employing in this book, we can see the play as insisting on the transactive relations that obtain among not only all citizens of the same city but all people in a given area of political competition. We can also identify, more precisely, a clash in the play among, first, traditional ideas of a paternalistic moral economy (invoked by the plebeians and by Menenius, and partly held by them), second, an idea of the city as a market economy to which competing interests come seeking profitable exchanges (invoked by the tribunes, Volumnia, and most of the patricians), and third, Coriolanus's idea of the city as the fosterer and appropriate object of noble loyalty as expressed by personal self-sacrifice in war. This chapter will thus show how throughout the play Coriolanus attempts to keep his idea of nobility from being compromised by a market economy; yet it will also suggest how Coriolanus might have made a place for himself in the paternalist moral economy of the plebeians that would have allowed his nobility to function in a way less intolerable to his convictions. I begin where the play begins, with the Roman crowd rioting over grain.

❦

The plebeian revolt with which the play opens differs from its source in Plutarch in order to more closely resemble Jacobean food riots which would have been familiar to the play's first audiences and to Shakespeare. The composition of *Coriolanus* is thought to have followed the Midlands uprising of 1607; Shakespeare alters Plutarch, according to whose account "there grewe sedition in the cittie, bicause the Senate dyd favour the riche against the people who dyd complaine of the sore oppression of userers,"[2] by making the revolt of the plebeians a matter of hunger in time of dearth: their inciter speaks "in hunger for bread, not in thirst for revenge" (1.1.24).[3] They seek to kill Caius Martius so as to "have corn at our own price" (1.1.9).

Recent historical study of English popular protests over food—and specifically over the price of cereals and bread—has taken its key ideas from E. P. Thompson.[4] Thompson claims that the "food riot," presented in the accounts of most previous historians as a spasmodic, disorganized, irrational, and usually futile popular response to hunger, was in fact a highly traditional, structured, and frequently successful popular intervention aimed at reducing grain prices and reasserting established popular rights in the socioeconomic order:

> It is of course true that riots were triggered off by soaring prices, by malpractices among dealers, or by hunger. But these grievances operated within a popular consensus as to what were legitimate and what were illegitimate practices in marketing, milling, baking, etc. This in its turn was grounded upon a consistent traditional view of social norms and obligations, of the proper economic functions of several parties within the community, which, taken together, can be said to constitute the moral economy of the poor. An outrage to these moral assumptions, quite as much as actual deprivation, was the usual occasion for direct action.
>
> While this moral economy cannot be described as "political" in any advanced sense, nevertheless it cannot be described as unpolitical either, since it supposed definite, and passionately held, notions of the common weal—notions which, indeed, found some support in the paternalist tradition of the authorities; notions which the people re-echoed so loudly in their turn that the authorities were, in some measure, the prisoners of the people. . . . The word "riot" is too small to encompass all this.[5]

Although most of Thompson's evidence is drawn from the eighteenth century, he shows that protests as late as the 1790s are consistent in form and aim—and in the spectrum of official response they provoked—with the Tudor and Stuart popular protests that elicited the influential "Book of Orders," originally written for Elizabethan magistrates and published in 1630. Thompson writes:

> these "insurrections" . . . exhibit a pattern of behaviour for whose origin we must look back several hundreds of years. . . . The central action in this pattern is not the sack of granaries and the pilfering of grain or flour but the action of "setting the price."
>
> What is extraordinary about this pattern is that it reproduces, sometimes with great precision, the emergency measures in time of scarcity whose operation, in the years between 1580 and 1630, were [*sic*] codified in the *Book of Orders*. . . . In Elizabeth's reign the magistrates were required to attend the local markets, . . . "resorte to the houses of the Farmers and others . . . and viewe what store and provision of graine theye have remayninge . . ." They might then order the farmers to send "convenient quantities" to market to be sold "and that at reasonable price." The justices were further empowered to "sett downe a certen price upon the bushell of everye kynde of graine."
>
> . . . The power to set a price upon grain or flour rested, in emergency, half-way between enforcement and persuasion.[6]

In many of the protests Thompson describes, the crowd acted to "set the price" for the poor at a lower rate than the one prevailing in markets and shops. Often there was little actual violence or destruction of property. Rather a crowd would stop a grain shipment or take a store of hoarded grain and sell it on the spot at the price they claimed was just, then would give the money to the farmer or carrier from whom the grain had been repossessed. In assessing the success of these protests, moreover, Thompson notes that when they involved seemingly gratuitous violence, the violence appears to have been aimed at particular enemies or disruptors of the moral economy the crowd sought to maintain: "very often the motive of punishment or revenge comes in."[7]

This account of crowd action bears on the opening scene of *Coriolanus* in ways to which criticism has not yet attended. Admittedly the Roman rising is an urban one, aimed apparently at the senate, but its central focus is hunger (specifically hunger for bread) as in the rural English risings, and the first claim of the people against the senate is that it plays the role of the hated badgers, regrators, and engrossers of early modern England in time of dearth. The senators, in the words of the Second Citizen, "Suffer us to famish, and their storehouses crammed with grain" (1.1.79).[8] Like the rural rioters discussed by

Thompson, and by John Walter and Keith Wrightson in their similar treatment of food protests between 1585 and 1660,[9] Shakespeare's Romans seek to regulate the price of grain and aim their violence at a specific opponent, "Caius Martius . . . chief enemy to the people" (1.1.6), who will, they expect, oppose their efforts: "Let us kill him, and we'll have corn at our own price. Is't a verdict?" (1.1.9).

Their language is legalistic: they "proceed" at 1.1.1 and 1.1.25, their leaders seek "verdicts," and they are eager to distinguish their proceedings from "revenge" at 1.1.24 and "malice" at 1.1.34. This suggests that they act within and are concerned to maintain their sense of legitimate social action. "Corn at our own price," which modern readers take to mean "the lowest price we can get," might well convey to a Jacobean "the customary time-honored just price." The discussion of revenge is particularly telling, since the First Citizen appears to censor his own revolutionary rhetoric: "the leanness that afflicts us, the object of our misery, is as an inventory to particularise their abundance; our sufferance is a gain to them. Let us *revenge* this with our pikes, ere we become rakes. For the gods know, I speak this in hunger for bread, *not* in thirst for *revenge*" (1.1.18; my emphases). That is, even though it may have targeted a particular enemy, the crowd's general motive is hunger, a human universal, and their intended victim needs to be justified by reference to a moral economy which he has flouted.

The crowd in an English food riot exploited a shared legitimating paternalist model of the economic community by showing the authorities that members of that community had been driven by desperate need to insist in an unseemly or disorderly way that attention be paid to them. However cruel the English economic system may in general have been, such protests were usually successful. Wrightson and Walter generalise: "Petitions preceded riots. Riots when they did occur were invariably successful in stimulating authoritative action to alleviate grievances."[10] Thompson is more specific:

> Riot may have been, in the short term, counter-productive [for the rioters], though this has not yet been proved. But, once again, riot was a social calamity, and one to be avoided, even at a high cost. The cost might be to achieve some medium between a soaring "economic" price in the market, and a traditional "moral" price set by the crowd. That medium might be found by the intervention of paternalists, by the prudential self-restraint of farmers and dealers, or by buying-off a portion of the crowd through charities and subsidies.[11]

The opening scene of *Coriolanus* exemplifies the patterns and aims of structured crowd behavior identified by Thompson, and the combination of threatening but at the same time legalistic rhetoric in the mouths of the leaders of the crowd also fits Thompson's idea that riots were a form of forcible appeal to a moral consensus—often an appeal to the gentry (justices of the peace) against yeoman farmers and middling grain entrepreneurs. According to Thompson, the protests of the poor opposed the introduction of laissez-faire pricing, and only when authorities accepted Adam Smith's view of the self-regulating market as "natural" did they systematically repress popular risings to "set the price." As a consequence, in the risings of the nineteenth century, unlike those of the early modern period, the paternalistic moral economy appealed to by the people no longer existed in the minds of the authorities, and so rioters were led by failure to a new analysis of their situation in terms of class conflict.[12]

The rioters in the opening of *Coriolanus* encounter a typical early modern response from the authorities—Menenius arrives, is recognized by the citizens as "one that hath always loved the people," and delivers his belly parable as a form of paternalistic admonition that is also reassuring, since it implicitly obliges the patricians to act to relieve dearth. Menenius suggests that the people should pray:

> For the dearth,
> The gods, not the patricians, make it, and
> Your knees to them, not arms, must help (1.1.71)

In doing this, Menenius not only diverts blame from the senate, but follows what Walter and Wrightson identify as a standard early modern explanation of famine:

> To meet the metaphysical problem posed by dearth there existed a body of explanation which rendered the arbitrariness of the weather intelligible if not predictable; a body of explanation that was principally the reserve of the church and of the more moralistic, especially puritan, laity. This was the doctrine of judgements.
>
> Judgements, the direct punitive actions of a jealous god, were in Gouge's words "consequents of sinne."[13]

But as soon as Caius Martius enters, bearing with him the news that the people have been granted magistrates of their own in the persons of the tribunes, it is clear that in Rome we are dealing with a state which is moving away from a paternalistic model of community, social stability, and charity toward marketlike representative government and is currently in a state of constitutional as well as social flux. The moral economy of consensus is giving way to a market economy of temporary profitable social contracts.

At the same time, however, the principle of loyalty to the monarch—which in Tudor and Stuart revolts (through early parts of the Civil War) could be counted on to unite both sides of any local dispute—is replaced in Rome by an inadequate rhetorical substitute. Menenius tries to overawe the plebeians by referring to the abstract destiny of the state:

> For your wants,
> Your suffering in this dearth, you may as well
> Strike at the heaven with your staves, as lift them
> Against the Roman state, whose course will on
> The way it takes, cracking ten thousand curbs
> Of more strong link asunder than can ever
> Appear in your impediment. (1.1.65)

If this invocation worked, it would show that all Romans share a sense of Rome's great future. But as a threat it rings hollow. Why should the "course" of the Roman state not include forced compromises with its hungry citizens? Since the senate responds to the food riot by a constitutional innovation granting the plebeians representation, it is clear that the Roman state is capable of changing course in mid-riot, especially when a renewed threat of war necessitates cooperation between patricians and plebeians. As a unifying center for popular loyalty, then, Menenius's view of Rome as an organism with the senate as its stomach is ineffective.

But his offer of the fable is in itself a gesture which grants the people importance. It is one of the gestures of social interdependence which, instead of money or credit, circulate in *Coriolanus* and serve as the most important currency in exchange between patricians and plebeians. Menenius offers his ideological fable of the body politic, the most general and prominent of these gestures, in explicit exchange for delay, quiet, and willingness to be ruled (or at least spoken to) from the people—the usual exchange value of such fictions: "If you'll bestow," says Menenius, "a small (of what you have little) / Patience awhile, you'st hear the belly's answer" (1.1.124). A parable of organic unity in the state, which casts the senate as an unglamorous organ, buys plebeian quiescence.

Volumnia, during the consulship crisis, reproaches her son for failing to make a similar exchange:

> You will rather show our general louts
> How you can frown, than *spend* a fawn upon 'em
> For the *inheritance* of their loves . . . (3.2.66, my emphases)

The crises of the play occur in the marketplace, identified by Coriolanus as the stage on which he is forced to play false roles:

> Must I
> With my base tongue give to my noble heart
> A lie that it must bear? Well, I will do't:
>   . . . To th' market-place!
> You have put me now to such a part which never
> I shall discharge to th'life. (3.2.99)

The Roman economy is centered, then, in a theatrical marketplace
where political gestures, rather than goods or money, are offered in
exchange. This gives the play an economic focus even though it takes
no interest in the glamor of wealth and includes no merchants, little
money, no buying or selling of goods, and only casual references to
credit. It portrays economic choices clearly, nonetheless. Caught between a paternalist and a protocapitalist moral economy, the plebeians
are pulled in various directions which both serve and frustrate what
modern Marxists would think of as their class interest.[14]

ぎ

The play presents Roman politics in economic terms, as the exchange
of one value for another in a public consensual market, and Coriolanus
sets himself and his nobility against precisely this aspect of his world.
Having established, from the viewpoint of the plebeians, some of the
ways the Roman polity is figured as an economy in *Coriolanus*, I turn
to the hero himself.

Before discussing his failure, let us look at what is valuable about
him. Early republican Rome, like the Greek city-states contemporary with it, was in a constant state of war with its neighbors, and
its survival and growth—in economic as well as political terms—
depended on its success in war. Rome's success was unparalleled, and
that success was attributed in the Renaissance to its institutions, among
them the warlike, pious, and temperate patrician elite which devoted
itself to the city's welfare.

Coriolanus, like Achilles, is a warrior whose individual prowess
decides the fate of cities.[15] His martial accomplishments suggest that
he is closer to the gods than other men, and his greatness makes him
difficult to rule. Unlike Achilles, he individually battles against a city
full of enemies and wins when he is shut into Corioli. But he also has
(again unlike Achilles) an all-too-human mother who ultimately faces
him with a choice in which there is no heroic option. He resembles
Achilles again when he is withheld from battle by a political quarrel
in which his services are undervalued; but unlike Achilles he has no
interest in tangible spoils and hates praise. The comparison, however
complex, suggests what is valuable about Coriolanus and what makes

him an incommensurable factor in the political equations of Rome, both in practical and in imaginative terms. Practically, he is uniquely important because his presence in battle guarantees victory and his absence risks defeat. Imaginatively he is important because he is focussed on greatness in action rather than in the opinions of others and is thus an example, potentially inspiring, of a different kind of Roman civic identity and leadership which might make the city deserve divine favors. That is, he forces the materialistic pragmatism of the rest of the characters to acknowledge that supreme practical effectiveness may be tied to beliefs in immaterial substances or goals. His value must be remembered as we turn to a discussion of his failure.

The most persuasive critical accounts of the play have followed the cue provided by Coriolanus's unsparing argumentative rigor and treat it as a parable in which his failure can be read to yield a clear, if complex, message. The message is something like this: Certain kinds of personal independence are impossible, and the pursuit of extreme independence claims leads the claimant to self-destruction. Membership in families and cities cannot be voluntarily abandoned; man is a social being by nature and history rather than by individual choice and cannot easily turn himself into a beast or a god. As a language user, Coriolanus, if he wishes to mean anything at all, is bound to communities. As Volumnia's son, he cannot escape psychological patterns established by his upbringing which determine his desires and limit his possibilities. As a patrician, he is implicated in the political strategies of his class and can only retain his nobility by continuing to act in ways which favor patrician dominance in Rome, even if such actions run counter to patrician ideals of behavior. Such are the messages found in *Coriolanus* by Stanley Fish, Janet Adelman, and Paul Cantor, who discuss the play in terms which allow respectively less precise moralizations as the critics more closely approximate the play's own terms of discourse.[16]

Language use entails an acceptance of the interdependence of members of the language community, Fish argues, and Coriolanus, by his misuse of speech acts (notably "I banish you"), tries to use language against the Roman community while retaining a linguistic authority that only communities can confer. This attempt is doomed, since no individual can meaningfully set him or herself against a community except as the representative of another community: thus Coriolanus cannot be revenged on Rome except as a Volscian. Coriolanus's contrastive double, Aufidius, understands this: "I would I were a Roman; for I cannot / Being a Volsce, be that I am," he says when Coriolanus has beaten him. Aufidius, indeed, anticipates a number of Fish's key critical positions by several millennia—most notably, of course, in the claim that our virtues lie in the interpretation of the time. Aufidius survives, and thrives, by recognizing that he is limited to membership in one interpretive community or another, whereas Coriolanus goes from one community to the other vainly striving to prove that he is free of community.

Adelman offers a parabolic account of the play which is lengthier, richer, and correspondingly more difficult to summarize than Fish's. She presents Coriolanus as a man acting out masculine fantasies of autonomy through strategies of violence, self-starvation, and denial of need, strategies that Volumnia has inculcated in him by denying him nurture. In doing this, Adelman argues, Coriolanus seeks, above all, independence from the dominance of Volumnia.[17] Thus when she presents herself to be killed at Rome's gates in act five she makes Coriolanus's deepest desires uncomfortably clear to him. He cannot face what he really wants—nor could he, if he were to face this hidden desire, reconcile it to patrician codes of family reverence. So, defeated, he turns away from the sack of Rome to go knowingly to his own death. Adelman implies in closing that Coriolanus's cry, "O mother, mother! What have you done," expresses his recognition of the psychological trap in which she has held him.

In both of these accounts of the play, as a linguistic and a psychological parable, Coriolanus is someone who does not understand the rules of the game he perforce is in and thus loses it. On one level hapless and a bit pathetic, on another he poses a real threat to cherished values—he disrupts community solidarity, espouses violence as a method of resolving disagreements, exacerbates class conflict, and becomes in some sense a traitor.[18]

Cantor's more extended reading of the play in political terms offers us a Coriolanus who understands somewhat more about his own situation, but whose articulation of problems is itself a danger to him and to the state. In Cantor's view, Coriolanus's truth telling and truth seeking disrupt the operation of the Roman political system. Coriolanus's pursuit of truth and his contempt for self-protective dissimulation and compromise arise ironically enough from his exceptionally complete or radical acceptance of Roman teachings, so that Coriolanus in effect tries to expose contradictions in the Roman system and is thus a demystifying threat as well as an embarrassment to the Roman patrician regime. "The city cannot allow men to think on their own," Cantor comments, "if that independence means that they will see through the deceptions politics makes necessary, for these deceptions work better if no one recognizes them for what they are."[19] Again

Coriolanus refuses to play the game by the rules, but in Cantor's account he understands, at least sporadically, the nature of his disagreement with them.

I see Coriolanus as a quite conscious representative of nobility as he understands it; he himself articulates the opposition between a market economy of value and a hierarchical society in which the value of martial nobility will be fixed, recognized, and nonnegotiable. His stature increases, I think, as we recognize the extent to which he sets himself against the value market he is in because of principles to which he tries to remain consistent. An account of the play which brings out this aspect of its hero helps explain why *Coriolanus* has a power to disturb (and why Coriolanus himself has a claim on admiration) beyond what the accounts of Fish, Adelman, and Cantor would suggest. In some ways my account of the play as a clash of economies combines their readings (which are themselves bound up, of course, in the opinions of other critics):[20] each of them offers an account of the play which shows that an aspect of social reality which Coriolanus would like to see as fixed and stable is in fact a dynamic economy.

The play itself is preoccupied with critical evaluation of Coriolanus. It ends with Aufidius standing on Coriolanus's body, telling the Volscian senate that, for reasons to be announced later, his murder is a good thing:

> My lords, when you shall know (as in this rage,
> Provok'd by him, you cannot) the great danger
> Which this man's life did owe you, you'll rejoice
> That he is thus cut off. (5.6.135)

The scene offers an uncomfortable emblem for critics who see the action of the play as the necessary victory of a social order over an individual who makes outrageous claims for himself. While they may not present Coriolanus's death as cause for celebration, they do of necessity "cut [him] off" and build their own designs atop his at last static and contained meaning. If, moreover, tragedy is a genre in which a hero's meaning, or the meaning of the action which consumes the central figure, is *not* contained or cut off by his or her death, then such readings oblige us to discount *Coriolanus*'s claim to be a tragedy.[21] Taking the play as the clash of different ideas of economy, as I do here, offers a more encompassing and satisfying way of talking about it, and as we pursue it we should find less occasion to mutter, with Aufidius, that Coriolanus "has a merit / To choke [our assessment of him] in th' utt'rance" (4.7.48).

Certainly Coriolanus makes some impossible autonomy claims; these come, however, as expressions of his awareness that he has reached an impossible position. He identifies certain key structures around him as primary constraints in order to renounce them. He renounces his city, obviously, but also his family and, at key moments, what he regards as his own instinctual (what we would probably call his genetic) nature. Thus at Rome's gates, on the brink of his intended revenge, his family comes to plead with him, and he says:

> my young boy
> Hath an aspect of intercession which
> Great Nature cries, "Deny not." Let the Volsces
> Plough Rome and harrow Italy; I'll never
> Be such a gosling to obey instinct, but stand
> As if a man were author of himself
> And knew no other kin. (5.3.31)

At this point in the play Coriolanus knows he is in a desperate situation in which impulses which should cohere are at odds with one another. But his desperation forces him to sketch very clearly oppositions which are latent in his sense of himself throughout. To be the sort of man he wishes to be, he must *deny:* deny Nature, deny "intercession" by others he loves, and deny his own history of being programmed by his mother, which with savage humor he likens to the imprinting of a newly hatched gosling which causes it to follow and imitate the first moving thing it sees. In order to deny he must *stand* as if alone not only at present but from the start, not only sui generis but self-generated, with an audience of gods alone if no people are noble enough to understand him.

That this extreme autonomy claim registers Coriolanus's desperate modification of a more reasonable notion of noble standing is shown by his blessing of his son a few lines further on:

> The god of soldiers,
> With the consent of supreme Jove, inform
> Thy thoughts with nobleness, that thou mayst prove
> To shame unvulnerable, and stick i'th'wars
> Like a great sea-mark standing every flaw
> And saving those that eye thee! (5.3.70)

As Coleridge's "Frost at Midnight" and Yeats's "A Prayer for My Daughter" and countless less eloquent and public statements attest, people strive to bless their children with felicities they themselves have found unattainable, and in their blessings they articulate parts of their theories of the good. Coriolanus here wishes for his son a sequence of development—less mechanical or obsessive than the imprinting of goslings—which will proceed as he feels his own should have done. To paraphrase tendentiously: May you be formed according to my

own value system, nobility, in which ideals of soldierly behavior dominate with the consent and approval of a stable and worthy authority
(Mars under Jove); and may this value system work for you (as it has
not for me) so that you prove "unvulnerable" to shame, fixed and stable
in vicissitudes, and useful as an example to others.

The nobility Coriolanus wishes for young Marcius is neither socially
useless nor self-generating: it devolves from divine example through
just such parental admonitions as the one Coriolanus delivers. Coriolanus himself has received such advice from Volumnia, who loaded
him "with precepts that would make invincible / The heart that conn'd
them" (4.1.9). The key presence of the gods in the ideal constitution
of nobility requires some further comment, however.

A. C. Bradley remarked that *Coriolanus* has little "atmosphere,"
meaning that neither nature nor fate nor the gods appear in this play
as they do in other Shakespearean tragedies: mysterious, involved,
present as "vaster fellow-actors and fellow-sufferers" with the characters.[22] Partly, of course, this is a feature shared with the other Roman
plays; *Coriolanus*, however, is particularly Roman in that piety in the
play is civic and is intimately related to public conduct. Romans make
frequent rhetorical use of the gods in persuading or browbeating others
(Volumnia freely assumes that the gods second her in any request),
but the gods are rarely seriously invoked as guides to personal behavior
in this play except by Coriolanus himself. Menenius's comment to
Sicinius on the pointlessness of prayer to avert Coriolanus's revenge
on Rome shows both the use of gods to condemn others and the common belief that Coriolanus is in a special relation to them: "No, in.
such a case the gods will not be good unto us. When we banished him,
we respected not them; and, he returning to break our necks, they
respect not us" (5.4.31). Coriolanus's own belief and behavior seem
almost to create what relation there is between the gods and the patrician community.

His own comments about the gods show their use to him as props
for his ethical independence from other human beings. His son must
believe in them to "inform [his] thoughts with nobleness"; the plebeians
waste such instruction, as Coriolanus says during a revealing brief
exchange with Menenius on his way to show his scars in the market:

Cor: What must I say?—
    "I pray, sir,"—Plague upon't! I cannot bring
    My tongue to such a pace. "Look, sir, my wounds!
    I got them in my country's service, when
    Some certain of your brethren roar'd and ran
    From th'noise of our own drums."

Men: O me, the gods!
  You must not speak of that; you must desire them
  To think upon you.
Cor: Think upon me? Hang 'em!
  I would they would forget me, like the virtues
  Which our divines lose by 'em. (2.3.52)

Coriolanus feels that his own example will be as misused or wasted on the plebeians as the moral instruction offered by the state, but he also shrinks from being assimilated into such public moral or intellectual exchanges. Menenius gets at the heart of the matter in saying "You must desire them / To think upon you," thus pointing out that the scar-showing exists to display patrician desire for plebeian goodwill; Coriolanus's response, surly as it is, makes the counterclaim that it is through preserving their difference from and indifference to the plebeians that the patricians maintain the moral superiority which, if anything can, justifies their power. Thus Coriolanus's comment that virtues are lost in transmission is not merely dismissive, but part and parcel of the way he thinks about civic value.

Although, as Bradley says, the gods are absent as actors or even as centers of numinous belief in this play, they occupy through Coriolanus a key set of cultural occasions in which reference to them is made, occasions in which the noble individual needs guides to behavior (or audiences for it) more reliable or objective than the interests of the community. Thus when Volumnia tells Coriolanus to go back to the plebeians in the marketplace and "Repent what you have spoke," he replies, "For them? I cannot do it to the gods, / Must I then do't to them?" (3.2.37). Prayer for Coriolanus has a proto-Protestant privacy; it divides him from immediate audiences and their interested responses. Coriolanus wishes all his speech to suit divine ears, and this wish props his refusal to tailor his discourse to local exigencies.

In pointing to these instances of Coriolanus's resistance to social structures, I do not argue that Coriolanus's "nobility" escapes the pragmatism of the play. It cannot in fact be separated from the economy he renounces. In the play's treatment of the constitution of subjects in the economies which surround and sustain them, nobility plays a peculiar, and not entirely asocial, role. It is an aspect of social structure itself, as the idealized behavior of a ruling elite. The play shows the social inculcation of that elite in process (this is one of the few plays in Shakespeare that shows three generations in a process of familial transmission of values).[23] Indeed, *Coriolanus* seems intentionally comprehensive in its perusal of different public and private aspects of the noble role.[24] Philosophically, however, a preoccupation with noble behavior which gets its warrant from a commitment "To imitate the graces of the Gods" (5.3.150), as Volumnia puts it with partial satire aimed at her son's hubristic tendencies, results in a kind of ethical self-regard which may lead the noble individual to stand out even from the social norms and best interests of his own class. Such at any rate is Coriolanus's-interpretation of "nobleness." For him it is the maintenance of virtue in indifference to its social reception; it involves the tacit claim that virtue is not socially constituted, but has a transcendent audience which is, however, in this play expected neither to participate in virtue nor to reward it after death.

❦

Shakespeare, then, centers his play on an opposition between nobility and market systems.[25] In elaborating this opposition I will focus on Coriolanus's repudiation of exchange systems involving the Roman crowd. "You must think," says the Third Citizen as Coriolanus clutches his burlap vestments to withhold his scars from view, "if we give you anything, we hope to gain by you" (2.3.72). The "gain" they hope for is merely that Coriolanus will "think" of them and acknowledge this principle of exchange, with its implication of mutual dependence.

CORIOLANUS: Well then, your price o'th'consulship?
FIRST CITIZEN: The price is, to ask it kindly. (2.3.74)

"Kindly" here means both "with goodwill" and "in a natural manner": they request him to respect the idea of exchange for mutual benefit, and his subsequent satiric statements amount to a refusal.[26]

An earlier remark by the Third Citizen shows that the exchange will consist of a distribution of precisely what Coriolanus tries hardest to keep to himself, his nobility: "if he show us his wounds and tell us his deeds, we are to put our tongues into those wounds and speak for them. So if he tell us his noble deeds, we must also tell him our noble acceptance of them" (2.3.5). This promiscuous tonguing will take nobility from Coriolanus's mouth and put it in that of the plebeians, as nobility becomes a communal project rather than an individual possession. Communal exchanges of food, words, and reputation, or regard for merit, are bound together in the play in passages such as the one above. Coriolanus constantly and violently attempts to dissociate himself from them, often by imagery of starvation. "Better it is to die, better to starve, / Than crave the hire which first we do deserve" (2.3.112), he says of his scar-showing in the marketplace, recognizing that he is participating in a quid pro quo exchange, but violently repudiating any desire for it or acceptance of its appropriateness. Coriolanus repeatedly announces and acts out his preference for death—often through a variety of kinds of "famishment"—to communal exchange. At times he imagines himself being deprived of food; at others (as implicitly above) he is turned into nourishment, being eaten up by the people (as the people claim they are "eat[en] . . . up" by the rich and the wars at 1.1.84). Very often his "famishment" will be connected with his being talked of, with his public reputation, and thus, by a pun which rarely comes to the surface in the play but brings together two of its major ideas, "fame" becomes a kind of "famishment" for him. He is in the mouths of others; eaten by them and unable to keep himself to himself, he will "famish" through "fame."

When Coriolanus refuses to circulate his accomplishments, he rightly sees the rhetoric of praise, a basic function of the Roman state, as a way of making his actions into public commodities. Cominius gives an account of this circulation and its purposes at the end of a battle which is in effect a marketing plan:

> If I should tell thee o'er this thy day's work,
> Thou't not believe thy deeds; but I'll report it,
> Where senators shall mingle tears with smiles,
> Where great patricians shall attend, and shrug,
> I'th'end, admire; . . .
>   . . . where the dull tribunes,
> That with the fusty plebeians hate thine honours,
> Shall say against their hearts, "We thank the gods
> Our Rome hath such a soldier." (1.9.1)

Coriolanus responds to this plan of politic praise by saying that even his mother's rhetorical exploitation of him, which he cannot prevent, disturbs him deeply.

>   Pray now, no more. My mother,
> Who has a charter to extol her blood,
> When she does praise me, grieves me. (1.9.13)

His resistance to praise becomes vehement later in this scene. After he refuses a hero's share of the spoils of battle, the trumpets utter "a long flourish" and the common soldiers fling their caps in the air. Marcius, enraged that they should interpret his refusal of wealth as a play for popularity, shouts:

> May these same instruments, which you profane,
> Never sound more! When drums and trumpets shall
> I'th'field prove flatterers, let courts and cities be
> Made all of false-fac'd soothing!

. . . No more, I say!
For that I have not wash'd my nose that bled,
Or foil'd some debile wretch, which without note
Here's many else have done, you shout me forth
In acclamations hyperbolical,
As if I lov'd my little should be dieted
In praises sauc'd with lies. (1.9.41)

Although cities are full of flattery and convert deeds into words, Coriolanus believes that a soldierly decorum should free the field of battle
from such displays.

Coriolanus opposes the peculiarly Roman publicization of morality
and exaltation of civic service, what Menenius calls the practice of "our
renowned Rome, whose gratitude / Towards her deserved children is
enroll'd / In Jove's own book" (3.1.288). Coriolanus wishes to "reward /
His deeds with doing them" (2.2.127), and thereby to evade or preempt
the conversion of actions into reputation. This bespeaks a stoic reserve
toward the value of reputation that links Coriolanus to a tradition
expressed by Montaigne: "It might perhaps be excusable for a painter
or another artisan, or even for a rhetorician or a grammarian, to toil
to acquire a name by his works; but the actions of virtue are too noble
in themselves to seek any other reward than from their own worth,
and especially to seek it in the vanity of human judgments."[27]

In adhering to this tradition, Coriolanus obsessively yet thought-
fully rejects the implication that one's social acts must aim at a social
reception. Such a detachment is more easily maintained by a retiree
like Montaigne than a political leader like Coriolanus; in conversation
with his mother, however, Coriolanus claims that he does not seek the
social power she so passionately desires:

VOLUMNIA: I have liv'd
   To see inherited my very wishes,
   And the buildings of my fancy:[28] only
   There's one thing wanting, which I doubt not but
   Our Rome will cast upon thee.
CORIOLANUS: Know, good mother,
   I had rather be their servant in my way
   Than sway with them in theirs. (2.1.196)

Coriolanus's resistance to praise and to evaluation thus forms itself
in opposition to the consensual Roman market of public regard. His
resistance often expresses itself, as I have shown, in terms involving
food and starvation: he would rather starve than eat if eating signifies

exchange with a community—he will deny economy at its root. These strands—linguistic exchange, social interdependence, and bargaining for mutual benefit—converge in Coriolanus's last speech before the tribunes sentence him to banishment:

> Let them pronounce the steep Tarpeian death,
> Vagabond exile, flaying, pent to linger
> But with a grain a day, I would not buy
> Their mercy at the price of one fair word,
> Nor check my courage for what they can give,
> To have't with saying, "Good morrow." (3.3.88)

Forced to recognize that the people have power to give and to withhold, he refuses the possibility of exchange with them. To "check his courage" here would be to compromise his nobility by saying what he believes to be untrue.

The plebeians recognize his resistance for what it is. At the opening of the play, they seek to sacrifice him in the belief that he is their chief economic obstacle, but it soon appears that they also object to him because he repudiates the moral economy that gives them a political hold on him:

> 2ND CIT: Consider you what services he has done for his country?
> 1ST CIT: Very well, and could be content to give him good report for't,
>   but that he pays himself with being proud. (1.1.29)

Coriolanus bypasses the customary exchange of their praise and good-will for his services. In fact, Coriolanus accomplishes what the First Citizen indignantly describes as an economic short circuit: he *pays himself* by being "partly proud . . . even to the altitude of his virtue" (1.1.38), and thus repudiates public estimates of his worth.

Coriolanus cannot agree even with his fellow patricians about nobility, however. The consulship crisis brings on a brilliant debate between Coriolanus on one side and Volumnia and Menenius on the other about the nature of nobility: she takes its essence to be the maintenance of power in the community, he takes it to be the preservation of personal integrity, courage, and honest discourse. For Coriolanus power in the community should flow from these qualities, and from a willingness to unleash personal violence to support noble claims. His solo victory in Corioli shows that, if anything, he underestimates when he comments that "on fair ground / I could beat forty of [the plebeians]" (3.1.240); nonetheless, for Coriolanus the purity and consistency of noble action are prior to power, whereas for Volumnia and Menenius nobility is an aspect of the power of a ruling class, and nobility without social power is wasted. This opposition rises to view when Volumnia tries to persuade him to return to the marketplace:

> CORIOLANUS: Would you have me
>   False to my nature? Rather say I play
>   The man I am.
> VOLUMNIA: O sir, sir, sir.
>   I would have had you put your power well on
>   Before you had worn it out. (3.2.14)

But as Coriolanus's last speech to the tribunes suggests, his nobility consists not merely in being indifferent to all external constraints, including death, but also in preserving an ethical system from contamination by particular occasions. Coriolanus announces to Sicinius that if

> Within thine eyes sat twenty thousand deaths,
>   . . . I would say
> "Thou liest" unto thee, with a voice as free
> As I do pray the gods. (3.3.70)

Nobility, as Coriolanus sees and embodies it, opposes itself to the social economy recognized by all other Romans, patrician and plebeian alike, in which personal qualities, deeds, or scars are commodities to exchange for "voices" or other tokens of communal power or goodwill.[29] Coriolanus's nobility implies a single standard for discourse (he tries always to speak in a "voice as free / As I do pray the Gods") and a single standard for behavior. He persistently short-circuits exchange systems by self-regard, refusing to "surcease to honor mine own truth" (3.2.121). Far from being in a game whose rules he does not understand, Coriolanus performs an almost impossible role whose principles he is alone in comprehending, articulating a nobility that opposes itself to the dominant economy which constitutes and reinforces the identities of all those around him. This emerges in a telling exchange at the end of one of his key tirades in the senate. He objects to the magistracy of the tribunes:

> CORIOLANUS: O good but most unwise patricians: why,
>   You grave but reckless senators, have you thus
>   Given Hydra here to choose an officer?
>   . . . .
>   You are plebeians
>   If they be senators; and they are no less
>   When, both your voices blended, the great'st taste
>   Most palates theirs. . . .
>   By Jove himself,

It makes the consuls base; and my soul aches
To know, when two authorities are up,
Neither supreme, how soon confusion
May enter 'twixt the gap of both and take
The one by th'other.
COMINIUS: Well, on to th'marketplace. (3.1.90)

The marketplace is indeed the next social stage, as well as the site in which, to Coriolanus's mind, nobility and commonality will take on a mutually contaminating relation. In the strife which follows the plebeians' repudiation of their vote in Coriolanus's favor, this mutual relation, which consists in the wide (and from Coriolanus's viewpoint debased) distribution of "nobility," ennobles the tribunes. Menenius pleads with Sicinius for an opportunity to talk Coriolanus into negotiation:

MENENIUS: Give me leave,
I'll go to him, and undertake to bring him
Where he shall answer by a lawful form—
In peace—to his utmost peril.
FIRST SENATOR: *Noble* tribunes,
It is the humane way. . . .
SICINIUS: *Noble* Menenius,
Be you then as the people's officer. (3.1.320, my emphasis)

The term "noble" is exchanged between senators and tribunes, and Sicinius ensures that it becomes attached to the state of being "the people's officer."

Coriolanus is multiply appropriable for varying political purposes.[30] Yet it insists both that politics must take the perspectives of all sectors into account and that elite strategies of autonomy and self-regarding nobility will be undone, both in general by pragmatic conditions of meaning and in particular by the onset of market economies. This insistence points to an area of possible topicality, in that it casts some light on James I's struggle with his parliaments toward the end of the first decade of the seventeenth century. The play is still more clearly topical—though again in a carefully displaced way—in bringing nobility pervasively and explicitly into the marketplace, and in making Coriolanus so disgusted at the practice. From before his coronation James's prolific creation and sale of knighthoods was matter for public comment.[31] Shakespeare himself, who appears to have paid for a coat of arms for his father in 1596 with the suggestive motto "Non Sanz Droict," can hardly have failed to reflect on ways people purchase the improvement of their blood. By selling knighthoods and peerages (and, soon after, baronetcies, which were invented in order to be sold), James ran into a problem noted by Conrad Russell: "the crown could only provide patronage by discrediting itself. Pym argued that since honour in the State was a divine thing, the sale of offices or titles was simony."[32] Coriolanus's objections to the marketing of his deeds and the bringing of nobility to the marketplace address this issue from the other end, and the play illustrates that such practices sit ill with desires for autonomy in either nobility or monarchy.

Coriolanus's own sense of nobility could, of course, seem to depend on his own uniqueness, and thus to be self-regard in a pejorative sense of self-preoccupation or narcissism. Against this view should be set his interest in Aufidius. From the opening of the play he mistakes Aufidius for a kindred spirit, another person who sets noble behavior above social goals:

Marcius: They have a leader,
    Tullus Aufidius, that will put you to't.
    I sin in envying his nobility;
    And were I anything but what I am,
    I would wish me only he.
Cominius: You have fought together!
Marcius: Were half to half the world by th'ears, and he
    Upon my party, I'd revolt to make
    Only my wars with him. (1.1.227)

These last four lines can be read in opposite ways, to mean that Marcius would revolt to oppose Aufidius or that (as he in fact does) he would revolt to make Aufidius a comrade; in either case, he implies that his sense of kinship-in-opposition to Aufidius is stronger than his allegiance to his city.

As a kind of joke, Marcius here also confesses himself a sinner who would like to take away Aufidius's nobility even as he values it. In another of the play's ironies of situation, this is exactly what Marcius does, since after the fight for Corioli, Aufidius exclaims:

                        Mine emulation
    Hath not that honor in't it had: for where
    I thought to crush him in an equal force,
    True sword to sword, I'll potch at him some way,
    Or wrath or craft may get him. (1.10.12)

Marcius's insistence on their mutually noble conflict, and his constant victories, end in driving his only rival in nobility, Aufidius, away from honor to an insistence on success by any means. There is an odd parallel in this to Coriolanus's son, who runs "after a gilded butterfly,

and when he caught it, he let it go again, and after it again, and over
and over he comes, and up again, catched it again; or whether his fall
enraged him, or how 'twas, he did so set his teeth and tear it" (1.3.60).
The parallel works both ways, as each warrior pursues the other, finds
the nobility of the other to be fragile, and succeeds in destroying it.
Perhaps the most poignant instance of Coriolanus's reliance on
Aufidius to mirror his idea of nobility comes after that idea has been
forced into double inconsistency, when Coriolanus has capitulated to
Volumnia at Rome's gates. He turns to Aufidius for solace, repeating
his name like a charm:

> Aufidius, though I cannot make true wars,
> I'll frame convenient peace. Now, good Aufidius,
> Were you in my stead, would you have heard
> A mother less? or granted less, Aufidius? (5.3.190)

The double sense of "I'd revolt, to make / Only my wars with him"
(an ambiguity Marcius himself may sense, since he proceeds to explain
his relation to Aufidius by saying "He is a lion / That I am proud to
hunt") typifies a prevalent kind of irony in *Coriolanus* caused by his
special value to the state and his unusual relation to discourse. Brutus
and Sicinius, the tribunes, have listened to Marcius's comments on the
Volscian, and when the nobles leave the stage, they comment:

SICINIUS: Was ever man so proud as is this Martius?
BRUTUS: He has no equal. (1.1.251)

Brutus means "he's the proudest person in Rome," but he could also
mean that he is proud *because* "he has no equal," and this estimate of
his merit would yield a logical defense of his pride. Self-regarding
nobility shows its incommensurability by undercutting, or choking off,
the political language of evaluation.

Throughout the play, then, Coriolanus rejects or attempts to distance himself from exchanges in the public market involving his reputation: this is a constant feature of his nobility. Under stress he also
makes declarations of his intent to behave as if absolutely autonomous;
this is a tragic deformation of his nobility, which in its extremity is
vulnerable to both logical and political attack. Volumnia shows how
different she is from her son when she tells him:

> You are too absolute.
> Though therein you can never be too noble,
> But when extremities speak. (3.2.39)

For her, gestures towards absolute self-reliance are appropriate parts
of the rhetoric of nobility when things are going well; for Coriolanus,

they become necessary when things deteriorate and structures that support the self have given way.

⛭

The most important of these structures is the family. It plays a crucial role in traditional claims of nobility, since genetic continuity props the fiction that one class of people is better than another. I want to look particularly closely at the way the family structure enters into the conflict between opposed systems of value in *Coriolanus*. The play reflects Renaissance theories about how genetic inheritance actually functions: Coriolanus calls Volumnia "the honour'd mould / Wherein this trunk was fram'd" (5.3.22), echoing the belief that women simply provided a receptacle for the paternal seed; Volumnia reiterates this view, while making her own role a more grammatically active one, a few lines further on: "Thou art my warrior: / I holp to frame thee" (5.3.62).

Volumnia takes credit for her son's traits, justifying her claims by appeal to the supposed character-forming powers of mother's milk, "Thy valiantness was mine, thou suck'st it from me" (3.2.129), and to her influence over his education, "as thou hast said / My praises made thee first a soldier" (3.2.107). Volumnia's milk, of course, is flavored by some singular maternal attitudes, as she declares to Virgilia:

> The breasts of Hecuba
> When she did suckle Hector, look'd not lovelier
> Than Hector's forehead when it spit forth blood
> At Grecian sword contemning. (1.3.40)

Volumnia not only expresses a perverse aesthetic judgment here, but, if the passage is taken in the context of her other claims about nurture, she makes hero-suckling into a martial art in its own right.[33] Volumnia further implies that her own martial-erotic relation to her son takes precedence over that of Virgilia: "If my son were my husband I should freelier rejoice in that absence wherein he won honour, than in the embracements of his bed, where he would show most love" (1.3.2).

The value preferences she thus inculcates are part of a public economy, as she shows in describing her maternal specialty: hypothetical exchanges of her son's presence, safety, and love for "that absence wherein he won honour."

> When yet he was but tender-bodied, and the only son of my womb; when youth with comeliness plucked all gaze his way; when, for a day of kings' entreaties, a mother should not sell him an hour from her beholding; I, considering how honour would become such a person— that it was no better than picture-like to hang by th' wall, if renown

made it not stir—was pleased to let him seek danger where he was like
to find fame. (1.3.5)

Alhough she imagines herself resisting "kings' entreaties" to "sell him
an hour from her beholding," she cannot resist the republican opportunity to let him endanger himself in the field for "fame." Virgilia, silent
all this while, asks the obvious question: "But had he died in the business, madam, how then?" (1.3.19). Volumnia's reply defines the trap
in which Coriolanus has grown up:

> Then his good report should have been my son, I therein would have
> found issue. Hear me profess sincerely: had I a dozen sons, each in my
> love alike, and none less dear than thine and my good Martius, I had
> rather had eleven die nobly for their country, than one voluptuously
> surfeit out of action. (1.3.20)

Given that Volumnia sees reputation and her son's life as interchange-
able, there is a ghastly appropriateness in the fact that Coriolanus ends
the play dead at a distance and Volumnia ends the play in a triumphal
entry to Rome—an unprecedented event in the history of this sexist
republic and one invented by Shakespeare.[34]

Coriolanus's hatred of the invariable translation of his deeds into
"good report" may well stem in part from resentment of his mother's
declared willingness to exchange him for it. Coriolanus's dislike of the
mechanisms of fame also resists Volumnia's evident desire to take
credit for whatever good report he receives and, through him, to
achieve the civic glory she cannot, as a woman, directly seek. He has
been brought up on the idea that a bad report would make his mother
wish him dead. This upbringing also explains his one apparently favor-
able reference to public evaluation in the play, when he asks for volun-
teers among the soldiers outside Corioli:

> If any such be here—
> As it were sin to doubt—that love this painting
> Wherein you see me smear'd; if any fear
> Lesser his person than an ill report
> . . . .
> Let him alone, or so many so minded,
> Wave thus . . . (1.6.67)

Since Volumnia raised Coriolanus to seek maternal love by painting
himself with blood and to feel that an ill report would make her wish
him dead, it is no wonder that he exhorts his men with the fear of ill
report rather than desire for good. Throughout the play, Coriolanus
both resents public discourse about his actions and is immediately

furious if they are misinterpreted to his public discredit—notably when he is called a traitor in Rome and in Corioli. Both the resentment and the anger are reactions against the economy in which he was brought up.

The play's attention to his nurture undercuts any implicit claims he makes to generate his own value. Even his most distinctive characteristic—his resistance to public demands and public approval—has been shaped, after all, by Volumnia's demands and her conditions for approval. Volumnia's translation of her son's experiences and pain into marketable commodities reaches a peak of grotesque comedy in the discussion of his wounds somewhat later in the play. Menenius and Volumnia take a kind of census:

> MENENIUS: Where is he wounded?
> VOLUMNIA: I'th'shoulder and i'th'left arm: there will be large cicatrices to show the people when he shall stand for his place. He received in the repulse of Tarquin seven hurts i'th'body.
> MENENIUS: One i'th'neck, and two i'th'thigh—there's nine that I know.
> VOLUMNIA: He had, before this last expedition, twenty-five wounds upon him.
> MENENIUS: Now it's twenty-seven: every gash was an enemy's grave.
>   (2.1.144)

Coriolanus shows extreme reluctance to display his body to the people, and his reluctance stems in part from this distasteful advance marketing. He resists his mother's vicarious participation in the social marketplace just as he resists that of the plebeians.

> To brag unto them, thus I did, and thus,
> Show them th'unaching scars which I should hide,
> As if I had receiv'd them for the hire
> Of their breath only! (2.2.147)

But when Coriolanus is banished, his rhetorical relation to his own nobility changes. Cast loose from his family, he also loses the civic usefulness that made his self-regarding nobility a public as well as a private asset. He mentions neither gods nor nobility when he comes disguised to offer service to Aufidius: rather, alone on the streets of Antium, he reflects with self-irony on the bad bargain he has struck, the "dissension of a doit" (4.4.17), the "trick not worth an egg" (4.4.21), which has divorced him from Rome and given his love to the Volsces. He invites Aufidius to an exchange of benefits:

> so use it
> That my revengeful services may prove
> As benefits to thee, for I will fight

> Against my canker'd country with the spleen
> Of all the under fiends. (4.5.89)

The supreme test of ethical self-reliance would be to sustain oneself without external confirmation of value, human or divine, as Coriolanus himself says (rather knottily) on leaving Rome:

> fortune's blows
> When most struck home, being gentle wounded craves
> A noble cunning. (4.1.7)

Evidently Coriolanus's nobility has failed this test, since he has distanced himself from the gods, compared himself to fiends, and offered Aufidius a profitable exchange.

Aufidius, however, embraces him as though he recognized and admired Coriolanus precisely for that nobility which Coriolanus feels he has given up:

> If Jupiter
> Should from yond cloud speak divine things,
> And say "'Tis true," I'd not believe them more
> Than thee, all-noble Martius. . . .
> [I] do contest
> As hotly and as nobly with thy love
> As ever in ambitious strength I did
> Contend against thy valor . . . .
> . . . .
> Why, thou Mars! (4.5.104)

After this confirmation, coming from the one man he acknowledges as an equal, of precisely the aspects of himself which his banishment and his incapacity to sustain his values in isolation had led him to doubt— that is, his nobility and his special relationship with the gods—it is no surprise that Coriolanus should imagine his own recovery and exclaim, "You bless me, Gods!" (4.5.136). He can again direct his attention upward and inward and reject the world of bargains and exchanges around him, as Aufidius notes during the campaign a few weeks later:

> He bears himself more proudlier
> Even to my person than I thought he would
> When first I did embrace him. Yet his nature
> In that's no changeling . . . (4.7.8)

But Coriolanus cannot, of course, sustain this autonomy in the face of his family's opposition, for he has not abandoned the notion that his nobility is partly a familial matter, nor does he exempt his family from the special relation to the gods that comes with nobleness, as we have already seen in his blessing to his son. When he estimates Virgilia's value, he sets it at a transcendent level: "What is that curtsy worth? or those dove's eyes, / Which can make gods forsworn? I melt . . . " (5.3.27) When he comes to his mother, the identification with his own nobility seems complete, though his language becomes less intimate and more formal:

> You gods! I prate,
> And the most noble mother of the world
> Leave unsaluted. (5.3.48)[35]

Having identified his family with his own nobility, and being told by Volumnia that his conduct, among other privations, prevents their prayers to the gods, Coriolanus cannot maintain his ethical autonomy: he is contradicted by someone who speaks to the gods, and for them, with the same apparent force as he. At a crux in her speech of persuasion, Volumnia threatens him with their displeasure, while in the same phrase accusing him of ignobility. She urges the mutual benefit of a peace to Romans and Volsces, and continues:

> Say my request's unjust,
> And spurn me back; but if it be not so,
> Thou art not honest, and the gods will plague thee
> That thou restrain'st from me the duty which
> To a mother's part belongs. He turns away.
> Down ladies: let us shame him with our knees. (5.3.164)

The gods, dishonesty, and shame: Coriolanus proves not "unvulnerable" to this combination aimed unerringly at the sources of his claims to autonomy, and gives in. His words betray his sense that he has been false, ridiculously so, to the gods he has tried to support, and from whom he has expected support in turn:

> O mother, mother!
> What have you done? Behold, the heavens do ope,
> The gods look down, and this unnatural scene
> They laugh at. (5.3.182)

At what do the gods laugh? Partly at the spectacle of a noble opponent of the market who, in pursuit of his just price, has circulated himself like a commodity, found among the Volsces a site where he is in demand, and then returned home with gloriously enhanced worth to be devalued by the mother/merchant who pushed him into circulation in the first place. Coriolanus takes pains to indicate that this circulation has not affected him in all ways, and that he has retained domestic commitment to Virgilia: "that kiss / I carried from thee, dear; and my true lip / Hath virgin'd it e'er since" (5.3.46). But he is well aware that his travels in search of a better market for his virtues have made his claims to absolute value impossible.

His nobility thus abandoned, it is fitting that Coriolanus should be murdered in an equivocation over the returns to the Volsces from the Roman war: Aufidius maintains that Coriolanus has given "away / The benefit of our levies, answering us / With our own charge" (5.6.66), while Coriolanus asserts that

> Our spoils we have brought home
> Doth more than counterpoise a full third part
> The charges of the action. (5.6.77)

Against this haggling (in which we assume that the truth lies on Coriolanus's side, though we cannot know), Coriolanus can summon up only the memory of his single-handed victory at Corioli. He dies attempting to reinvoke the terms of his now compromised nobility, goaded by taunts that show how shrewdly Aufidius has taken his measure. "Hear'st thou, Mars?" asks Coriolanus in outrage; "Name not the god, thou boy of tears," Aufidius replies, striking like Volumnia at his claims to nobility and to privileged discourse with the gods. Coriolanus responds, of course, with a reference to history, that vindicator of nobility in the gods' absence:[36]

> If you have writ your annals true, 'tis there,
> That, like an eagle in a dovecote, I
> Flutter'd your Volscians in Corioles.
> Alone I did it. Boy! (5.6.113)

Even to the end, then, Coriolanus consciously and deliberately, as well as passionately and vulnerably, holds up his end of a debate between the claims of a noble subject and those of the various structures (redescribed by Shakespeare as essentially economic in their operation) which reconstitute and diminish that nobility by making it part of cycles of social exchange for mutual benefit. His tenacity partly explains, I believe, the sense of loss he leaves behind him in viewers and readers. He fights to have agency on his own terms. In a play in which the transcendent is absent, both in that the gods are distant or fictive and that no character is much interested in anything beyond his immediate perspective, Coriolanus's belief in a self-regarding noble ideal and in the special relationship of his nobility to the gods comes to bear an enormous weight. It is, moreover, the sole alternative source of value which might offer more stability than markets of social exchange. Markets, of course, need not be unstable, and the food riot at the opening of the play, which happens because of the failure of markets, also alludes to a paternalist economy more reassuring than the one the play explores. In the Rome of the play, however, markets are fickle and hungry, consuming value rather than generating it. The Rome of *Coriolanus* is to that of the other Roman plays (especially *Antony and Cleopatra*) as the sonnets to the dark lady are to those to the young man: a poorer market, a deflationary economy.

Even while Coriolanus's behavior has been hopelessly compromised by the extremes to which he is driven, he becomes an increasingly poignant and distant example of nobility to all around him. "Let him be regarded / As the most noble corse that ever herald / Did follow to his urn" (5.6.142), says a Volscian lord when he is safely dead. Coriolanus becomes the subject of nostalgia for a lost nobility before his body is cold.

༃

At the opening of this chapter, before introducing the paternalistic moral economy of the Roman crowd, I suggested that Coriolanus might have had a place in this version of the Roman economy (one superseded in the course of the play), though he refuses this too. A state in which everything is in negotiation offers opportunities to a charismatic individual, and early in the play Coriolanus seems to be "called" toward a central position in Rome. As sourly reported by the tribunes, the triumph Coriolanus is given on his return from Corioli demonstrates the extent to which Coriolanus has the charisma which could re-center Rome:

> Brutus: All tongues speak of him, and the bleared sights
>   Are spectacled to see him . . . .
>   . . . stalls, bulks, windows
>   Are smother'd up, leads fill'd and ridges hors'd
>   With variable complexions, all agreeing
>   In earnestness to see him . . . .
>   . . . Such a pother,
>   As if that whatsoever god who leads him
>   Were slily crept into his human powers,
>   And gave him graceful posture. (2.1.203)

Brutus surely does not think Coriolanus a quasi-divinity, yet even he notes the centering attraction his extraordinary deeds have given him. Both Brutus and the tribunes expect this public attraction to be converted immediately into political authority of a kind that they have not had to fear from the senate up to this point:

Sicinius: On the sudden,
   I warrant him consul.
Brutus: Then our office may,
   During his power, go sleep. (2.1.218)

According to Clifford Geertz, social centers of charisma "are essentially concentrated loci of serious acts; they consist in the point or points in a society where its leading ideas come together with its leading institutions to create an arena in which the events that most vitally affect its members' lives take place. It is involvement, even oppositional involvement, with such arenas and with the momentous events that occur in them that confers charisma."[37] Geertz concludes: "It is not, after all, standing outside the social order in some excited state of self-regard that makes a political leader numinous but a deep, intimate involvement—affirming or abhorring, defensive or destructive—in the master fictions by which that order lives."[38] Coriolanus, who incarnates *virtus*, cannot help being charismatic in a Rome where, as Cominius puts it, "It is held / That valour is the chiefest virtue" (2.2.83), but Coriolanus repudiates the unstable negotiation of countless exchanges necessary to maintain or use his charisma.

Neither Coriolanus's view of a proper moral economy (in which his elite should be allowed to stand in a "state of self-regard") nor that of the plebeians (in which the elite should guarantee a paternalist moral economy against profiteering) obtains in the Rome of this play. But Coriolanus has no desire himself to fill the gap by supplying the state with a charismatic center, even though he alone among the patricians has the apparently essential excellence that might allow him to become such a center. To be valued (and thus useful) in an inevitable communal market, but at the same time to be convinced that your value does not derive from this set of negotiations (but instead allows the negotiations to transmit genuine value from its essential source to those who lack it) is the role open to a self-regarding noble in such a state. Coriolanus's oppositional stance might enhance his charisma, if he were merely playing very hard to get, but he insists on withholding himself and on loudly registering his anger at forced compromises.

According to the most authoritative sources Shakespeare had for a generalized historical view of Rome, the creation of the tribunes, and the formation of a balanced or mixed state, was a progressive move. Anne Barton, basing her argument on Livy and on Machiavelli's commentary on Livy in the *Discourses*, has recently claimed that in *Coriolanus* Shakespeare "looked attentively at the young Roman republic delineated by Plutarch and by Livy, and chose to emphasize what was hopeful, communal and progressive in it, when writing his interpretation of the time."[39] Insofar as the play tells a story of successful innovation in Roman political economy, this is true. But republican Rome may also have fascinated Shakespeare because its communal ideal threw all values into interdependence and because there was no charismatic center to the state. At sixteen, Coriolanus struck down the last king of Rome; by his own obstinate resistance to market economies, he foregoes opportunities to become a charismatic ruler himself.

ĕ

Some of Shakespeare's heroes are born pragmatists, some achieve pragmatism, and some have pragmatism thrust upon them. *Coriolanus* offers a key instance of the forced acceptance, by its hero, of both his city and his own identity as economies rather than fixed systems. In resisting this acceptance he faces a choice between destroying his city and family on the one hand and himself on the other, and he chooses his own destruction after a brief attempt to turn himself into a bargainer. From his point of view, then, pragmatism brings with it a tragic loss. For the plebeians, however, the marketplace is a site of hope, where their voices, like their labor and their wares, are needed. Though both Voscian and Roman nobles express nostalgia for Coriolanus, the demystification of the noble should cause little nostalgia among the plebeians.

Coriolanus is, moreover, probably the most persistently ironic, rather than nostalgic, of Shakespeare's tragedies: statements and actions, as we have seen, change significance and escape the control of speakers and actors, and Coriolanus himself can hardly say a word that does not reverberate hollowly against his coming fate. Irony is an affective mode. It occurs when a word or phrase or gesture or situation can be revalued from a different perspective. We could say that irony consists of the recognition that language is an economy: that words have meaning only when they come to market, when they have been brought into a situation in which they can be evaluated or accepted, but that an unexpected or hostile market may reverse the value a speaker intends. A completely noble world would be inimical to irony, and for Coriolanus, a noble person avoids, or tries to avoid, situations in which his words can be misconstrued or separated from his deeds. But, of course, his very efforts to immunize himself in this way set him up for one ironic fall after another.

As I have also argued, however, irony paradoxically sometimes works *for* Coriolanus and against his denigrators, precisely because his asserted self-difference creates an alternative sphere for evaluation. Moreover, because Coriolanus attempts to live in a different world of his own construction—with an audience of gods who, until they look down with ironic laughter at his capitulation to his mother, are not themselves given to irony at the expense of mortals—his untenable nobility acquires magnitude and charisma, despite the manifold ironies to which the play subjects him.[40] Bradley could feel "it is not only his faults that make him impossible . . . there is bound up with them a nobleness of nature in which he surpasses everyone around him."[41] I have tried to show what Bradley does not say: that Coriolanus's nobility not only surpasses, but is different in substance from that of the other patricians around him.

The play scrutinizes not only the constituents of nobility, but the social economy which sustains, undermines, and ironizes it, with relentless rigor. Coriolanus's banishment and death remove a major impediment to a world in which the public's main aim will be "to have corn at our own price," and in which that price will be set by no agreed-upon moral economy, but by the politics, both progressive and cruel, of the market. The asymmetry between Coriolanus and his environment casts in question the capacity of a market world to generate or sustain the nobility for which, as the play also shows, it continues—residually and temporarily—to hunger. Coriolanus does not, of course, wait passively for others to define his value for him; he actively recognizes and resists the market world that surrounds him, and his resistance itself is what finally defines his nobility.[42] As I have tried to show, Coriolanus's nobility defines itself around (and destroys itself through) impatience with determining systems—language, community, and family—in which illusions, claims, and gestures of originality in self-fashioning must find their floating ground. It is unprofitable to be entirely scornful of what works, yet those who matter do so because they modify what works, sometimes through contagious scorn. Both halves of this pragmatic observation fit Coriolanus.

9

Plasticity and Politics in
Antony and Cleopatra

৵

Coriolanus thought he lived in a state, and found, to his cost, that he inhabited an economy. The political tension between expectations based on fixed systems and practices constrained by dynamic economies has been explored throughout this book, particularly in the two previous chapters. But what happens when rulers believe that their task is to shape or ride an economy rather than to conform to and exemplify a fixed set of values? *Antony and Cleopatra* explores this peculiarly modern problem: how to shape the political self in a changing world without firm rules.

Antony and Cleopatra eludes precise formulations, generic and moral. Norms for tragedy, even those derived from Shakespeare's varied practice elsewhere, do not fit it well, and it subverts rules of conduct which might be (and often are) invoked in judging it. Janet Adelman, at the end of an indispensable account of the play published in 1973, comments on its unwillingness to conform tidily to our systems of explanation, and concludes that "the play achieves a fluidity of possibility far more akin to our actual experience than any of our systems can be."[1]

It would be easy, two decades later, to turn on this humanist formulation, with its inclusive predication of subjective richness and freedom. Adelman herself does not celebrate literature in just these terms any longer, and like many other contemporary cultural critics, sees individual subjectivity less as a dependable reservoir of exciting variety and more as a constituted nexus of ideological pressures and discursive habits. Adelman's landmark essay on *Coriolanus*, "Anger's My Meat," marks a shift in her work toward emphasis on the construction of the subject within systems of constraint.[2] Such a critical turn against the humanist emphasis on autonomous will shaping idiosyncratic identity, however, finds itself anticipated and to some extent forestalled by *Antony and Cleopatra*, with its extraordinary variety of perspectives resisting hierarchization, its peculiarly sophisticated internal audience for the theatrics of rule, and its bracketing of imposed and highlighting of self-imposed violence.[3] Even about death, characters in the play make choices among an array of elaborately discussed possibilities. This chapter returns to the issue, first raised in connection with Stanley Fish and then with *Hamlet*, of relative freedom and constraint, and argues that *Antony and Cleopatra* works pragmatically with large questions about the scope and limits of human agency. In *Hamlet* the thought-experiment concerning discourse and agency focused on the individual subject; in *Antony and Cleopatra*, I will argue, the play's inquiry focuses on the freedom for self-remaking of whole political communities.

Adelman's comment that *Antony and Cleopatra* "achieves a fluidity of possibility far more akin to our actual experience than any of our systems can be" suggests that an increase in freedom, an awareness of the fluid possibilities around us, is available through critical reading and thinking (in this case about *Antony and Cleopatra*, which is seen to achieve subjective possibility like that we may experience). The New Critical notion that literature is more varied and fluid than "systems" (what might then have alternatively been called "theories") has, since she invoked it here, largely been turned around, on the one hand by the ascendency of extremely literary, antisystematic, edifying theorists, especially Nietzsche, Foucault, and Derrida, who may seem to liberate or otherwise expand our thinking at least as energetically as most canonical literary texts, and on the other by the idea (not tied to these Europeans, who show no particular desire to democratize reading lists) that close reading of classic texts, far from liberating us, instead carries with it an ideology of socially conservative canon-maintenance. But what Adelman means by "systems" is quite different from what contemporary readers experience as "theory." "Systems," as Adelman uses the word, seems to refer to structural explanations of a necessitarian cast. And her suggestion that something about *Antony and Cleopatra* opposes itself to structural explanations of history and human behavior seems to me very right. I shall in this chapter take up Roberto Unger's polemic against the validity and social force of deep-structural social explanation and argue that *Antony and Cleopatra* provides a Shakespearean examination of historical plasticity, of a moment in ancient history in which social systems are in flux and widely recognized to be so.

This interest in historical plasticity—and in the liberating possibilities the recognition of such plasticity may bring—puts me in some conflict with the tendency in contemporary cultural criticism, associated with Foucault or Althusser, to locate subjectivity in tight disciplinary fields of constraint or as subject to directive ideological callings or "interpellations." Yet such a criticism, too, however pervasively negative, seeks to emancipate, though not by attributing emancipatory power directly to classic works. Emancipation comes instead as a kind of utopian coda to the documentation of actual or local limits. The emancipatory idea becomes the recognition that human social life is a human artifact, that systems of contextual constraint are historically specific, subject to critique, overthrow, and evolution, and that recognizing them as such is a step toward changing them. Critics who emphasize constraint and devote themselves to a series of unmaskings may regard it as foolishly optimistic to assert, but probably at some level believe, that, as Roberto Unger puts it, "the relation of our context-revising freedom to the contexts we inhabit is itself up for grabs."[4] Unger is saying that our cultural criticism might feed into a new politics which will restructure the contingent in ways we have not yet been daring enough to imagine, but he also, in specific criticism of the dark determinism of Foucauldian poststructuralists, urges intellectuals not to disempower themselves by overstating the power of structure over subject in their criticism. The assertion of contingency, Unger feels, furthers political plasticity and the revision of unsatisfactory constraining contexts.[5]

Antony and Cleopatra dramatizes a historical juncture in which everyone is aware that contexts are subject to revision and that traditional constraints need either reassertion or revision. This is partly to say that *Antony and Cleopatra* is preeminent among Shakespeare's tragedies in representing widespread authoritative acceptance of the contingency of values and institutions—acceptance, that is, by all major voices in the play (not excluding Octavius) that there is nothing more certain or stable than social agreement (whether enforced or spontaneous) in conferring value on persons, acts, objects, or states. Leaders in the play have internalized, to greater or lesser degrees, the Shakespearean redescription of fixed structures as dynamic economies, but the political consequences of this internalization differ. The play isolates political vocabularies in which the malleability of historical processes and social orders to particular, often idiosyncratic, human purposes is articulated; these vocabularies compete with (and manipulate) others which articulate the dominance of natural law or the omnipotence of divine will or the momentum of historical process. The question is, What style of leadership, what political vocabulary, will emerge to shape the future world?

The Renaissance itself is a period of self-conscious context revision, and I want to frame my discussion of *Antony and Cleopatra* by first treating two other English Renaissance texts in which political and social contexts are subject to radical revision by a successful leader: Marlowe's *Tamburlaine* and Marvell's "An Horatian Ode upon Cromwell's Return from Ireland." I put them in relation to Machiavelli's *The Prince*, the key Renaissance exposition of the contingency of political legitimation. In developing this comparison I shall also argue that whereas *Tamburlaine* and the "Horatian Ode" adopt a clearly masculinist model for the politics of rule, in which a powerful male imposes his will on a female fortune, in *Antony and Cleopatra* one of the several suggested models for rulership (and the most provocative one) is best read according to a specifically feminist model in its endorsement of a differential and contestatory style of leadership involving collaboration in rule between males and females. Read as a political partnership involving a new public style, the relationship between Cleopatra and Antony compels us also to reconsider the historically proximate coming of Christ—an event hinted at, though in deconsecrating ways, throughout *Antony and Cleopatra*. Christ's leadership, with its ultimate political importance, offers, like the leadership of Antony and Cleopatra, a context-revising politics that is neither Machiavellian nor masculinist. This juxtaposition of Christ and Cleopatra, though audacious, makes sense in terms of Shakespeare's persistent pragmatism about the historical flux of world views, political systems, and leadership styles. He sees them as terms in a dynamic economy. *Tamburlaine* and the "Horatian Ode," then, though powerful and original in their political art, are less extraordinary than *Antony and Cleopatra* in their treatment of context revision; this framing provides a ground from which the more thoroughgoing legitimation of contingency in leadership that I see in Shakespeare's play will emerge.

Machiavelli, Marlowe, Marvell: Leadership Style and Male Mastery of Contingency

An overheard phrase sparks one of the most audacious steps in Tamburlaine's rise to empire. He has just won a battle as Cosroe's field commander and given him the imperial crown of his ineffectual elder brother Mycetes. Cosroe, making the recent shepherd/brigand Tamburlaine his lieutenant general and regent of Persia, prepares for his investiture, and is addressed by his counselor Menaphon:

> MENAPHON: Your Majesty shall shortly have your wish,
>   And ride in triumph through Persepolis. *Exeunt.*
>   *Manent Tamb. Tech. Ther. Usum.*
> TAMBURLAINE: And ride in triumph through Persepolis?
>   Is it not brave to be a King, Techelles?
>   Usumcasane and Theridamas,
>   Is it not passing brave to be a King,
>   And ride in triumph through Persepolis?
> TECHELLES: O my Lord, tis sweet and full of pompe.

USUMCASANE: To be a King, is halfe to be a God.
Theridamas: A God is not so glorious as a King:
    I thinke the pleasure they enjoy in heaven
    Can not compare with kingly joys in earth.
. . . .
Tamburlaine: . . . presently Techelles here shal haste,
    To bid him battaile ere he passe too farre.[6]

This moment of inspiration or improvisation is only the most famous of a series of unlikely contingencies that Tamburlaine exploits in starting his career as world-historical individual. The capture of Zenocrate and her treasure (which leads him to throw off his shepherd's garb in order to proclaim himself a fit wooer), the prompt use Tamburlaine makes of his spoils in the conversion of Theridamas (he dazzles Theridamas's followers with newly acquired wedges of gold), and the subsequent seizure of Mycetes and overthrow of Cosroe, all display a swift capture of fortune by a will that improvises on, even as it asserts the fatedness of, its own repeated victories.[7]

This kingship of vertiginous ascent rather than settled legitimacy, according to the philosophic Theridamas, offers pleasures unobtainable in heaven (where, we must presume, contingencies of this kind can have no place). Certainly the claim that kings are superior to gods unsettles any transcendental notions of divine right: Marlowe here anticipates, less provocatively, the claim of the prologue "Machevil" in *The Jew of Malta:*

> I count Religion but a childish Toy,
> And hold there is no sinne but Ignorance.
> Birds of the Aire will tell of murders past;
> I am asham'd to heare such fooleries:
> Many will talke of Title to a Crowne.
> What right had Caesar to the Empire?
> Might first made Kings, and Lawes were then most sure
> When like the Dracos they were writ in blood.[8]

Tamburlaine offers a particularly clear focus (for which *The Jew of Malta* credits Machiavelli and cites the Roman transition from republic to empire) on what J. G. A. Pocock describes as the contest of male "virtue" and female "fortune" for the prize of secular power. In the absence of a supervening providential understanding of historical contingency, this contest offered a mode of explanation of historical process inherited by early modern Europe via Boethius from antiquity:

> in opposing virtue to fortune Boethius was appealing to a long-standing tradition of discourse, which, however, he proceeded to set in a Christian

context. In the senatorial ethos of republican and imperial Rome, *fortuna* had rather the meaning of luck than of chance . . . but the element of chance was acknowledged in the recognition that luck could not be counted upon. . . . The *baraka, mana,* or *charisma* (to use terms from other cultures) of the successful actor thus consisted both in the quality of personality that commanded good fortune and in the quality that dealt effectively and nobly with whatever fortune might send. . . . This opposition was frequently expressed in the image of a sexual relation: a masculine active intelligence was seeking to dominate a feminine passive unpredictability which would submissively reward him for his strength or vindictively betray him for his weakness.[9]

Tamburlaine's alternation of impressive gravity with infectious zest is a study, more subtle than it is usually credited with being, of how such charisma might interact with the menu of opportunities it meets. Moreover, Tamburlaine's style of leadership is clearly masculinist and feminizes those male characters such as Theridamas whom he persuades or seduces to become his followers. In consonance with Pocock's observations about the gendering of virtue and fortune, we may note that Zenocrate *is* Tamburlaine's fortune, as his rise begins with her capture and is crowned by their marriage in part 1, and his decline in part 2 begins with her death, followed by Tamburlaine's murder of his son, declaration of enmity to Mahomet, and burning of the Koran.

Marlowe's interest in the leadership style of a context-revising historical individual thus finds expression in a charismatic non-Christian leader whose attitude to gods and providence is deliberately defiant and whose success lasts only as long as his domination of the woman who confers on him both luck and legitimacy. *Tamburlaine* might, indeed, be read as an approving lesson on how to gain what Machiavelli calls "new principalities acquired by one's own arms and skill,"[10] but a lesson which emphasizes male autonomy less than Machiavelli does and stresses the role of women more:

But let us consider Cyrus and the others who have acquired and founded kingdoms; you will find them all admirable. . . . And examining their deeds and their lives, one can see that they received nothing but the opportunity from Fortune, which then gave them the material they could mold into whatever form they desired; and without that opportunity the strength of their spirit would have been extinguished, and without that strength the opportunity would have come in vain.[11]

We can discern in this passage Pocock's shadowy genders (here as part of a traditional tendency to gender the dichotomy of form and matter), as the union of strength of spirit with opportunity brings forth new kingdoms. Hanna Fenichel Pitkin, in her study of gender in

Machiavelli's thought, calls this embodiment of masculine self-imposition on history "the Founder," and defines him as "a male figure of superhuman or mythical proportions, who introduces among men something new, good, and sufficiently powerful so that it continues beyond his lifetime on the course he has set."[12] Pitkin goes on to comment that the "point is never just getting others to do what you want, but changing them, introducing new patterns of action and of relationship."[13] But these new patterns must be imposed on a shifting medium of contingent human relations in time, and Pitkin demonstrates that for Machiavelli this medium was hostile and feminine:

> The seemingly exclusively masculine world of Machiavelli's political writings, where men contend in the arena of history, is acutally dominated or at least continually threatened from behind the scenes by dimly perceived, haunting feminine figures of overwhelming power. The contest among the men turns out to be, in crucial ways, their shared struggle against that power. The feminine constitutes "the other" for Machiavelli, opposed to manhood and autonomy in all their senses: to maleness, to adulthood, to humanness, and to politics.[14]

Tamburlaine collaborates successfully with this "other," though his style of leadership is Machiavellian in its insistence on autonomy and domination.

Marvell's Cromwell offers a more complex case of Machiavellian context revision. Complementing Marlowe's tragic glass, Marvell's tragic scaffold marks a convenient and hallowed, if obviously arbitrary, end point for the arc of English Renaissance dramatic representations of context-breaking historical change. For Jonathan Dollimore and Walter Cohen the revolution and regicide of the 1640s supply a telos for subversive or radical tendencies in Renaissance drama; for Leonard Tennenhouse they supply evidence that Stuart absolutism needed whatever support the drama could give it.[15] As long ago as 1955, Patrick Cruttwell chose the "Horatian Ode" as the last balanced utterance of *The Shakespearean Moment*.[16]

Blair Worden, in a persuasive and detailed article on the "Horatian Ode," argues that it reflects, in a much more sober way, the same kind of Machiavellian reflection on virtue and contingency in a time of the breaking of nations that I have found in *Tamburlaine*.[17] There are obvious differences, of course. Marvell, though not writing for immediate publication, treats events with nearly the immediacy of a pamphleteer, and the events he describes have grave consequences for himself and all his own previous commitments, while Marlowe dramatizes an exotic career at an historical and geographic distance; Marvell's writing does not aim to please a public (we know almost nothing about the reception of the "Horatian Ode"),[18] while Marlowe's takes up and transforms stage traditions with huge popular success. But Marvell's poise and Marlowe's in-your-face brashness both present us with a rule-breaking career and, in effect, ask us what new rules we can find in it:

> View but his picture in this tragic glass
> And then applaud his fortunes as you may.[19]

The open question about the "Horatian Ode" has been: How should we applaud Cromwell's fortunes? Partly, it would seem, by seeing in them an emblem of the relative fragility of institutions and the creative/destructive power of a truly Machiavellian new prince, who could

> by industrious valour climb
> To ruin the great work of time,
>> And cast the kingdoms old
>> Into another mould.
> Though justice against fate complain,
> And plead the ancient rights in vain:
>> But those do hold or break
>> As men are strong or weak.[20]

Marvell's equivocal handling of Cromwell's providential understanding of his victories evokes Machiavelli on Moses:

> But to come to those who, by means of their own skill and not because of Fortune, have become princes, I say that the most admirable are Moses, Cyrus, Romulus, Theseus, and the like. And although we should not discuss Moses, since he was a mere executor of things ordered by God, nevertheless he must be admired, if for nothing but that grace which made him worthy of talking with God. But let us consider Cyrus and the others . . . if their deeds and their particular institutions are considered, they will not appear different from those of Moses, who had so great a guide.[21]

Machiavelli's implicitly skeptical transition from Moses, who is to be revered for conversing with God, to Cyrus, who achieved so much without God's help, is repeated by Marvell (with a similar effect of deniable skepticism or guarded irony about divine direction) as he moves from treating Cromwell providentially to treating him as a secular individual:

> 'Tis madness to resist or blame
> The force of angry heaven's flame:
>> And, if we would speak true,
>> Much to the man is due . . .

Machiavelli points us, as does Marvell, to the difficulty of distinguishing divine direction from the purely human virtue of a Cyrus or Tamburlaine—Moses and Cromwell deserve credit for both.

The "Horatian Ode," moreover, pragmatically investigates Cromwell's relation to God by describing its practical consequences in much the same way that Marlowe shows us the political efficacy of Tamburlaine's declared relation to fate, the stars, and the gods. Belief in a supernatural warrant may conceivably be a source of Tamburlaine's self-confidence, and belief in his special connection with the supernatural is surely a source of his power over his followers. He is, however, the instrument of no discernable plan, and his own attitude toward the the supernatural is capricious. There is nothing capricious about Cromwell, of course, but otherwise his providentiality is seen by Marvell as a parcel of his extraordinary fortunes, which force abstract questions of justification or right to give way to the accomplishments of power: "those do hold or break / As men are strong or weak" (39–40). Worden's description of the pamphlet literature that swirled around Cromwell in 1650 makes it clear that his claims to be a divine instrument were vigorously contested.[22] And Pocock comments that Marvell "introduces into his *Horatian Ode* a number of . . . unmistakable images of Cromwell as a Machiavellian prince-legislator akin to Romulus in the necessary illegality and ruthlessness of his proceedings"—images, that is, of Cromwell as a Founder whose creativity involves violent revision of established contexts.[23]

Following Pitkin, I have been suggesting that we can expect to find in such a Machiavellian Founder an underlying troubled relation to sexual difference, and any reader of Marvell's poetry will expect this from Marvell. Though there are no women in the "Horatian Ode," there is a series of hints that a context reviser like Cromwell must set aside feminine interests in order to masculinize himself, and that this process may at times involve violence against women, even a kind of matricide. The "forward youth" turns away from love songs and his "muses dear" to arm himself for war, thus turning toward masculinity and taking up what may perhaps be his father's rusty "corslet" (1–8). Cromwell's own rise, which the youth will attempt to imitate, is conceived more violently:

> So restless Cromwell could not cease
> In the inglorious arts of peace,
>   But through adventurous war
>   Urgèd his active star.
> And, like the three-forked lightning, first
> Breaking the clouds where it was nursed,

> Did thorough his own side
> His fiery way divide.
> (For 'tis all one to courage high
> The emulous or enemy:
> And with such to inclose
> Is more than to oppose.) (9–20)

Here Cromwell urges on the star (presumably of his nativity) to exceed itself, and then breaks the clouds which had contained him, an image which suggests an explosion or cleavage in the womb and thus a Caesarian birth with violent consequences for the mother. Cromwell divides his fiery way through his own side; with such as he, "to enclose / Is more than to oppose."[24] So Cromwell emerges not simply as a context smasher, but also as a matrix smasher, a man who recasts the "mould" (36) in which he himself was shaped.

This historical relation is also cast as a kind of rape to which the virginal victim (Charles I, as well as his "helpless right") accedes. At the scaffold, Charles

> Bowed his comely head,
> Down, as upon a bed.
> This was that memorable hour
> Which first assured the forcèd power.
> So when they did design
> The Capitol's first line,
> A bleeding head where they begun,
> Did fright the architects to run. (63–70)

My interpretation of Cromwell in these phallic terms, and of the "bleeding head" as a violated maidenhead, resonates with other Livyan stories of the foundation of the Roman republic in the rapes of the Sabine women and of Lucrece (who then bloodily divided her own side). Blair Worden agrees: "[r]egicide seemed to have been both a divine punishment for national sins and an act of constitutional rape, so traumatic that no one before Marvell could write adequately about it."[25] Cromwell's phallic representation is reinforced when the Picts "from this valour sad / Shrink underneath the plaid" (107–8). At the poem's close Cromwell, mothered not by a human woman but by war and fortune, is urged to maintain the violent readiness which has brought him to this point:

> But thou, the Wars' and Fortune's son,
> March indefatigably on,
> And for the last effect
> Still keep thy sword erect:

> Besides the force it has to fright
> The spirits of the shady night,
>   The same arts that did gain
>   A power, must it maintain. (113–20)

E. E. Duncan-Jones points out that this passage alludes to the *Odyssey*.[26] Among the shades whom Odysseus held off with his sword while waiting for Teiresias to tell him his fate was that of his mother Antikleia, whose name in Greek means "against glory." Cromwell must keep his phallic sword up against his mother, and against his matrix, to retain his power and gain the glory he has won by masculinist violence.

At one point in the "Horatian Ode" Cromwell is imagined as female, and the very incongruity of the image suggests the instability of the relation of dependence it figures. The image is framed by lines which deal ambiguously with the likelihood that Cromwell will take over the government on his return to England.[27]

> And now the Irish are ashamed
> To see themselves in one year tamed:
>   So much one man can do,
>   That does both act and know.
> They can affirm his praises best,
> And have, though overcome, confessed
>   How good he is, how just,
>   And fit for highest trust:
> Nor yet grown stiffer with command,
> But still in the Republic's hand:
>   How fit he is to sway
>   That can so well obey. (73–84)

The next lines show Cromwell voluntarily subjecting his male valor to a female House of Commons:

> He to the Commons' feet presents
> A kingdom, for his first year's rents:
>   And, what he may, forbears
>   His fame, to make it theirs:
> And has his sword and spoils ungirt,
> To lay them at the public's skirt. (85–90)

Then suddenly the genders are reversed:

> So when the falcon high
> Falls heavy from the sky,
> She, having killed, no more does search

> But on the next green bough to perch,
> Where, when he first does lure,
> The falc'ner has her sure. (91–6)

The double gender reversal, in which Cromwell, the autonomous "one man . . . that does both act and know," becomes female and the skirted public at whose feet he has placed his sword becomes the male falconer, underlines the unlikeliness that Cromwell will remain in this feminized position for long.

In both *Tamburlaine* and the "Horatian Ode," then, a Machiavellian masculinist prince revises the world at the expense of legitimists who plead ancient rights in vain. In both texts, as, less insistently, in *Antony and Cleopatra*, much literary power emanates from the claim to historical truth: this is how it was, applaud it as you may. The "Horatian Ode," moreover, is partly modelled on Horace's Ode 1.37, which rejoices in Augustus's male triumph over Cleopatra and her effeminate Egyptians but praises her resolution in suicide. It has, then, an underground or indirect relation to *Antony and Cleopatra*, in that it suggests a partial parallel between Cromwell's triumph over Charles and the events of that play, even though in constitutional terms *Antony and Cleopatra* marks the final transformation of republic into empire, while the years 1648–50 in England saw what appeared to be the reverse transformation.

But *Antony and Cleopatra* differs from these other two texts in that it focuses on a contest among self-aware world revisers, virtually all of whom accept the contingency of politics and seek support from no settled principle of legitimacy—and one of whom is a woman. It approaches the problem Machiavelli raised for political thought in the Renaissance as if it were solved. In the world of *Antony and Cleopatra* no one who matters is anything but Machiavellian in accepting the idea that morality in politics has no extrahuman force and is a weaker human force than is conventionally or rhetorically claimed. Moreover, *Antony and Cleopatra* examines the possibility, excluded in Machiavelli, that world revising might successfully be done by enlisting, rather than subduing, the feminine.

Responses to Plasticity in *Antony and Cleopatra*

All our major problems in the understanding of society arise from the same source. They have to do with the difficulty of accounting for the actions of a being who, individually and collectively, in thought and relationship, might break through the contexts within which he ordinarily moves. The perennial temptation in the understanding of society

and personality is to equate the very nature of explanation with an
explanatory style that treats people's actions and thoughts as governed
by a describable structure. When we make this mistake, we deny the
power to discover truth and establish association beyond the limits of
the available contexts. Or we treat these episodes of structure breaking
as if they were themselves governed by metastructures. . . . To disengage
the idea of explanation from the exclusive hold of these styles of explanation is the beginning of insight in social thought. Indeed, for the theorist
of society it is the most exacting and delicate of tasks.[28]

℥

It somehow became possible, toward the end of the nineteenth century,
to take the activity of redescription more lightly than it had ever been
taken before. It became possible to juggle several descriptions of the
same event without asking which one was right—to see redescription as
a tool rather than a claim to have discovered essence. It thereby became
possible to see a new vocabulary not as something which was supposed
to replace all other vocabularies, something which claimed to represent
reality, but simply as one more vocabulary, one more human project,
one person's chosen metaphoric.[29]

These two passages from Roberto Unger and Richard Rorty are
markedly contemporary in tone and application: both of them describe
what they take to be a distinctively modern mode of intellectual liberation, which Rorty (taking his examples from literature) says has taken
place and Unger (discussing social theory) thinks is still to be fully
achieved. Both Unger and Rorty attribute liberatory power to the recognition that formative contexts, or habits of description, are human
artifacts, contingent regularities in a dynamic economy. I agree that
this is something that needs perpetually to be rediscovered, and also
something that theorists began insisting on relatively recently. But
throughout this book I have attempted to demonstrate that Shakespeare
persistently redescribes formative contexts of various kinds—both social and intellectual—as human economies, and I will suggest that
Antony and Cleopatra is particularly bold in this regard. Though both
Tamburlaine and the "Horatian Ode" acknowledge the fragility of contexts, and (in the comparison the "Horatian Ode" sponsors between
Cromwell and Charles I) Marvell's poem suggests that contrasts in
style of leadership may be intimately involved in hugely consequential
changes in the social order, neither of the texts considered above tries
to imagine a world in which it is *accepted* that formative contexts are
up for grabs, and in which a talent for recontextualization is itself an
attribute of charismatic leadership.

Antony and Cleopatra marks an especially extensive Shakespearean prefiguration of aspects of a modern pragmatist agenda. Shakespeare's play concerns a historical episode of structure breaking and of the reimposition of new structures; of all his plays, it presents the greatest number of competing irreconcilable descriptions of "the same event."[30] One can imagine a good essay on the play beginning "It somehow became possible, in the early seventeenth century, to take the activity of redescription more lightly than it had ever been taken before," and so on. To say this does not refute Rorty's comment on the redescriptive freedom of Nietzsche and Proust and Freud; it simply underscores the claim, made in the Introduction, that the intellectual situation at the beginning of the seventeenth century offered opportunities for the juggling of world views similar to those taken up by modernists and postmodernists, and that *Antony and Cleopatra* exhibits a zest in redescription similar to theirs. I shall argue that the most innovative of the political vocabularies that compete in *Antony and Cleopatra* itself fits Rorty's account of new-found modernist freedom and serves Unger's overriding end of disengaging the project of historical explanation from the idea of the discovery of controlling contexts or metacontexts.

Antony and Cleopatra is couched in the language of contingent evaluative activity. Indeed, the whole play turns on a series of hyperbolic value claims and the challenge to customary evaluations they pose. Thus Antony after Actium:

> Fall not a tear, I say, one of them rates
> All that is won and lost: give me a kiss,
> Even this repays me. (3.11.69)[31]

The grand gestures of the principals occur, moreover, against a background of lesser acts of evaluation. At moments the transactive aspect of these evaluations appears with startling, almost epigrammatic clarity:

MENAS: You and I have known, sir.
ENOBARBUS: At sea, I think.
MENAS: We have, sir.
ENOBARBUS: You have done well by water.
MENAS: And you by land.
ENOBARBUS: I will praise any man that will praise me, though it cannot be denied what I have done by land.
MENAS: Nor what I have done by water. (2.6.83)

This exchange illustrates two of the major distinguishing features of the play: its internal audience of sophisticated insiders, experienced judges of one another and of the principal actors, and its basis in competition. Everyone seems to know everybody else:

CANIDIUS: Who's [Caesar's] lieutenant, hear you?
SOLDIER: They say, one Taurus.
CANIDIUS: Well I know the man. (3.7.77)

Cleopatra, Antony, and Octavius compete for the approval and loyalty of this class of professional soldiers and administrators. Such a group, which knows social power intimately and is close to its prime wielders, but can evaluate them and if necessary shift allegiances, converses in a vocabulary of political contingency, sometimes with a Machiavellian focus on the seizure of fortune's favors:

ENOBARBUS: We came hither to fight with you.
MENAS: For my part, I am sorry it is turned to a drinking.
    Pompey doth this day laugh away his fortune.
ENOBARBUS: If he do, sure he cannot weep't back again.
MENAS: Y'have said, sir. (2.6.101)

ℭ

VENTIDIUS: Who does i' the wars more than his captain can,
    Becomes his captain's captain: and ambition,
    The soldier's virtue, rather makes choice of loss,
    Than gain which darkens him.
    I could do more to do Antonius good,
    But 'twould offend him. (3.1.21)

ℭ

MENAS: I'll never follow thy pall'd fortunes more.
    Who seeks and will not take, when once 'tis offer'd,
    Shall never find it more. (2.7.81)

Antony and Cleopatra stands out from other political plays—including *Troilus and Cressida*, the *Henriad*, and *Coriolanus*—because in it all the major responses to the complex historical moment it dramatizes recognize that the moment calls for the revision of contingent contexts.

The historical moment *Antony and Cleopatra* enacts is transitional: either the last act in the corruption of the Roman Republic in its descent toward empire (this might be the reading of a republican like the Machiavelli of the *Discourses*) or the first act in the highly successful establishment of an empire which fell into tyranny only after Augustus's own long principate, and whose imperial institutions would survive for half a millenium in Rome and up to the twentieth century elsewhere (this might be the reading of the Machiavelli of *The Prince*).[32]

Or it might be seen in Hegelian terms as part of an even larger drama of transformation, involving not only the internal politics of Roman rule but also the channelling of Hebraic and Hellenic influences toward the Christian West through the consolidation of the empire and its eventual adoption of Christianity. On any of these latter views Augustus's rule was a huge success. Reestablishing republican forms while forging an imperial system, Augustus himself acted as a prudent, temperate, and indeed philosophic ruler. His reign was equivocally celebrated and given legitimacy in the *Aeneid* (a poem itself so temperate in the passions it endorses that it seems deliberately to court inclusion in the select curriculum of Plato's republic). Yet at the same time Augustus's rule separated formal republican institutions from actual power in ways that had hardly been seen before in Rome, and this disjunction was exacerbated by the outrageous cynicism of his heirs. Plutarch summarized Augustus's career as a master of contingency in terms that foreshadow Marvell's Cromwell:

> This is to be noted in him, that so young a man having so small beginnings, coming out of a meane house in comparison of others, hath excelled all other young and old men in wisedome and greatnesse of courage: should rise so high. . . . It is a wonderful thing that he could winde himselfe out of so many great affaires and warres, that he could within foure and twenty yeares of age, restore againe into so good estate the commonwealth of Rome, turmoiled and troubled with so many proscriptions and civill warres as it was. And that afterwards so long as he commanded alone, he did so firmely establish this Monarchie, that notwithstanding the infinite troubles received under other Emperours, yet it stood upright and in so great prosperities for so many hundred yeares.[33]

In this probable source for Shakespeare's play, Octavius is credited not only with an extraordinary rise but also with posthumous powers of stabilization; yet the rise itself illustrates the plasticity of the historical medium he molded.

Neither republicans nor absolutists could prefer Antony and Cleopatra to Caesar as rulers. A Machiavellian perspective helps us to appreciate the opportunities for creative exercise of virtue afforded by the play, but something more is needed to see Antony and Cleopatra as exemplars of an admirable political style. Quotations from the progressive pragmatists Rorty and Unger, who feel that public understanding, and indeed celebration, of context revision and redescription are to be encouraged, have suggested some of what is needed. Herbert Marcuse supplies something more: "In the great historical revolutions the imagination was, for a short period, released and free to enter into the projects of a new social morality and of new institutions of freedom; then it was sacrificed to the requirements of effective reason."[34] I will suggest that *Antony and Cleopatra* is a play about such a "short period," and that Cleopatra and Antony enter into such a "project."

The central contest in the play is one of differing stylistic and strategic responses to a sense of the openness or plasticity of history. These differences are exhaustively teased out through a series of political oppositions, each focussed on intensely and then discarded: the triumvirate vs. Pompey, with his appeals to the just gods; Antony and Octavian vs. Lepidus, with his sentimental appeals to loyalty and good nature; Cleopatra vs. Enobarbus, with his appeal to reason and soldiership and maleness; Octavian vs. Antony; Octavian vs. Cleopatra. One can identify three main positions. First (the ideologically dominant position in the Renaissance, though one everywhere cast in question by Shakespeare), that the appearance of contingency or plasticity is unreal because there are divinely sanctioned universals governing outcomes. Second (a position associated with Octavius Caesar), that history is contingent, and the plasticity of the current juncture is real but undesirable and temporary. Third, that contingency and plasticity are real, desirable, and to be endorsed as continuing conditions of life. This last, of course, is the position I want to mark as exceptional and identify with Antony and Cleopatra as leaders.

Members of the group of professionals who surround the major figures in the play discuss contingent choices with one another in the name of political reason, as do Antony's generals after the naval battle at Actium:

> CANIDIUS: Toward Peloponessus are they fled.
> SCARUS: 'Tis easy to't, and there I will attend
>   What further comes.
> CANIDIUS: To Caesar will I render
>   My legions and my horse, six kings already
>   Show me the way of yielding.
> ENOBARBUS: I'll yet follow
>   The wounded chance of Antony, though my reason
>   Sits in the wind against me. (3.10.31)

Enobarbus's "reason" is the "effective reason" of Marcuse, which here is beginning to harden the plasticity that Antony and Cleopatra represent and celebrate. But for a time, even in Enobarbus, the "erotic" power (as I shall describe it) of Antony and Cleopatra remains a countervailing force. Enobarbus's conflict suggests the extent to which the play explores a contest between different *kinds* of political reason.

The position that contingency is an illusion because a providential order is at work receives extraordinarily little representation in *Antony and Cleopatra*. What it gets comes from Pompey:

> If the great gods be just, they shall assist
> The deeds of justest men. (2.1.1)

This conditional assertion is undercut both by Pompey's precipitous failure and by his immediate shift to a language of local political contingencies:

> Mark Antony
> In Egypt sits at dinner, and will make
> No wars without doors. Caesar gets money where
> He loses hearts: Lepidus flatters both,
> Of both is flatter'd: but he neither loves,
> Nor either cares for him. (2.1.11)

The insignificance of the providential position in *Antony and Cleopatra* marks it off not only from official culture in the Renaissance but also from most other plays by Shakespeare. In *Macbeth*, for instance, not only is a moral order invoked against the protagonists, but a supernatural antimoral order is invoked in preparation for crimes by Macbeth and Lady Macbeth themselves. This may signal the primitive state of Scottish culture in the play, but providential positions are also strongly entertained in *Hamlet* and *Lear*, and even in *Coriolanus* the hero seems characteristically serious about prayer.

The position that plasticity is real but undesirable, or at any rate desirable only insofar as it allows the reimposition of rules which will stabilize it and guarantee the power of the reimposer, is connected in the play with Octavius Caesar and, more generally, with Rome and the Roman stratum of soldiers and administrators that surrounds both Antony and Caesar. Thus, as he consolidates his power, Octavius strives for impersonality, efficiency, and an end to contests.

> Let our best heads
> Know, that to-morrow the last of many battles
> We mean to fight. (4.1.10)

Ꝯ

> The time of universal peace is near:
> Prove this a prosperous day, the three-nook'd world
> Shall bear the olive freely. (4.6.5)

Octavius, a typically masculinist Machiavellian Founder, insists on firm separation between genders and is both manipulative and contemptuous of women. He may genuinely care for Octavia, with her "beauty, wisdom, modesty" (2.2.241), but his use of her is characteristic of the man who will send Thidias to tempt Cleopatra with the comment:

> women are not
> In their best fortunes strong; but want will perjure
> The ne'er-touch'd vestal. (3.12.29)

As toward women, so toward love. I have already quoted Pompey on Caesar's politically dangerous tendency to acquire money and lose hearts. The play underlines the relevance to Caesar of the question raised in chapter 17 of *The Prince*, whether it is better for the ruler to be loved or feared. Machiavelli, notoriously, contends that fear is more reliable than love,[35] and on the face of it *Antony and Cleopatra* bears this out, but the play also takes frequent note of the political utility of love:

> every hour,
> Most noble Caesar, shalt thou have report
> How 'tis abroad. Pompey is strong at sea,
> And it appears he is belov'd of those
> That only have fear'd Caesar (1.4.34)

Octavius is younger than Antony, but his policies are old, and early on he criticizes Antony for failing in political maturity, conceived of as understanding the demands of one's time:

> to confound such time,
> That drums him from his sport, and speaks as loud
> As his own state, and ours,—'tis to be chid:
> As we rate boys, who being mature in knowledge,
> Pawn their experience to their present pleasure,
> And so rebel to judgment. (1.4.28)

Caesar says this at a moment when the audience knows Antony *has* been drummed from his sport and is on his way to Rome. Does one understand time better as a young man acting middle-aged or a middle-aged man acting young? Antony will refer to Caesar as "the young man" (3.11.62), but in a famous exchange which serves as a transition to the play's third position on plasticity, Antony endorses youth seen as a receptively festive response to the opportunities the world sets before one, while Caesar expresses his desire to master contingency:

> ANTONY: Be a child o' the time.
> CAESAR: Possess it, I'll make answer. (2.7.98)

The third position toward historical contingency in *Antony and Cleopatra* shows the play's political complexity and daring. Antony and

Cleopatra see political plasticity as real and desirable, and to embrace it properly is, for them, to make it a principle of personality and charismatic political appeal. This position is held by Antony and Cleopatra as joint possessors of an unusual style of leadership and speakers of an exceptional political language. It is erotic, daring, masculine *and* feminine, tolerant of the existence of competitors, generous, and extremely successful.

This description must contend, of course, with Octavius's defeat of Antony and Cleopatra and also with a standard moral response to their story which holds that Antony's aims are like Octavius's (though his nature is different) until he is corrupted or misled by Cleopatra—she is said to activate or magnify faults in his nature. This is Plutarch's view and one that receives ample expression in the play, even from Antony himself.

Yet Antony and Cleopatra together exemplify a kind of leadership we do not find elsewhere in Shakespeare and rarely in history. And the result is far from the appalling consequences we are led to imagine as a consequence if, say, Hal had put the laws of England at Falstaff's command. The response of leaders to historical plasticity varies, but in Cleopatra, and to a less consistent but still preponderant degree in Antony, it takes the form of leadership through excess or transgression, through embracing the unexpected, through always staying ahead of one's followers. We are used to this kind of leadership in the arts and intellectual life, but not in politics. People follow Antony and Cleopatra out of interest, desire for novelty or discovery, need for invigoration, as well as for more conventionally self-interested motives. Antony and Cleopatra lead from the avant-garde and issue what amount to challenges to the world to keep up with them, even as they offer such challenges to one another:[36]

> Here is my space,
> Kingdoms are clay: our dungy earth alike
> Feeds beast as man; the nobleness of life
> Is to do thus: when such a mutual pair,
> And such a twain can do't, in which I bind,
> On pain of punishment, the world to weet
> We stand up peerless. (1.1.34)

This may be, as Cleopatra immediately says, an "excellent falsehood" (1.1.40) insofar as it is a statement about Antony's plans, but it is an innovation in the gendering of leadership which we should not underrate, and in its call for the world's attention and admiration, it offers the mutual creative love contest as a kind of governing principle. The Nile, which overflows its own boundaries and fertilizes the flats around it, symbolizes Antony and Cleopatra's relation to the culture around them. They do not measure, direct, and repress; instead they exceed, and their peerlessness itself transforms the clay and dung that surround and set it off.[37] Theirs is a leadership which, moreover, includes disorder and accepts the contestatory character of social experience by blurring the boundaries between seriousness and play.

Radical yet practical innovations in leadership frequently involve a deliberate flouting of boundaries. Roberto Unger calls attention, for instance, to Gandhi's strategic insistence on self-defilement:

> Consider the aspect of [Gandhi's] activity that comes closest to the status of cultural revolution: not passive disobedience against the imperial master but the attempt to form a man who can be the citizen of a single nation, capable of common allegiance and even compassionate solidarity, across the frontiers traced by the norms of caste and ritual purity. . . . The most cultural-revolutionary aspect . . . was his practice of defilement and his recruitment of others to share this practice with him: to reach out to the forbidden person, to undertake the most humiliating work, to touch the dirtiest thing. . . . The empowered person was the person who had emancipated himself, through repeated practice, from the fixed hierarchies of value that stood in the way of mutual responsibility.[38]

We hear from Octavius approvingly of Antony's capacity to drink horse urine, eat strange flesh, and browse tree-bark (1.4.61) as soldierly stoicism, a questionable description, and disapprovingly of his tippling with slaves and standing the buffet with stinking knaves (1.4.19); we hear from Enobarbus that Cleopatra makes vile things becoming, so that priests bless her when she is riggish (2.2.238). Both Antony and Cleopatra are leaders who in their gestures transmute or embrace the socially defiled, and while they are otherwise unlike Gandhi they offer the same kind of enlargement of the social sphere of legitimate empowerment (in reaction to the same kind of imperial austerity and exclusiveness).

In this regard, at least, it makes sense to call Cleopatra's mode transgressive. But it is more centrally contestative, as Cleopatra engages in gamelike competitive transactions in which the rules of the game are subject to change during play: a mode of leadership which accelerates the dynamism of the economy she inhabits. Here her greatest interest as a leader lies. She contests everything and is endlessly committed to competitions that do not aim at the elimination of contestants. Hence the games in which she takes part (billiards, angling, drinking, cross-dressing, etc.), her constant "wrangling" (1.1.48) with Antony, and the far from hypocritical shock she expresses when a contest in which she is participating ends in the death of her opponent: "Can Fulvia die?" (1.3.58). She has participated in Roman history by consorting with the greatest Romans at their height of fortune and competes with them to increase their greatness as well as hers, just as she sees Rome as her partner in a collaborative rule which includes perpetual stylistic competition, rather than as her opponent in a death-struggle of antithetical principles. Such transgressive, hierarchy-disrupting contestation is theorized as a feminine mode in much feminist criticism of both poststructuralist and humanist types, most notably perhaps in Jane Gallop's *The Daughter's Seduction*. Gallop suggests in psychoanalytic terms a "con-centric" (French pun intended) way of opposing phallocentric dominance that serves to generalize Cleopatra's continual generation of subversive attitudes and her refusal to live in a phallic world.[39]

Michael Grant, attempting to do justice not only to the historical Cleopatra's personal sexual attractiveness but also to her ideas, suggests that partnership in difference with Rome was her political aim:

> there seems to have emerged from [Cleopatra's] association [with Julius Caesar and then Mark Antony] a genuine and viable concept of a new sort of Greco-Roman world. Cleopatra . . . envisaged that this whole vast territory, together with the external regions dependent upon it, should no longer be under the sole, exclusive domination of Italians, as it had been hitherto. Instead it should be a partnership, in which the Greek and Hellenized orientals who inhabited the regions east of the Adriatic were to be associates of the Romans rather than merely their subjects, enjoying a status almost equal to theirs. This was an aim for which her whole upbringing and natural inclination prepared and encouraged her.
>
> It was also, however, an aim which presents us today, if we are trying to study her career, with a very serious problem. For the Romans appreciated, not altogether clearly perhaps but quite clearly enough, what she was about; and it terrified them.[40]

The result of Roman awareness of this serious political purpose was a reactive wave of vituperative propaganda, reflected in the Roman view of Cleopatra as it appears in the play. "Name Cleopatra as she is call'd in Rome" (1.2.103), says Antony to the messenger he is encouraging not to mince words with him.

Cleopatra's "corruption" of Antony, then, consists in getting him to adopt this style of leadership, which means getting him to accept her as a true political partner. She contests his subordination of politics to love in their first conversation in the play:

CLEOPATRA: I'll set a bourn how far to be belov'd.
ANTONY: Then must thou needs find out new heaven, new earth.
                    Enter an Attendant.
ATTENDANT: News, my good lord, from Rome.

ANTONY: Grates me, the sum.
CLEOPATRA: Nay, hear them, Antony:
   Fulvia perchance is angry; or who knows
   If the scarce-bearded Caesar have not sent
   His powerful mandate to you, "Do this, or this;
   Take in that kingdom, and enfranchise that;
   Perform't, or else we damn thee."
ANTONY: How, my love? (1.1.16)

Throughout this conversation, Cleopatra both forces on Antony's attention the political aspects of his love for her and disallows his strategy of treating that love as an excuse for not taking politics seriously ("Let Rome in Tiber melt," etc.). She continues:

> You must not stay here longer, your dismission
> Is come from Caesar, therefore hear it, Antony.
> Where's Fulvia's process? Caesar's I would say. Both?
> Call in the messengers. As I am Egypt's queen,
> Thou blushest, Antony, and that blood of thine
> Is Caesar's homager: else so thy cheek pays shame
> When shrill-tongued Fulvia scolds. The messengers! (1.1.26)

Cleopatra insists that women and sexual relations are part of the fabric of politics, and that she will not "seem the fool I am not" (1.1.42) by accepting Antony's plea to treat love as a separate realm:

ANTONY: Now for the love of Love, and her soft hours,
   Let's not confound the time with conference harsh:
   There's not a minute of our lives should stretch
   Without some pleasure now. What sport to-night?
CLEOPATRA: Hear the ambassadors. (1.1.44)

Though Antony will not give in here, but sweeps her off with him while paying tribute to the attraction he finds in her contestatory energy ("Fie, wrangling queen! / Whom everything becomes" [1.1.48]), she succeeds in making him share her erotic politics. In his relations with Cleopatra, Antony embraces and accepts conflict and adopts a style of leadership that not only puts up with but requires rivals. Thus, when the soothsayer warns Antony to stay away from Caesar and avoid direct contests with him, the advice coincides not only with Antony's desire for Cleopatra but also with his willingness to share the world with Caesar and to accept the uncertainty of his own preeminence. Caesar has no such willingness, and in this he displays not only a Machiavellian desire to secure his power, but also a monological male Romanness which cannot tolerate the dialogic of culture, race, and gender that Cleopatra and Antony together have made into a potentially world-transforming style of leadership.

The erotic quality of their leadership is obvious. But while there is much sexuality in the play, there is very little sex. The sexuality tends to halo relationships rather than to focus on acts, and thus helps to construct a social environment rather than belonging to particular couples. This environment enshrines Cleopatra and Antony and radiates from them, underwriting, as it were, the special force they exert on their followers. Consider the preponderance of unpaired characters. Enobarbus, Pompey, Charmian, Iras, Octavia, Maecenas, Agrippa, even Octavius, all forego specific gratification of sexual desire and deflect erotic interest toward the central pair. Antony in Plutarch has several children by Octavia, but in Shakespeare he has "[his] pillow left unpress'd in Rome, / Forborne the getting of a lawful race, / And by a gem of women" (3.13.106), for Cleopatra's sake. Mardian the eunuch's comment could be generalized to fit most characters in the play:

> I can do nothing
> But what indeed is honest to be done:
> Yet have I fierce affections, and think
> What Venus did with Mars. (1.5.15)

Even Antony and Cleopatra, the Mars and Venus of the play (under the net in its second half), make love less and talk about it more than might have been expected.[41] One might redescribe this by saying that sexuality is constituted in the play by language and gesture. To return to Gallop's vocabulary, eros in the play pulls people con-centrically into orbits rather than fixing them hierarchically through phallocentric acts, and the space around the central pair becomes rather crowded. Antony and Cleopatra's talk, like that of others, tends moreover to cement relations between the erotic and the political: they kiss publicly and bind the world to weet they stand up peerless.

Their sexual desire for each other is part of the "imaginative command" over others that Michael Goldman describes as central to their greatness:

> The sexual magnetism which Antony and Cleopatra exert on each other is very similar to the magnetism of great leaders and great actors, perhaps indistinguishable from it. What binds Cleopatra and Antony sexually is not unlike what binds the world to them and binds us to the attractive presences of the actor and actress who impersonate them. . . . Antony and Cleopatra are most actor-like in that they exhibit a magnetism that is culturally suspect. Paramount among the vile things

they make becoming to the audience are the particular vices of glamorous actors. Cheapness and self-indulgence, narcissism and whoredom, hover about all their gestures.[42]

Goldman's concentration here and elsewhere on the transgressive charisma of the actor describes the transformative dynamics of avant-garde leadership, which I have associated with a strong view of historical plasticity and contingency, an awareness of politics as a dynamic economy. Political commitments to Antony and Cleopatra are suffused with the erotic: Iras, Eros, Charmian, and Enobarbus all share in the *Liebestod* of Antony and Cleopatra, and they elect it more cleanly than do the principals. Iras and Enobarbus die onstage of broken hearts, a strained fact only the play's generally unflinching commitment to real outcomes could ballast.[43] By the same token, political disaffection with Antony and Cleopatra takes the form of a critique of the erotic.

Erotic Politics and History

Antony and Cleopatra does not merely record different positions toward a historical moment in Roman time; it also offers, albeit in obscure glimpses, an anticipation of the coming Christian Era. This gives a final unexpected twist to the context in which Cleopatra and Antony's relationship is to be viewed and, more importantly, allows us to see their redescriptive politics as more successful and historically powerful than it might otherwise seem.

The hints of Christ's imminence come when characters register the historical plasticity of their moment. Even Cleopatra's women, who, like Caesar's men Maecenas and Agrippa, seem more fixed in their loyalties than do the servants of Antony, can easily entertain the idea of reversals of fortune:

> CHARMIAN: Good now, some excellent fortune! Let me be married to three kings in a forenoon, and widow them all: let me have a child at fifty, to whom Herod of Jewry may do homage. Find me to marry me with Octavius Caesar, and companion me with my mistress.
> SOOTHSAYER: You shall outlive the lady whom you serve. (1.2.25)

This is a particularly interesting passage, since it suggests Alexandrian speculation on Octavius's ultimate victory from the very start of the play, while nonetheless demonstrating that even with the world at her feet Charmian would not wish to live without Cleopatra (though she can imagine reversing roles and having Cleopatra as her servant). But finally it hints at the arrival of a miraculous child who, in connection with three kings, will once again transform the power relations of the east. Charmian's words specifically recall the prophecy of the wise men that disturbs Herod in Matthew 2:3 and leads him to the massacre of the innocents in Matthew 2:16; with others, the reference to Herod forcibly reminds viewers of the play that the birth of Christ is forthcoming.

ALEXAS: Good majesty,
    Herod of Jewry dare not look upon you,
    But when you are well pleas'd.
CLEOPATRA: That Herod's head
    I'll have: but how, when Antony is gone,
    Through whom I might command it? (3.3.2)

One of the problems with the thesis that Antony and Cleopatra are avant-garde leaders is that their perceived impact on political history is slight, and their example has contributed rather to an unfortunate patriarchal opposition between political and erotic realms. But there is a variety of odd hints in the play that their erotics of rule should be seen in light of the historically imminent arrival of Christ, the context-breaking, charismatic, ultimately self-sacrificial prophet of love who would be carried to Egypt to flee the very Herod whose head Cleopatra would have. By this I do not mean to imply that the play has a providential logic or that it is in any way Christian in outlook.[44] As I have already suggested, *Antony and Cleopatra* is exceptionally free from providential thinking. But there are links between the idiosyncratic political style of Cleopatra and Antony and the peculiar plasticity of their historical moment in the Mediterranean world. The dominant institutions that emerged from that moment were Imperial Rome and Christianity, and when the second is considered as a political style, it has many of the same qualities as the leadership of Antony and Cleopatra and may therefore be imaginatively subordinated in the play to the leadership they represent. Christianity bound Greek, Hebrew, and Roman traditions together. Its messiah allowed himself to be defiled among the wretched. It endorsed male and female communities bound together by love. As a political force, it in the end subdued the monologic Romanness of an Octavius.[45]

The hints about the coming of Christ in the play, then, support the plausibility of a different kind of empire ruled in a collaborative and contestatory political style by Antony and Cleopatra *and* Octavius. In other words, they remind us of Christ's imminence in order to show that Cleopatra and Antony were trying out a new style of leadership at a ripe moment for such a style. These hints are not confined to the references to three kings and a child to whom Herod will do homage.

Antony serves his own followers at a last supper, making them weep. He habitually surrounds himself with loving commoners, and is happy

> To give a kingdom for a mirth, to sit
> And keep the turn of tippling with a slave,
> To reel the streets at noon, and stand the buffet
> With knaves that smells of sweat . . . (1.4.18)

This resembles at least one English Renaissance attempt to characterize the oddity of Christ's lordship:

> I . . . knowing his great birth,
>   Sought him accordingly in great resorts;
>   In cities, theatres, gardens, parks, and courts:
> At length I heard a ragged noise and mirth
>   Of theeves and murderers: there I him espied,
>   Who straight, *Your suit is granted*, said, & died.[46]

As his end comes near, Antony's chief follower denies him and repents that denial. The bloody weapon used to kill Antony is carried as a talisman of imperial power to Caesar (like the apocryphal lance Joseph of Arimathea carried to Britain), even as Antony's dying body is ministered to by three women.

There is nothing conclusive about such affinities, but they supply a context in which Cleopatra's posthumous portrait of Antony can seem to point toward the coming god-man:

> His face was as the heavens, and therein stuck
> A sun and moon, which kept their course, and lighted
> The little O, the earth.
>
> . . . .
>
> His legs bestrid the ocean, his rear'd arm
> Crested the world: his voice was propertied
> As all the tuned spheres, and that to friends:
> But when he meant to quail, and shake the orb,
> He was as rattling thunder. For his bounty,
> There was no winter in't: an autumn 'twas
> That grew the more by reaping: his delights
> Were dolphin-like, they show'd his back above
> The element they lived in: in his livery
> Walk'd crowns and crownets: realms and islands were
> As plates dropp'd from his pocket. (5.2.79)

This recalls the comment made to Enobarbus in Caesar's camp, when Antony has sent Enobarbus's treasure after him: "Your Emperor / Continues still a Jove" (4.6.28). It is as a continuing overflowing source of joy and value that Antony is remembered, and he remains such after his death:

> CLEOPATRA: Think you there was, or might be such a man
>   As this I dreamt of?
> DOLABELLA: Gentle madam, no.
> CLEOPATRA: You lie up to the hearing of the gods.
>   But if there be, or ever were one such,
>   It's past the size of dreaming: nature wants stuff
>   To vie strange forms with fancy, yet to imagine
>   An Antony were nature's piece, 'gainst fancy,
>   Condemning shadows quite. (5.2.93)

Antony's enlarging effect exceeds that of fancy; it transforms and expands the possibilities of living. He is a hero of plasticity who after death assumes the role of a god, the god he was as Cleopatra "dreamt of" him, or the god who "might be" a guide to life along the lines Antony imperfectly laid out in Cleopatra's imagination. As Graham Bradshaw comments, "[h]er 'dream' is the most intense actualisation of her sense not only of Antony's and indeed her own potentialities, but of the mysterious and illimitable potentialities in life itself. . . . By so courteously setting limits . . . Dolabella's 'Gentle Madam, no' deflects the real challenge of Cleopatra's 'Thinke you there was, *or might be* . . . ?' "[47] We can be more specific about the life-potentialities Cleopatra sees in Antony, or in her dream of Antony; they are connected both to the mode of political originality she and Antony shared and to the imminent context-revising advent of Christianity.

Just as Antony's erotic leadership resonates with hints about the coming of Christ, such hints thicken around Cleopatra as she dies, imprisoned in a monument in which she will manage to elude Roman justice, hugging the serpent to her bosom (which will make an unpolicied ass of Caesar), hailed as the "eastern star" (5.2.307), kissed fatally by a disciple, yet armed in death with the power to catch more men in her "strong toil of grace" (5.2.346). Although Antony and Cleopatra have not quite known what to do with the politics of eros and the power to make life and love out of death that politics brings, they bear an uncanny resemblance to someone who will. The asp that kills her is an odd worm: "his biting is immortal" (5.2.245).

Again, this is not to suggest that *Antony and Cleopatra* covertly endorses Christianity. Cleopatra's strong toil of grace is not identifiable with Christ's. Rather, the hints about Christianity serve to underwrite the otherwise unfulfilled historical claims the play entertains about a politics of erotic inclusiveness, childlike acknowledgement of desire, and the plasticity of human contexts. Both Antony and Cleopatra die amid an increasing pressure of transcendence claims. But this is a play in which transcendence claims are also seen as moves in a contingent politics of self-advancement. Antony and Cleopatra, making their grand gestures, are characters trying rhetorically to transmute political failure into imaginative success. But the play intimates ways in which the imaginative energies they have brought to politics, their articulation of an androgynous politics of inclusive empowerment, general plasticity, and erotic self-realization, open doors toward social hope through a politics of contingency which Octavius Caesar cannot permanently shut. The play renders unto Caesar what is Caesar's. But what remains remains political.

Coda

However exhilarating it may be to live by, plasticity is a hard thing to die for. Cleopatra, after Antony's death, imagines with characteristic concreteness what will happen to her in a Roman triumph and forecasts what she and Antony will mean as parts of a retrospective moralization serving Roman political ends:

> Saucy lictors
> Will catch at us like strumpets, and scald rhymers
> Ballad us out o' tune. The quick comedians
> Extemporally will stage us, and present
> Our Alexandrian revels: Antony
> Shall be brought drunken forth, and I shall see
> Some squeaking Cleopatra boy my greatness
> I' the posture of a whore. (5.2.213)

Their identities will be manipulated to serve the purposes of others. Symbols of a more comprehensive evanescence haunt the defeated Antony:

Antony: Eros, thou yet behold'st me?
Eros: Ay, noble lord.
Antony: Sometime we see a cloud that's dragonish,
    A vapour sometime, like a bear, or lion,
    A tower'd citadel, a pendent rock,
    A forked mountain, or blue promontory
    With trees upon't, that nod unto the world,
    And mock our eyes with air. Thou hast seen these signs,
    They are black vesper's pageants.
Eros: Ay, my lord.
Antony: That which is now a horse, even with a thought
    The rack dislimns, and makes it indistinct
    As water is in water.
Eros: It does, my lord.
Antony: My good knave Eros, now thy captain is
    Even such a body. (4.14.1)

His own commitments to plasticity, and the plasticity of the historical juncture that gave his actions huge significance, have turned on him, and everything now seems terribly fluid, as "indistinct / As water is in water."

It takes no gigantic failure, however, to bring on this characteristic pathos in Shakespeare. For it is the darker side of his pragmatist intuition, explored throughout this study, that human life does not have anchoring points of contact with absolute solidity, but instead moves in liquids of varying thickness; that plasticity varies in degree, but that there is no ultimate escape from it, and no certainty of one's own future shape within it. Conceiving social life as a dynamic economy brings the possibility of accumulation and the promise of change, but no strong solace for loss and death.

This pathos haunts all transactions over time in which values shift and touches not only the revision of politics Antony and Cleopatra attempt but also artistic creation and procreation. Prospero is jarred into famous expression of this Shakespearean pathos by the realization that Caliban has not been made part of the "harmoniously charming" (4.1.119)[1] vision he has woven for Ferdinand and Miranda.

> *Enter certain Reapers, properly habited: they join with the Nymphs in a graceful dance; towards the end whereof Prospero starts suddenly, and speaks; after which, to a strange hollow, and confused noise, they heavily vanish.*
>
> . . . .
>
> Ferdinand: This is strange: your father's in some passion
>   That works him strongly.
> Miranda: Never till this day
>   Saw I him touch'd with anger, so distemper'd.
> PROSPERO: You do look, my son, in a mov'd sort,
>   As if you were dismay'd: be cheerful, sir.
>   Our revels now are ended. These our actors,
>   As I foretold you, were all spirits, and
>   Are melted into air, into thin air:
>   And, like the baseless fabric of this vision,
>   The cloud-capp'd towers, the gorgeous palaces,
>   The solemn temples, the great globe itself,
>   Yea, all which it inherit, shall dissolve,
>   And, like this insubstantial pageant faded,
>   Leave not a rack behind. We are such stuff
>   As dreams are made on; and our little life
>   Is rounded with a sleep. Sir, I am vex'd;
>   Bear with my weakness; my old brain is troubled:
>   Be not disturb'd with my infirmity. (4.1.138)

Antony's vision of dissolution into a thin liquid returns in Prospero's attempt to make the intergenerational inheritance of blessings into a rational and genial transmission of a secure moral order, as if he were God and Miranda and Ferdinand Eve and Adam. It did not work in

Eden, and it does not work for Prospero. In both cases the frightening (but also conceivably hopeful) substitute is a view of life mutating endlessly toward a future we cannot see, one we perhaps could not understand if we did see it. Yet Prospero, facing his failure to impose chosen forms on the future, begins and ends with personal reassurances to the young who will survive him: "be cheerful, sir . . . Be not disturb'd with my infirmity." We are all "infirm," but we must transmit some cheer about our lack of lasting firmness to those who come after. How would they achieve their forms if we did not lose ours? So plasticity may be cause for communal hope even as it rules out individual permanence. But this cannot be hope for a particular social order, since no such order will arrest change.

Pragmatists renounce a sense of their own necessary participation in a permanent state of things, something Shakespeare shows Prospero experiencing. As Richard Rorty remarks, even in our own antitranscendental time this remains hard to do. By renouncing the belief that knowledge is representation of reality, and that enlightened social arrangements could ground themselves on immutable truths about human nature, pragmatists give up strong consolations:

> What is disturbing about the pragmatist's picture is . . . that it takes away two sorts of comfort to which our intellectual tradition has become accustomed. One is the thought that membership in our biological species carries with it certain "rights" . . . The second comfort is provided by the thought that our community cannot wholly die. The picture of a common human nature oriented towards correspondence to reality as it is in itself comforts us with the thought that even if our civilization is destroyed, even if all memory of our political or intellectual or artistic community is erased, the race is fated to recapture the virtues and the insights and the achievements which were the glory of that community.[2]

Shakespeare's picture of human participation in communities cannot be nostalgic for individual rights which would not be fully claimed until the Enlightenment, but it is, as I have suggested throughout, very alive to the historical mutation of social arrangements away from the forms of life to which individuals have pegged their own value and toward new forms that offer new opportunities. Shakespeare sees hope in such mutation as well as danger. It would be overstating my case to claim that, like Rorty, Shakespeare thinks that "whatever good the ideas of 'objectivity' and 'transcendence' have done for our culture can be attained equally well by the idea of a community which strives after both intersubjective agreement and novelty."[3] But this book has shown how closely Shakespeare's texts, in their own terms, explore the consequences of an outlook that does without absolutes. Shakespeare is anti-

transcendental; he locates the power to confer value and accept truth
in social economies; and he is interested in social experimentation. His
plays dramatize the uncertainties in experience which the new science
and philosophy of the later seventeenth century sought to contain, and
which twentieth-century pragmatists acknowledge.

The Western tradition in philosophy, and much Western literature
and literary criticism, have taught us to make a virtue of necessity—to
seek certainty, to pursue ineluctable causality, to justify knowledge.
Market economies, which exploit instability in value, react to historical
change, promote technical and political innovation, and prompt the
new appetites they serve, are from the point of view of this tradition
a low and incidental, rather than a dignified and central, feature of
human communities. Pragmatism, which tries to make a virtue of contingency, has obvious ties to market-like democratic institutions, but
it has, except in the path-breaking work of Barbara Herrnstein Smith,
avoided extended analysis of how central in human life it makes markets. In addition to advancing such discussion, I hope this book will
help to establish the capacity of pragmatic, market-oriented thinking
to produce a useful redescription of a notoriously enduring and chal-
lenging set of texts, deeply enmeshed with the ordinary operations of
their culture and yet penetratingly critical of those operations. Seen as
pragmatic cultural critic, Shakespeare exemplifies a profitable engagement with ongoing social transactions which also produces a powerful critical perspective on them. From the point of view of pragmatists, such examples are needed. For of the many bad associations
from which pragmatism suffers, the worst perhaps is complacent shal-
lowness, unwillingness to go very low or very high, willingness to
accept or indeed to endorse mediocre cultural and political compromises.[4]

As tools for the exploration of our contingent relations, Shakespeare's texts register unexpected (as well as expected) kinds of value.
As the objects of continuous and mutating critical attention, personal
investment, and social reverence (as well as hostility), they function as
a source of cultural energy beyond themselves. This book, of course,
is only another manifestation of that ongoing process. Its stance is more
flexible than many. But it takes a stand, nonetheless, in arguing that
Shakespeare studies and pragmatism have something to gain from each
other.

Notes

Chapter One

1. See Georges Bataille, "The Notion of Expenditure," in Allan Stoekl, ed. and trans., *Visions of Excess: Selected Writings, 1927–1939*, Theory and History of Literature, vol. 14 (Minneapolis: University of Minnesota Press, 1985), p. 123: "In the market economy, the processes of exchange have an acquisitive sense. Fortunes are no longer placed on a gambling table; they have become relatively stable. . . . Under these new conditions, the elementary components of *potlatch* are found in forms that are no longer as directly agonistic. Expenditure is still destined to acquire or maintain rank, but in principle it no longer has the goal of causing another to lose his rank.

"In spite of these attenuations, ostentatious loss remains universally linked to wealth, as its ultimate function."

2. W. V. O. Quine, "Two Dogmas of Empiricism," in *From a Logical Point of View* (Cambridge: Harvard University Press, 1961; reprinted New York: Harper & Row, 1963); see especially p. 43: "Any statement can be held true come what may, if we make drastic enough adjustments elsewhere in the system. . . . Conversely, by the same token, no statement is immune to revision."

3. Thomas Kuhn, *The Structure of Scientific Revolutions*, 2d ed. (Chicago: University of Chicago Press, 1970). See especially pp. 205–8 of the "Postscript," on relativism and on Kuhn's scepticism about the "is-ought" distinction.

4. Donald Davidson, "On the Very Idea of a Conceptual Scheme," *Inquiries into Truth and Interpretation* (Oxford: Oxford University Press, 1984).

5. See W. J. T. Mitchell, ed., *Against Theory: Literary Studies and the New Pragmatism* (Chicago: University of Chicago Press, 1985), pp. 11–30. For a self-distancing comment similar to mine, see Giles Gunn, *Thinking Across the American Grain: Ideology, Intellect, and the New Pragmatism* (Chicago: University of Chicago Press, 1992), p. 4: "The new pragmatism of which I speak here . . . thus bears comparatively little resemblance to the version recently introduced in literary studies that is known chiefly for its predisposition 'against theory.' On the contrary, the kind of pragmatism to which I refer contends that there is no such thing as a practice without theory; the only relevant question is deciding which theory we shall have: that which claims to immunize practice against theory by pretending that theory has no practical consequences, or that which presumes that the only way we can prevent practice from producing consequences we don't like is by developing better theories about practice."

6. *Pragmatism*, in *William James: Writings, 1902–1910*, ed. Bruce Kuklich (New York: The Library of America, 1987), p. 509.

7. Richard Rorty, "On Ethnocentrism," in *Objectivity, Relativism, and Truth: Philosophical Papers*, vol. 1 (Cambridge: Cambridge University Press, 1991), p. 209.

8. See Frank Lentricchia, "The Return of William James," *Cultural Critique* 4 (Fall 1986), p. 6.

9. For two interesting attempts to generalize Marxian economic thought so as to construct a description of language, social differentiation, and psychology in economic terms, see Jean Baudrillard, *For a Critique of the Political Economy of the Sign*, trans. Charles Levin (St. Louis: Telos Press, 1981), and Jean-Joseph Goux, *Symbolic Economies: After Marx and Freud*, trans. Jennifer Curtiss Gage (Ithaca: Cornell University Press, 1990).

10. If Quine's "gavagai" were under discussion because of a gestural offer to barter a handful of glass beads and a bottle of corrupt rum for it—not an implausible scenario, given the history of culture contacts—it would be a yet more striking instance of the indeterminacy of translation, since the whole exchange would teach the native a new meaning for "gavagai" as well: that which can be bartered for beads and drink. See W. V. O. Quine, *Word and Object* (Cambridge, MA: MIT Press, 1960), chapter 2.

11. See Ralph Waldo Emerson, "Shakspere, or the Poet," in Douglas Emory Wilson and Wallace E. Williams, eds., *The Collected Works of Ralph Waldo Emerson*, vol. 4, *Representative Men* (Cambridge, MA: Harvard University Press, 1987). This essay is well discussed by Michael Bristol in *Shakespeare's America, America's Shakespeare* (London: Routledge, 1990) pp. 123–30. The general importance of Emerson (but not Shakespeare) for pragmatists is argued by Cornel West in *The American Evasion of Philosophy: A Genealogy of Pragmatism* (Madison: University of Wisconsin Press, 1989).

12. Harold Bloom *Ruin the Sacred Truths: Poetry and Belief from the Bible to the Present* (Cambridge: Harvard University Press, 1989), pp. 8, 64.

13. See, for instance, Emerson, "Plato, or the Philosopher," *Representative Men*, pp. 24–25: "When we are praising Plato it seems we are praising quotations from Solon, and Sophron, and Philolaus. Be it so. Every book is a quotation; and every house is a quotation out of all forests, and mines, and stonequarries; and every man is a quotation from all his ancestors. And this grasping inventor puts all nations under contribution."

14. This is the subtitle of James's *Pragmatism*. See *William James: Writings, 1902–1910*, p. 479.

15. Stephen Toulmin, *Cosmopolis: The Hidden Agenda of Modernity* (New York: Free Press, 1990), pp. x–xi.

16. Stanley Cavell, *Disowning Knowledge in Six Plays of Shakespeare* (New York: Cambridge University Press, 1987), p. 3.

17. Toulmin himself acknowledges the pragmatism of his historical argument when he accepts the conclusions of Richard Rorty's *Philosophy and the Mirror of Nature* (Princeton: Princeton University Press, 1979).

18. Richard Rorty, "Habermas and Lyotard on Postmodernity," *Essays on Heidegger and Others: Philosophical Papers*, vol. 2 (Cambridge: Cambridge University Press, 1991), p. 172.

19. See Stanley Fish, *Doing What Comes Naturally: Change, Rhetoric, and the*

Practice of Theory in Literary and Legal Studies (Durham: Duke University Press, 1989), pp. 1–4.

20. On pragmatism's debt to Darwin, see Rorty, *Essays on Heidegger and Others*, pp. 3–4, and his "Just one more species doing its best," *London Review of Books*, 25 July 1991, pp. 3–4. See also Hilary Putnam, "James's Theory of Perception," in *Realism with a Human Face* (Cambridge: Harvard University Press, 1990), p. 234: "a good example of the temperament [William] James prefers [to that of the 'rationalist'] would be Charles Darwin. . . . Many things make Darwin an appropriate representative of the pragmatist temperament."

21. See Fish, *Doing What Comes Naturally*, chap. 14.

22. See, e.g., Barbara Herrnstein Smith, *Contingencies of Value: Alternative Perspectives for Critical Theory* (Cambridge: Harvard University Press, 1988), p. 221 n. 28; Gunn, *Thinking Across the American Grain*, pp. 187–91.

23. Rorty, "Just one more species doing its best," p. 5.

24. Barbara Herrnstein Smith urges us similarly to distinguish discourses "not absolutely . . . by virtue of their radically opposed claims to 'truth' or 'objective validity,' but as occupying different positions along a number of relevant continua" (*Contingencies of Value*, p. 101).

25. Thus, to take one example among many, Fish takes on H. L. A. Hart's Quinean description of the law as a negotiation space with a stable center and a contested periphery as a residual kind of essentialism, even while acknowledging that in practical terms legal practice does look like this. See Fish, *Doing What Comes Naturally*, pp. 512–13.

26. *Doing What Comes Naturally*, p. 458.

27. Ibid.

28. Ibid., p. 459, my emphasis.

29. Ibid., p. 21.

30. Ibid., pp. 32–33.

31. Stephen Greenblatt, *Shakespearean Negotiations* (Berkeley: University of California Press, 1988), p. 7.

32. Graham Bradshaw, *Shakespearean Scepticism* (1987; Ithaca: Cornell University Press, 1990), p. 39. The emphases are Bradshaw's.

33. Jean-Christophe Agnew, *Worlds Apart: The Market and the Theater in Anglo-American Thought, 1550–1750* (Cambridge: Cambridge University Press, 1986), pp. 97–98.

34. Fernand Braudel, *The Wheels of Commerce*, trans. Sian Reynolds (New York: Harper and Row, 1982), pp. 223–24.

Chapter Two

1. Thomas Greene, "Pitiful Thrivers: Failed Husbandry in the Sonnets," in Patricia Parker and Geoffrey Hartman, eds., *Shakespeare and the Question of Theory* (New York: Methuen, 1985), p. 231.

2. The rare references to public markets of exchange in the *Rime Sparse* are contemptuous and categorically separate the poet's love and his praise from market behavior: see Robert M. Durling, ed. and trans., *Petrarch's Lyric Poems* (Cambridge: Harvard University Press, 1976), nos. 7, 13, 223, 308.

3. Anne Ferry, *The "Inward" Language: Sonnets of Wyatt, Sidney, Shakespeare, and Donne* (Chicago: University of Chicago Press, 1983), p. 7.

4. Ibid., p. 210.

5. Joel Fineman, *Shakespeare's Perjured Eye: The Invention of Poetic Subjectivity in the Sonnets* (Berkeley: University of California Press, 1986), p. 47.

6. Ibid, p. 297.

7. For Shakespeare as Heidegger, see Fineman, *Shakespeare's Perjured Eye*, p. 333 n. 35: "What is novel about the Shakespearean is that it forswears this structure of polarity, not by reconciling contraries within a larger unity nor by exploiting the tension produced by their oxymoronic combination, but, specifically, by reiterating them in such a way as to put the concept and the consequence of polar opposition into question." For Shakespeare as Derrida, see ibid. p. 46.

8. Individual sonnets are quoted from Stephen Booth, *Shakespeare's Sonnets* (New Haven: Yale University Press, 1977), with their numbers given parenthetically after each citation.

9. See Sigmund Freud, "On the Universal Tendency to Debasement in the Sphere of Love," trans. Alan Tyson, *The Standard Edition of the Complete Psychological Works of Sigmund Freud*, ed. and trans. James Strachey, vol. 11 (New York: Norton, 1976), p. 181.

10. See John Bernard, "'To Constancie Confin'de': The Poetics of Shakespeare's Sonnets," *PMLA* 94 (1979).

11. Adena Rosmarin, "Hermeneutics versus Erotics: Shakespeare's *Sonnets* and Interpretive History," *PMLA* 100 (January, 1985), 30.

12. Archaic gift economies do defer returns, and gifts of poetic praise are generally well described in terms of this form of exchange. Shakespeare's poems are peculiar from this viewpoint too, however, in that they are reticent about name and lineage and largely silent about deeds, as I shall argue below. See Marcel Mauss, *The Gift: Forms and Functions of Exchange in Archaic Societies*, trans. I. Cunnison (New York: Norton, 1967).

13. This position is argued by John Bernard, "'To Constancie Confin'de.'" Bernard believes that the Sonnets perform a leap of faith: "Shakespeare's desire to isolate love's 'worth' from the physical and moral laws of nature impels him, then, to emphasize a 'constancy' in both beloved and poet that is increasingly metaphysical" (p. 80, see also pp. 88–89). Compare Ferry, *All in War with Time: Love Poetry of Shakespeare, Donne, Jonson, Marvell* (Cambridge: Harvard University Press, 1975), and Murray Krieger, *A Window to Criticism: Shakespeare's Sonnets and Modern Poetics* (Princeton: Princeton University Press, 1964), as quoted below.

14. See, however, Heather Dubrow, *Captive Victors: Shakespeare's Narrative Poems and Sonnets* (Ithaca: Cornell University Press, 1987), p. 218, for argument about the doctrinal issues involved in tears and ransom, which qualifies this claim by suggesting that the couplet invokes a kind of Christian economics rather than an escape from penury.

15. On this see W. G. Ingram and Theodore Redpath, eds. *Shakespeare's Sonnets* (London: University of London Press, 1964), p. 250: "we believe that

[lines 9–14] could also be understood to refer to the repeated formula of line 7." They feel, that is, that "eternal love in love's fresh case" may consist of repeating such appropriable human gestures as "thou mine, I thine."

16. See G. Wilson Knight, *The Mutual Flame: On Shakespeare's Sonnets and "The Phoenix and the Turtle"* (London: Methuen, 1955), p. 86.

17. Ibid, p. 86.

18. Booth, *Shakespeare's Sonnets*, p. 418.

19. Dubrow, *Captive Victors*, pp. 224–25, my italics.

20. Krieger, *A Window to Criticism*, pp. 141–42.

21. Krieger, typically pushing an endurance claim toward a transcendence claim, comments at the end of his discussion of 124 that "love . . . constitutes itself a body politic distinct and indissoluble, untouchable by all others and subject to none—finally beyond the 'state' of man (in all its senses) whose child it is not" (pp. 142–43). This seems to me quite wrong, but Krieger speaks for the majority of critics in making Shakespeare a kind of Platonist at moments like these.

22. Booth, *Shakespeare's Sonnets*, pp. 425–26; John Donne, "Farewell to Love," *Poetical Works*, ed. Herbert J. C. Grierson (London: Oxford University Press, 1971), p. 62.

23. See also Jonathan Dollimore, *Radical Tragedy: Religion, Ideology, and Power in the Drama of Shakespeare and His Contemporaries* (Brighton: Harvester, 1984), chap. 1, especially pp. 17–19, for evidence that Shakespeare's lifetime was one of vigorous anti-essentialist argument.

24. Wittgenstein, *On Certainty*, ed. G. E .M. Anscombe and G. H. von Wright, trans. Denis Paul and G. E. M. Anscombe (New York: Harper & Row, 1969), pp. 15e (nos. 94–97, 99) and 33e (no. 248). In subsequent quotations from this work, pages will be given parenthetically below.

25. On the relevance of these passages to *Anna Karenina*, see Martin Price, *Forms of Life: Character and Moral Imagination in the Novel* (New Haven: Yale University Press, 1983), pp. 178–80. For discussion of *On Certainty* in the context of the rest of Wittgenstein's work see Austin Quigley, "Wittgenstein's Philosophizing and Literary Theorizing," *NLH* 19 (Winter 1988), especially pp. 220–25.

26. Richard Rorty, *Consequences of Pragmatism* (Minneapolis: University of Minnesota Press, 1982), p. 158.

27. See Yukio Futagawa and Martin Pawley, *Frank Lloyd Wright: Public Buildings* (New York: Simon and Schuster, 1970), p. 119: "As the subsoil was liquid mud and the area itself subject to earthquakes Wright resolved to float the whole building on rafts of concrete linked by joints which would permit differential movement. . . . Wright . . . balanc[ed] each slab on a central pile bored deep into the subsoil so that the independent movement of each slab need not involve subsidence or cracking. . . . The success of these measures was dramatically demonstrated during the severe earthquake of 1923."

28. Quoted in Booth, *Shakespeare's Sonnets*, pp. 227–28, from the Loeb translation.

29. Quoted in Booth, *Shakespeare's Sonnets*, p. 554.

30. For interesting commentary on Shakespeare's allusions, see Jonathan Bate, "Ovid and the Sonnets; or, Did Shakespeare Feel the Anxiety of Influence?" *Shakespeare Survey* 42 (Cambridge: Cambridge University Press, 1990), p. 73.

31. Booth, *Shakespeare's Sonnets*, p. 229.

32. Donald Foster, "Master W. H., R.I.P.," *PMLA* 102 (January 1987): 42–54.

33. Shakespeare's sonnets, of course, attained canonical status after the institutionalization of his plays as socially central and at least partly as a result thereof; we can assume, then, that they were put to wide erotic use only in the late nineteenth and twentieth centuries, and thus that a particular historical account of their survival would not be entirely a story of continuity, though it would bear out the survival claims made in 55.

34. Ferry, *All in War with Time*, p. 19. Ferry creates what seems to me a false distinction between the lower-numbered sonnets, in which miracles take place (apparently through poetry's "creation of a nontemporal order where sequence is ruled by verbal necessity rather than by time" [p. 19]), and higher-numbered sonnets which, with "flattering falsity . . . actually insist that beauty, love, even poetry, belong to the timebound world in which the friend lives and the poet writes about him" (pp. 46–47). The differences in spirit which she sees between poems seem to me just that, differences in spirit, intent, or purpose: they don't denote a shift in the poet's idea of what is possible and impossible in poetry or in the world. Because Ferry believes that there are two views of poetry and time in the sonnets to the young man, the first idealistic and the second anti-idealistic, she tends to read the later time sonnets much more darkly than I do. She sees them as betrayals of early promises to work miracles: I see them as fulfillments of early suggestions that poetry can resist destruction by understanding time. Compare her accounts of sonnets 108 and 123 (pp. 48–52) with mine. See also Foster, "Master W. H., R.I.P.," p. 48 for a position anticipating mine.

35. Donne, *Poetical Works*, p. 45

36. Quoted in Booth, *Shakespeare's Sonnets*, p. 384.

37. See Booth, *Shakespeare's Sonnets*, pp. 388–89 for a splendidly characteristic account of how these lines "derive much of their power from being both simple and straightforward and simultaneously so complexly wondrous that beholder and beheld are indistinguishable from one another in a statement that makes their ordinary relationship quite clear."

38. Booth, *Shakespeare's Sonnets*, p. 386.

39. See C. T. Onions, *Shakespeare Glossary*, 3d ed., enlarged and revised by Robert D. Eagleson (Oxford: Clarendon Press, 1986), p. 106; compare Lear's "my poor fool is hang'd" (5.3.304).

40. See Philip Martin, *Shakespeare's Sonnets: Self, Love, and Art* (Cambridge: Cambridge University Press, 1972), p. 90, for a similar comment which is part of a very different account from mine of sonnet 116. See also Barbara Herrnstein Smith, "Fixed Marks and Variable Constancies: A Parable of Literary Value," *Poetics Today* 1 (1979): 13, for an account of her own sporadic view

of the poet of 116 attempting "to sustain the existence, by sheer assertion, of something which everything in his own experience denied."

41. See *OED* "bear" v1 3a.

42. Wordsworth, "Scorn Not the Sonnet," in Jack Stillinger, ed., *Selected Poems and Prefaces by William Wordsworth* (Boston: Houghton Mifflin, 1965), p. 433.

43. Joseph Pequigney, *Such Is My Love: A Study of Shakespeare's Sonnets* (Chicago: University of Chicago Press, 1985).

44. Eve Kosofsky Sedgwick, *Between Men: English Literature and Male Homosocial Desire* (New York: Columbia University Press, 1985).

45. On the alternative Wittgensteinian pragmatism offers to deconstruction, see Samuel C. Wheeler III, "Wittgenstein as Conservative Deconstructor," *NLH* 19 (Winter 1988).

46. John Kerrigan, "An Account of the Text," in Shakespeare, *The Sonnets and "A Lover's Complaint"* (London: Penguin, 1986), pp. 427–33. This evidence is much augmented by findings reported by Donald Foster in " 'Adde to thy Will / One Will of Mine': Rereading Shakespeare's Sonnets in the Light of W.S.'s *Funerall Elegy* for Will Peter" at the 1990 MLA session, "Interrogating Shakespeare's Sonnets."

47. Barbara Herrnstein Smith, *Contingencies of Value: Alternative Perspectives for Critical Theory* (Cambridge: Harvard University Press, 1988), p. 42. Citations will be given parenthetically henceforth.

48. It should also be noted that, though Herrnstein Smith is most interested in the behavior of professional humanists, her economic/pragmatic account of social interaction encompasses scientific communities as well as artistic or interpretive ones. That is, she describes truth as well as beauty pragmatically, as that which is efficient in the satisfaction of desires, and proceeds to display the economic structure of truth seeking within scientific communities which organize themselves around the evaluation of attempts to determine objective truth. Scientists experiment for the approval of audiences at least as much as painters paint for it.

49. See *Contingencies*, p. 5, where Herrnstein Smith comments that the history of her engagement with Shakespeare's sonnets "spans thirty-five years, during fifteen of which I professed them almost without interruption, sometimes every term, and during two years of which I prepared an edition. There is no other work or body of literature that I know so well."

50. David Simpson, "Literary Criticism and the Return to 'History,' " *Critical Inquiry* 14 (Summer 1988): 744–45.

Chapter Three

1. Richard Rorty, *Objectivity, relativism, and truth: Philosophical Papers*, vol. 1 (Cambridge: Cambridge University Press, 1991), p. 1: "By an antirepresentationalist account I mean one which does not view knowledge as a matter of getting reality right, but rather as a matter of acquiring habits of action for coping with reality." Theater, on such a view, is not representation but ther-

apy—a position, of course, approached in part by Aristotle when defending drama against the strictures of Plato, though Aristotle might be paraphrased as saying "not only representation (*mimesis*) but also therapy (*katharsis*)." It should be noted that Rorty here takes up arguments against representationalism originally put forward by Donald Davidson.

2. John Dewey, "The Construction of Good," originally published in *The Quest for Certainty* (New York, 1927), quoted from *Pragmatism: The Classic Writings*, ed. H. S. Thayer (Indianapolis: Hackett, 1982), p. 305.

3. Cornel West, *The American Evasion of Philosophy: A Genealogy of Pragmatism* (Madison: University of Wisconsin Press, 1989), p. 5.

4. For an account of Platonic antitheatricality, see Jonas Barish, *The Antitheatrical Prejudice* (Berkeley: U. of California Press, 1981), p. 7.

5. David Richard Jones, *Great Directors at Work* (Berkeley: University of California Press, 1986), pp. 89, 91. Quoted material here and in the epigraph from Konstantin Stanislavsky, *An Actor Prepares*, trans. E. R. Hapgood (New York: Theatre Arts Press, 1935).

6. Dewey, *Pragmatism*, p. 520.

7. *Brecht on Theatre*, ed. and trans. John Willett (London: Methuen, 1964), p. 225.

8. John Dewey, "The Practical Character of Reality," originally published in 1908, quoted from Thayer, *Pragmatism*, p. 279.

9. *Brecht on Theatre*, p. 205. One might also note the epigraph Willett chooses from Brecht for this book: "the inflexible rule is that the proof of the pudding is in the eating." Brecht uses the idea of "representation" continually, but always with a view to representing social situations as alterable by human action. He did, at least to some extent, believe that inevitable historical processes underlay the changes he wanted to sponsor (that is, his Marxism had a necessitarian side, and he did partly believe there was an underlying "reality" to represent and "get right"), but his ideas about theater were pragmatic ones.

10. See *Brecht on Theatre*, p. 95 and pp. 236–37, for Brecht's commentary on this feature in Stanislavsky: "practically every gesture is submitted for the public's approval"(95).

11. See, among many other works, David Bevington, *Action Is Eloquence: Shakespeare's Language of Gesture* (Cambridge: Harvard University Press, 1984), for thorough discussion of gesture, costume, and staging throughout Shakespeare's oeuvre, and Michael Goldman, *Acting and Action in Shakespearean Tragedy* (Princeton: Princeton University Press, 1985), for readings of tragedies which emphasize the actions of actors on the stage.

12. See Jonathan Goldberg, *James I and the Politics of Literature: Jonson, Shakespeare, Donne, and Their Contemporaries* (Baltimore: Johns Hopkins University Press, 1983). Goldberg's book attempts precisely this sort of placement but comments that "Shakespeare's relation to his culture remains difficult to summarize, not because he is apart from it, but because he assumes no fixed relationship to it. This has often made it possible to act as if Shakespeare was some timeless figure, a man for all times and yet of none. This is, palpably, erroneous. Yet, opposing attempts, for instance E. M. W. Tillyard's, to moor

his political and historical attitudes in a morass of Elizabethan commonplaces, have foundered. As [Stephen] Greenblatt says, it seems untrue to characterize Shakespeare as a Tudor propagandist, but equally unconvincing to speak of him as a Marlovian rebel; it is false, too, to locate him (with Jonson) on some *via media*. The space of Shakespearean representation is, Greenblatt concludes, radically unstable, a place of improvisation where all the beliefs of the culture are trotted out, tried on, but where none is ultimately adopted. This is not Keatsian negative capability exactly . . ." (p. 230). For a somewhat similar (though more philosophically and less politically inflected) comment on Shakespeare's exploration of groundlessness as a reproof to the quest for certainty in general and to Santayana's relative devaluation of Shakespeare in particular, see John Dewey, *Art as Experience* (1934; New York: Perigee, 1980), pp. 320–22. Dewey writes on p. 321, "Art that is faithful to the many potentialities of organization, centering about a variety of interests and purposes, that nature offers—as was that of Shakespeare—may have not only a fullness but a wholeness and sanity absent from a philosophy of enclosure, transcendence, and fixity."

13. Michel Foucault, "The Subject and Power," *Critical Inquiry* 8 (1982), 778, quoted in West, *American Evasion*, p. 224. Compare the late interview "On the Genealogy of Ethics" in *The Foucault Reader*, ed. Paul Rabinow (New York: Pantheon, 1984), pp. 340–44, where Foucault discusses his preoccupation with "techniques of the self."

14. Mikhail Bakhtin, *Problems of Dostoyevsky's Poetics*, ed. and trans. Caryl Emerson (Minnesota: University of Minnesota Press, 1984), p. 287.

15. The most poignant instance of this in my memory, now rendered yet more complex by posthumous revelations, was the memorial service at Yale for Paul de Man, in which distinguished fellow-deconstructors eulogized his disinterested nobility of character in a reversion to humanist terminology he would surely have found somewhat ironical as well as touching.

The kind of personal commitment involved in a desire to maintain agency is well articulated by Hilary Putnam in *Realism with a Human Face* (Cambridge: Harvard University Press, 1990). Putnam points out that there are two main groups of arguments for intellectual liberty: the Utilitarian and the Kantian. The Utilitarian argument is that "without freedom of thought and speech, any party and any government will harden into an exploiting class, a tyranny." (Foucault thinks that this more or less has happened anyway, though his formulation of the issue—as the creation of impersonal 'disciplines'—avoids the personalization implicit in Putnam's "ruling group.") The Kantian argument, Putnam continues, "is complementary to the Utilitarian one. The Kantian argument is that, quite apart from its value to society, intellectual liberty— Kant calls it autonomy—is absolutely indispensable to the integrity of the person. Why? If you are autonomous, if you think for yourself in moral and political matters, then that is not a real question for you. . . . Let me say, without further ado, that here I am a Kantian (as well as a Deweyan). Asking me 'But how do you *know* autonomy is a good thing?' in the familiar philosophical epistemological fashion is inviting me to provide a 'foundation' for my own integrity as a human being. Rather than do that, I have to say 'I have reached bedrock, and my spade is turned'" (pp. 202–3). Putnam's final quotation is from Wittgenstein's *Philosophical Investigations*, 3d. ed., trans. G. E. M. Anscombe (New York: Macmillan, 1953), no. 217. Pragmatic liberals share the view that autonomy is a good thing, even though they are less sure than classical liberals that it is an easy (much less automatic) thing to have.

16. See recent discussions of agency in Paul Smith's *Discerning the Subject* (Minneapolis: University of Minnesota Press, 1988); Roberto Mangabeira Unger's *Social Theory* (Cambridge: Cambridge University Press, 1987), especially chap. 5; and Cornel West's *The American Evasion of Pragmatism*. Both Lee and Annabel Patterson have for some time vigorously urged the need to retain, in radicalized forms, humanist interpretive categories, especially agency. See, for a general statement about authorship, the Introduction to Lee Patterson's *Chaucer and the Subject of History* (Madison: University of Wisconsin Press, 1991), and for a particular discussion of *Hamlet* which anticipates mine in several ways, Annabel Patterson, *Shakespeare and the Popular Voice* (Cambridge, MA: Basil Blackwell, 1989), chap. 5. Her idea of Shakespeare as an "intense skeptic" who becomes a "mature radical" seems to me complementary to the pragmatist Shakespeare I advocate.

17. See William Kerrigan and Gordon Braden, *The Idea of the Renaissance* (Baltimore: Johns Hopkins University Press, 1989), which explores the idea that the Renaissance is a time of enhanced commitment to selfhood, and Stephen Greenblatt, *Renaissance Self-Fashioning* (Chicago: University of Chicago Press, 1980). Greenblatt notes in a justly famous epilogue that all the self-fashioners he writes of, from More to Shakespeare, "do in fact cling to the human subject and to self-fashioning, even in suggesting the absorption or corruption or loss of the self. How could they do otherwise? What was—or, for that matter, what is—the alternative?" (p. 257).

18. Coleridge, lecture 12 from *The Lectures of 1811–12*, in Signet *Hamlet*, ed. Edward Hubler (New York: New American Library, 1963), pp. 190, 193.

19. See A. C. Bradley, *Shakespearean Tragedy* (1904; London: Macmillan, 1957), p. 85.

20. All quotations from the play are from the Arden *Hamlet*, ed. Harold Jenkins (London: Methuen, 1982).

21. For a fine account of the soliloquy as a meditation on the philosophical preconditions of action, see Goldman, "'To Be or Not To Be' and the Spectrum of Action," *Acting and Action in Shakespearean Tragedy*, chap. 2.

22. Hamlet thus promotes in Ophelia, both for therapeutic purposes and because he himself is suffering from it, the kind of disjunction Troilus experiences as a terminal crisis when he says "This is and is not Cressid." Ophelia's "O, what a noble mind is here o'erthrown" speech, which ends "O woe is me / T'have seen what I have seen, see what I see" (3.1.152) might be paraphrased, "This is and is not Hamlet."

23. See Arden *Hamlet*, pp. 493–96.

24. There is, of course, some question about what Hamlet means by "relative." Jenkins ("cogent, material") and David Bevington ("cogent, pertinent")

more or less agree with G. B. Evans in the Riverside Shakespeare ("closely related [to fact], i.e. conclusive"), but as G. R. Hibbard (who glosses it as "relevant, cogent") points out in the Oxford *Hamlet* this is the first use of the word with this meaning that the OED records, and the only such use of it in Shakespeare. Hilda Hulme suggested (and Onions and Eagleson accept in *A Shakespeare Glossary*) "able to be related," noting that in Shakespeare the suffix "-ive" seems equivalent to the modern suffix "-able" (as in "unexpressive she" or "uncomprehensive deeps"). See Hulme's *Explorations in Shakespeare's Language* (New York: Barnes and Noble, 1962), pp. 30–34. The main pre-Shakespearean use of the adjective "relative" recorded in OED, however, is as a grammatical term, meaning "relating to or referring to an antecedent term", that is, not standing alone, not referential to something outside the discursive context but rather relating two parts inside it. Thus there is philological plausibility to the claim that Hamlet intends a productive philosophical oxymoron in the "grounds more relative" he invokes—he will seek confirmation not by building on an external certainty, but by bringing a discourse and a subject into relation and examining the result. There is also a pun on Claudius as Hamlet's "relative," of course.

25. Marjorie Garber, *Shakespeare's Ghost Writers: Literature as Uncanny Causality* (New York: Methuen, 1987).

26. I would not want my comparison of Hamlet in act 5 to a relatively serene patient at the end of a fairly successful analysis to be taken as a claim that he is always calm. Fresh versions of old issues bring fresh intensities (therapy is not lobotomy)—thus Hamlet's "tow'ring passion" (5.2.80, referring to 5.1.247–87) at Laertes for reminding him of the histrionics of vengefulness in relation to slain fathers.

Chapter Four

1. René Girard, "'To Entrap the Wisest': A Reading of *The Merchant of Venice*," in Edward Said, ed., *Literature and Society* (Baltimore: Johns Hopkins University Press, 1980), p. 101–2.

2. The Arden Shakespeare, *The Merchant of Venice*, ed. John Russell Brown (London: Methuen, 1955). I incorporate line references parenthetically.

3. See Walter Cohen, "*The Merchant of Venice* and the Possibilities of Historical Criticism," *Journal of English Literary History* 49 (1982), 765–85, incorporated into his *Drama of a Nation: Public Theatre in Renaissance England and Spain* (Ithaca: Cornell University Press, 1985), pp. 195–211, for persuasive argument that the play invokes both English and Italian responses to the onset of credit economies. I shall suggest that Cohen could find much more detailed support for his views in the plot of the play.

4. See Leonard Tennenhouse, "The Counterfeit Order in *The Merchant of Venice*," in Murray Schwartz and Coppélia Kahn, eds., *Representing Shakespeare: New Psychoanalytic Essays* (Baltimore: Johns Hopkins Press, 1977), pp. 54–69, for persuasive argument on these lines.

5. Lawrence Danson, attempting in what is generally an extremely helpful

account of the play to fend off a homoerotic interpretation of Antonio's melancholy, comments that "two monosyllabic expletives might seem a slender basis on which to build a character's motivations, but it can be done," cites performances of Antonio as homosexual which give a tragic twist to the final scene (he is left alone onstage when all the heterosexual couples leave it), and concludes that "what is crucial to decide . . . is whether those otherwise innocuous 'fies' in the first scene should actually lead to Antonio's exclusion and a final dying fall" for the play. But there is much more than a couple of "fies" to suggest erotic causes for Antonio's melancholy. See Danson, *The Harmonies of The Merchant of Venice* (New Haven: Yale University Press, 1978), pp. 37–38.

6. See Marc Shell, "The Wether and the Ewe: Verbal Usury in *The Merchant of Venice*," *Kenyon Review*, n.s., 1, no. 4 (Fall 1979): p. 66 for a summary of financial relations between Antonio and Bassanio which in some ways anticipates this one. Shell calls Antonio "a zealot [against interest-taking] who seems to condemn even marine insurance" (p. 70). See also Marianne Novy, *Love's Argument* (Chapel Hill: University of North Carolina Press, 1984), p. 69, for the interesting suggestion that Antonio "behaves like the altruists described by Anna Freud who have given up to another person, with whom they identify, the right to have their instincts gratified."

7. Eve Kosofsky Sedgwick, "Sexualism and the Citizen of the World: Wycherley, Sterne, and Male Homosocial Desire," *Critical Inquiry* 11 (December 1984): 227. For a more extended account of homosocial desire, see the introduction to Sedgwick's *Between Men: English Literature and Male Homosocial Desire* (New York: Columbia University Press, 1985).

8. *Between Men*, p. 50.

9. Lawrence Stone, *The Crisis of the Aristocracy, 1558–1641* (Oxford: Clarendon, 1965), pp. 520–21.

10. See Stone, *Crisis of the Aristocracy*, p. 530.

11. Shylock's line on first seeing Antonio, "How like a fawning publican he looks!" (1.3.36), which has always puzzled commentators because Antonio can hardly be said to be "fawning" in his relations with Shylock, may be explicable in these terms. If we assume that Shylock sees Antonio as fawning on Bassanio (certainly the only person we see Antonio prone to fawn on), then the notion that Antonio is like a Roman tax gatherer who abuses those below him—especially Jews—in order to ingratiate himself to those above, shows Shylock's insight into the kind of emotional "interest" we have seen Antonio exacting from his own loans.

12. G. K. Hunter, "The Theology of the Jew of Malta," *Journal of the Warburg and Courtauld Institutes* (1964), p. 216.

13. Genesis 25:23, the Geneva Bible (1560), lightly modernized. All subsequent biblical quotations are from the Geneva Bible.

14. See Arnold Williams, *The Common Expositor* (Chapel Hill: University of North Carolina Press, 1948), pp. 169–72, and Danson, *Harmonies*, pp. 72–76, where these contexts are drawn together to support a different argument.

15. For a different reading of it, turning on the distinction in Jewish law between "brothers" and "others," see Shell, "The Wether and the Ewe," pp. 68–70.

16. *Crisis of the Aristocracy*, p. 542.

17. R. H. Tawney, *Religion and the Rise of Capitalism* (New York, 1926), p. 151, quoted in Danson, *Harmonies*, p. 142.

18. "*The Merchant of Venice* and the Possibilities of Historical Criticism," p. 771.

19. Ibid., p. 774.

20. *Crisis of the Aristocracy*, p. 633.

21. See Arden *Merchant*, Appendix 5, p. 173.

22. Sigurd Burckhardt, in *Shakespearean Meanings* (Princeton: Princeton University Press, 1968), p. 210, comments: "As the subsidiary metaphors of the bond and the ring indicate, *The Merchant* is a play about circularity and circulation; it asks how the vicious circle of the bond's law can be transformed into the ring of love." As will soon become clear, I do not feel that the "rings of love" at play's end offer a qualitative transformation of the earlier "bonds."

23. "Sexualism," p. 229.

24. Compare Novy, *Love's Argument*, pp. 76–80, for an account, which in several ways anticipates this one, of how "the victory goes to Portia" at the end of the play. See also Richard Wheeler, *Shakespeare's Development and the Problem Comedies* (Berkeley: University of California Press, 1981), p. 168, for an argument that, from the point at which she apparently submits to Bassanio, "Portia's self-appropriated power orders the movement of the play."

25. Bernard Williams, "Moral Luck," in *Moral Luck: Philosophical Papers, 1973–1980* (Cambridge: Cambridge University Press, 1981).

26. Williams himself suggests that Richard Rorty's pragmatism may have important uses in the study of moral issues: see his "Auto-da-Fé: Consequences of Pragmatism," in Alan R. Malachowski, ed., *Reading Rorty: Critical Responses to Philosophy and the Mirror of Nature (and Beyond)* (Oxford: Basil Blackwell, 1990), p. 36: "[Rorty's] kind of questioning has great force in a field that he himself does not take up, that of moral philosophy."

27. "Moral Luck," p. 21.

28. Ibid., p. 21.

29. Ibid.

30. Ibid.

31. Ibid.

32. Portia's generosity is bounded by race, as she shows in her sentiments toward Morocco (though not in her face-to-face treatment of him); this is simply another way that the play underlines the "moral" advantage of being in the socially empowered category in terms of race as well as rank, religion, and wealth.

33. *Drama of a Nation*, p. 205.

34. Fernand Braudel, *Civilization and Capitalism*, vol. 3, *The Perspective of the World*, trans. Siân Reynolds (New York: Harper and Row, 1984), p. 142.

35. Arden *Merchant*, p. 93, quoting Thomas, *History of Italy* (1549), Z1.

36. Richard Rorty, "On Ethnocentrism," in *Objectivity, relativism, and truth: Philosophical papers*, vol. 1 (Cambridge: Cambridge University Press, 1991), p. 209.

37. Thomas Nagel, "Moral Luck," in *Mortal Questions* (New York: Cam-

bridge University Press, 1979), p. 35. Nagel's essay began as a response to an earlier version of Williams's—this is why they have the same title—and it attempts to offer a rationale for the idea of moral autonomy.

38. The term "agent-regret" is Williams's; it denotes the special feeling of regret for a bad outcome that comes with a sense of having been an agent (perhaps only by passivity when one could have been active) in the chain of causes that led to the outcome. See Williams, "Moral Luck," p. 27.

39. *Mortal Questions*, p. 31.

Chapter Five

1. For a similar argument about the *Henriad*, see Sandra K. Fischer " 'He Means to Pay': Value and Metaphor in the Lancastrian Tetralogy," *Shakespeare Quarterly* 40:149–64. I came to her essay after I had drafted this chapter. My general conclusions are also anticipated by H. R. Coursen, *The Leasing Out of England: Shakespeare's Second Henriad* (Washington D.C.: University Press of America, 1982).

2. Parenthical references are to the A. R. Humphrey's New Arden editions of *King Henry IV, Part One* (London: Methuen, 1960) and *King Henry IV, Part Two* (London: Methuen, 1966).

3. Richard Rorty, "The Contingency of Selfhood," *Contingency, irony, and solidarity* (Cambridge: Cambridge University Press, 1989), p. 41.

4. The most influential argument to this effect is Stephen Greenblatt's "Invisible Bullets," which appears in its final form as chapter 2 of *Shakespearean Negotiations*. I discuss Greenblatt's essay below.

5. Quotations from Peter Ure's New Arden edition of *King Richard II* (London: Methuen, 1951) are cited in parentheses.

6. I am partly anticipated in this line of argument by C. L. Barber, though Barber is concerned to identify ritual rather than exchange patterns in the plays. See *Shakespeare's Festive Comedy* (Princeton: Princeton University Press, 1959), p. 201.

7. See Arden *1 Henry IV*, appendix 3, p. 177. It does not seem likely that Shakespeare knew that the historical Henry of Monmouth (i.e., Prince Hal) was taken in by Richard II and shown great kindness during Bolingbroke's banishment.

8. The king mentions his father only once in all of *Henry V*, while wooing Katherine: "Now beshrew my father's ambition! he was thinking of civil wars when he got me: therefore was I created with a stubborn outside, with an aspect of iron, that when I come to woo ladies I fright them" (5.2.236). Here and below I cite J. H. Walter's New Arden *King Henry V* (London: Methuen, 1954).

9. The issue of why Hal has to go on being a prodigal is raised provocatively in Jonathan Crewe's "Reforming Prince Hal: The Sovereign Inheritor in *2 Henry IV*," *Renaissance Drama*, n.s. 21 (1990): 225–42. My own description of the agon between Hal and Henry IV first arose as a response to a draft of his essay, and though my explanation differs from his both in details and vocabulary, it is also in his debt.

10. The play's treatment of parricide has long been of interest to psychoanalytic critics, starting with Ernst Kris, "Prince Hal's Conflict," *Psychoanalytic Quarterly* 17 (1948). For an able summary with references to other authors, see Richard Wheeler, *Shakespeare's Development and the Problem Comedies* (Berkeley: University of California Press, 1981), pp. 158–67, esp. p. 163.

11. Jean-Pierre Vernant, "Tensions and Ambiguities in Greek Tragedy," in Vernant and P. Vidal-Naquet, *Tragedy and Myth*, trans. Janet Lloyd (Atlantic Highlands, NJ: Humanities Press, 1981), pp. 36–37.

12. *Shakespeare's Development*, p. 163. I think Wheeler must mean "flout his father."

13. Phyllis Rackin, *Stages of History: Shakespeare's English Chronicles* (Ithaca: Cornell University Press, 1990), p. 97.

14. There are also, of course, moralistic critics for whom Falstaff is a genuine misleader of youth. For pre-War criticism see John Dover Wilson, *The Fortunes of Falstaff* (Cambridge: Cambridge University Press, 1943). David Bevington comments with mild satire on the perspective shared by, for example, E. M. W. Tillyard and Lily Campbell, "Hal's rejection of Falstaff is not priggishness but inevitable triumph over sin, signifying an end to England's morality-like soul struggle" (*Tudor Drama and Politics* [Cambridge, MA: Harvard University Press, 1968], pp. 244–45).

15. One of the most influential representations of this view is C. L. Barber's chapter "Rule and Misrule in *Henry IV*," in *Shakespeare's Festive Comedy*.

16. A. C. Bradley, "The Rejection of Falstaff," in *Oxford Lectures on Poetry* (London: Macmillan, 1909), pp. 262–3.

17. W. H. Auden, "The Prince's Dog," in *The Dyer's Hand* (London: Faber and Faber, 1963), p. 190.

18. Ibid., p. 192.

19. William Empson, "They That Have Power to Hurt," in *Some Versions of Pastoral* ([1935]; New York: New Directions, 1974). Auden, incidentally, may well have been reading his uncorrected edition of Empson alongside Shakespeare while composing "The Prince's Dog." Like Empson (who corrects himself in a note to the 1974 reprint), Auden carelessly assumes that Falstaff's comment that "if the rascal have not given me medicines to make me love him, I'll be hanged" (2.2.17) refers to Hal rather than Poins, and in general he follows the line of homoerotic pathos—and cross-reference between the *Henriad* and the sonnets—pioneered by Empson. Compare Empson pp. 106–9 with Auden pp. 191–92.

20. "The Rejection of Falstaff," p. 273.

21. Stephen Greenblatt, "Invisible Bullets," *Shakespearean Negotiations* (Berkeley: University of California Press, 1988), pp. 42–43.

22. "The Rejection of Falstaff," 254. On this see Empson, *Essays on Shakespeare*, ed. David Pirie (Cambridge: Cambridge University Press, 1986), p. 69: "Their separation, says Bradley, might have been shown in a private scene rich in humour and only touched with pathos; a remark which shows how very different he would like the characters to be."

23. "Invisible Bullets," 58.

24. "The Rejection of Falstaff," pp. 257, 259–60.

25. Bradley is also subtly registering reactions of his own that he finds difficult to accept here.

26. *Shakespearean Negotiations*, p. 41, quoting Mack's introduction to the Signet Classic *1 Henry IV* (New York: New American Library, 1965), p. xxxv. For Mack's possible debt to Bradley, see "The Rejection of Falstaff," p. 256: "Both as prince and as king [Hal] is deservedly a favourite, and particularly so with English readers, being, as he is, perhaps the most distinctively English of all Shakespeare's men." This becomes a more substantial and less sentimental claim when Empson points out that Henry V was believed in the sixteenth century to be the first English-speaking English king (since Harold), an argument intelligently extended by Steven Mullaney in *The Place of the Stage* (Chicago: University of Chicago Press, 1988), pp. 80–87.

27. "Invisible Bullets," p. 41.

28. On this see Alan Liu, "Wordsworth and Subversion, 1793–1804: Trying Cultural Criticism," *Yale Journal of Criticism* 2, no. 2 (Spring 1989), especially pp. 55–56 and 87–88.

29. See Mikhail Bakhtin, *Rabelais and His World*, trans. Helene Iswolsky (Bloomington: Indiana University Press, 1984), p. 158.

30. See Arden *1 Henry IV*, pp. 234–35.

31. For such an opposition, see Barber, *Shakespeare's Festive Comedy*, p. 195: "The relation of the Prince to Falstaff can be summarized fairly adequately in terms of the relation of holiday to everyday."

32. On the festive calendar, see François Larocque, *Shakespeare's Festive World*, trans. Janet Lloyd (Cambridge: Cambridge University Press, 1991), part 1. See also p. 244, where Larocque notes Shakespeare's "reluctance to portray popular festivity in any way other than as under the control of the aristocracy."

33. *Andrew Marvell: The Complete Poems*, ed. Elizabeth Story Donno (Harmondsworth: Penguin, 1972), p. 58.

Chapter Six

1. Harold Bloom, *The Anxiety of Influence* (New York, Oxford University Press, 1973), p. 11.

2. *Selected Prose of T. S. Eliot*, ed. Frank Kermode (London: Faber & Faber, 1975), p. 40

3. My pronouns emphasize the extent to which this is a male-based account of influence. For a feminist revision of this Oedipal account of influence, see Sandra Gilbert and Susan Gubar, *The Madwoman in the Attic* (New Haven: Yale University Press, 1979), part 1. Feminist theory also seeks to replace or supplement Freud's Oedipal *agon* with Nancy Chodorow's account of the continuance of prelinguistic intimacy between mothers and daughters. See, for discussion of Chodorow as a corrective to Freud and Lacan, Margaret Homans, *Bearing the Word: Language and Female Experience in Nineteenth-Century Women's Writing* (Chicago: University of Chicago Press, 1986), chap. 1.

4. Since I am generalizing here about a wide field of writing, any specific

citations will probably seem rather arbitrary. See, however, Jonathan Dollimore, "Introduction: Shakespeare, Cultural Materialism, and the New Historicism," in Dollimore and Alan Sinfield, eds., *Political Shakespeare: New Essays in Cultural Materialism* (Manchester: Manchester University Press, 1985), where influence studies are not so much contested as ignored, and Stephen Greenblatt's opening chapter, "The Circulation of Social Energy," in *Shakespearean Negotiations* (Berkeley: University of California Press, 1988), which uses a paradigm of exchange to introduce essays that juxtapose contemporary or near-contemporary texts and treat them as comparable responses to currents of social energy. Survey articles on New Historicism and cultural materialism include: Walter Cohen, "Political Criticism of Shakespeare," in Jean E. Howard and Marion F. O'Connor, eds., *Shakespeare Reproduced* (New York: Methuen, 1987), pp. 18–46; Dollimore, "Introduction," *Political Shakespeare*, pp. 2–17; Jonathan Goldberg, "The Politics of Renaissance Literature: a Review Essay," *Journal of English Literary History* 49 (1982): 514–42; and Jean E. Howard, "The New Historicism in Renaissance Studies," *English Literary Renaissance* 16 (1986): 13–47.

5. Harold BLoom, *Ruin the Sacred Truths* (Cambridge: Harvard University Press, 1989), p. 54.

6. In citing this, I am not attempting to evaluate Bloom's characteristically bold historical claim that Chaucer should be thought of as a complete pioneer in this regard (one thinks of Ovid or Euripides, for instance, or, closer to hand, the speaker in *Astrophil and Stella*). Rather, I point out that attempts to generalize about Shakespeare's method or his singularity often come up with partial formulations of the general pragmatic substitution I offer as Shakespeare's throughout this book.

7. Many others make this claim in various, sometimes qualified, forms. See, for example, David Daniell, "Shakespeare and the Traditions of Comedy," in S. Wells, ed., *Cambridge Companion to Shakespeare Studies* (Cambridge: Cambridge University Press, 1986) pp. 108–9; Anne Barton in the *Riverside Shakespeare*, ed. G. Blakemore Evans et al. (Boston: Houghton Mifflin, 1974) p. 217 ("An extraordinary synthesis of material which, in itself, is challengingly diverse"); C. L. Barber, *Shakespeare's Festive Comedy*, p. 124 ("a more inclusive release of imagination"); Wolfgang Clemen, in the Signet Classic *Midsummer Night's Dream* (New York: New American Library, 1963), p. xxiii ("combines for the first time totally disparate worlds into one unified whole"); David Young, *Something of Great Constancy* (New Haven: Yale University Press, 1966), p. 33 ("Shakespeare was trying to improve on his own earlier efforts and those of his predecessors. The amalgam of styles and means indicates a conviction that the key to improvement was inclusiveness."); or, in a different idiom, but one which makes even larger claims for the play as a locus for diverse areas of signification, Louis Montrose, "The Shaping Fantasies of Elizabethan Culture," in M. Ferguson et. al., eds., *Rewriting the Renaissance* (Chicago: University of Chicago Press, 1986), p. 87 ("[*MND*] also creates the culture by which it is created"); Jonathan Crewe, *Hidden Designs* (New York: Methuen, 1986), pp. 134–35 ("without ceasing to do the work or relinquishing the specific goals

of either [*Errors* or *Shrew*] . . . , *MND* embodies revised and above all qualified (mitigated) versions of the projects embodied in both").

8. See Ann Thompson, *Shakespeare's Chaucer* (New York: Barnes and Noble, 1978), chap. 3 passim; Harold F. Brooks, Arden *Midsummer Night's Dream* (London: Methuen, 1979), lviii–lxxxviii; Geoffrey Bullough, *Narrative and Dramatic Sources of Shakespeare*, vol. 1, *Early Comedies* (New York: Columbia University Press, 1957), 367–84; E. Talbot Donaldson, *The Swan at the Well: Shakespeare Reading Chaucer* (New Haven: Yale University Press, 1985), chap. 1 and 2 passim.

9. *Shakespeare's Chaucer*, p. 16. See, for evidence that 1594–96 is a period of strong influence, Thompson's appendix of allusions, 220–21.

10. See Thompson, *Shakespeare's Chaucer*, pp. 58 and 83, for dismissals of the influence of the fabliaux on Shakespeare and English Renaissance drama generally. Donaldson, Brooks, and Bullough do not mention "The Miller's Tale," nor does Kenneth Muir in *The Sources of Shakespeare's Plays* (New Haven: Yale University Press, 1978). The one partial exception I have found to this is an essay by James Andreas, "From Festivity to Spectacle: The *Canterbury Tales, Fragment I* and *A Midsummer Night's Dream*," *Upstart Crow* 3 (Fall 1980): 19–28. Though Andreas "suspends" source study to "pursue a comparative investigation," he anticipates several general points about the "Miller's Tale"/ "Knight's Tale" alignment and *MND* I make below, and he notes that Bottom offers a "verbal echo" of the "anality" of the "Miller's Tale," though he draws the line at that point (see esp. p. 25).

11. Francis Beaumont's epistle is unmentioned by Donaldson and receives no detailed discussion from Ann Thompson or from Alice Miskimin in *The Renaissance Chaucer* (New Haven: Yale University Press, 1975). As far as I can tell, no one has previously commented on its presentation of Chaucer as an original for the progress of Elizabethan comedy in the 1580s and 1590s. This may be because Caroline Spurgeon omits most of Beaumont's discussion of Latin comedy, though Derek Brewer includes all of it. See below, notes 13 and 23.

12. "To His Very Loving and assured Good Friend, Mr. Thomas Speght," *The Works of our Ancient, Learned, & Excellent English Poet, Jeffrey Chaucer* (London, 1598; reprinted 1602, 1687).

13. See Derek Brewer, *Chaucer: The Critical Heritage* (London: Routledge and Kegan Paul, 1978), 1: 135–36.

14. *The Works of our Ancient . . . English Poet*, sig. A4r. We do not, unfortunately, know the identity of the learned Chaucer lover at Cambridge, nor of "that worthy learned Man your good Friend in *Oxford*" who is mentioned in the next sentence as upholding the "most high Reputation" of Chaucer at the other university.

15. Compare these with the same lines in the *Riverside Chaucer*, 3d ed., ed. Larry D. Benson et al. (Boston: Houghton Mifflin, 1987): "Ye knowe ek that in forme of speche is chaunge / Withinne a thousand yeer." In fact Speght's editorial work consisted not only of glossing, but of altering old words himself.

16. "To His Very Loving and Assured Good Friend," sig. A3r and v.

17. Ibid., sig. A3v.

18. Sidney includes "our *Chaucer's* Pandar" in a list with "the *Terentian Gnato*" in his *Apology*, and Nashe also puts the two together in a sentence about witty language, but neither of these is a comment on Chaucer as a source for Elizabethan comic drama. Otherwise I can find no comparison between Chaucer and Plautus or Terence in the sixteenth-century allusions prior to Beaumont recorded by Spurgeon.

19. "To His Very Loving and Assured Good Friend," sig. A3v.

20. Ibid., sig. A4r.

21. See Northop Frye, "The Argument of Comedy," in D. Robertson, ed., *English Institute Essays, 1948* (New York: Columbia University Press, 1949).

22. Charles Muscatine, *The Book of Geoffrey Chaucer: An Account of the Publication of Geoffrey Chaucer's Works from the Fifteenth Century to Modern Times* (San Francisco: Book Club of California, 1963), p. 23.

23. Muscatine, *Book of Chaucer*, p. 29. This is relevant in part because my quotations from the "Miller's Tale" below are taken from McFarlin Library's 1687 reprint of Speght's 1602 edition.

24. Sir John Harington, "An Apologie of Poetrie," prefixed to *Orlando Furioso* in English translation, 1591. Quotations from *The Cobler of Canterbury*, *Greene's Vision*, and Harington taken from Caroline Spurgeon, *Five Hundred Years of Chaucer Criticism and Allusion* (Cambridge: Cambridge University Press, 1925), 1: 131–32, 137–38, 138, and 134.

25. Quoted in Spurgeon, *Five Hundred Years*, p. 144–45. Note also this exchange from the anonymous *Returne from Parnassus*, where the dispute is over the propriety for poetry of the word "jape": *Ingenioso*: "Sir, the worde as Chaucer useth it hath noe unhonest meaninge in it, for it signifieth a jeste." *Gullio*: "Tush! Chaucer is a foole, and you are another for defending of him." The expression "Chaucer's jest" does not appear in *OED*, Eric Partridge's *Dictionary*, B. J. and Helen Whiting's *Proverbs, Sentences, and Proverbial Phrases*, either of R.W. Dent's collections, F. P. Wilson's *Oxford Book of English Proverbs*, or M. P. Tilley's *A Dictionary of Proverbs in England in the Sixteenth and Seventeenth Centuries*.

26. George Whetstone, *The Right Excellent and Famous Historye of Promos and Cassandra*, in W. C. Hazlitt, ed., *Shakespeare's Library* (New York: AMS Press, 1965), 6, 215. See Brewer, *Chaucer*, p. 114; see also Spurgeon, *Five Hundred Years*, p. 116.

27. Brewer, *Chaucer*, p. 120, quoting John Higins, *The Nomenclator or Rembrancer of Adrianus Iunius Physician* . . . (1585), p. 34.

28. See *The Riverside Chaucer*, p. 67, where the word is glossed as "elegant, pleasing (thing); i.e. pudendum."

29. See "quaint" in John S. P. Tatlock and Arthur G. Kennedy, *A Concordance to the Complete Works of Geoffrey Chaucer* (Gloucester, MA: Peter Smith, 1963), p. 719. There are of course many uses of "quaint" as an adjective meaning "ornate" or "crafty" or "particular"—thirty seven, to be exact, including the rhyme word in the "Miller's Tale": "As clerkes ben full subtill and queint, / And privily he caught her by the queint." I quote from the 1687 reprint of Speght's Chaucer.

30. Talbot Donaldson complains that modern Shakespeareans do not, for

the most part, appreciate Chaucer's complexity, so that when they make the comparison they disable it. See *The Swan at the Well*, pp. 2–3.

31. My comparisons between Shakespeare and Lyly follow G. K. Hunter's chapter in his *John Lyly: The Humanist as Courtier* (Cambridge: Harvard University Press, 1962).

32. Chaucer, *Works*, Speght ed., p. 28.

33. Ibid., p. 31.

34. Ibid., pp. 31–32.

35. *Hamlet* 3.4.211.

36. Discussions of the sources of an interest in sleeping and waking in *A Midsummer Night's Dream* tend to attribute it to the influence of John Lyly, who, like Puck in the epilogue, asks auditors of his court plays to imagine that they have dreamed what they have seen, and who in his *Endimion* has the title character sleep through much of the play, be pinched by fairies, and so on. In his extended comparison of Lyly and Shakespeare, G. K. Hunter comments that "the very profusion of Lylian motifs in [*Dream*] might seem to turn it into a cento, were it not that this profusion is in itself unLylian. . . . Shakespeare's play acquires a density of meaning which Lyly never achieved and probably never aimed at" (*John Lyly*, p. 319). Hunter sums up the contrast with references to Titania's embrace of Bottom and to the performance of "Pyramus and Thisbe": "the performance of the Pyramus and Thisbe play is only the fullest example of a tendency apparent throughout the play to interlace the episodes in a way unknown to Lyly. Even when Shakespeare does not implicate his themes in one another, he is prepared to use the tension of a possible clash as a dramatic device: the tense proximity of the fairy queen and the mechanicals is preserved throughout 117 lines till 'the shallowest thickskin of that barren sort' is fitted with his grossest form and only then are the opposites allowed to embrace" (p. 321). Hunter, then, admits Shakespeare could not have learned this sort of juxtaposition from Lyly—but he could have learned it from the "Miller's Tale."

37. Shakespeare's use of the adverb "obscenely," which also occurs in *Love's Labor's Lost*, is the first recorded in the *OED*. He is also the first recorded user of the adjective "obscene," in *Richard II*. It seems possible that by a dubious etymology Shakespeare connects the word with that which is not to be represented on the stage (Latin "scaena")—this would make sense of Bottom's use of the word, which may more simply be explained by his taste for novel expressions.

38. E. K. Chambers, *The Elizabethan Stage* (Oxford: Clarendon, 1923), 4: 286. Henceforth cited as Chambers.

39. Chambers, p. 288. This may be why the dramatists showed overt interest only in Chaucer's sage and serious works. See Thompson, *Shakespeare's Chaucer*, p. 58: "the type of story that attracted the dramatists' attention is significant since it shows an interest in the serious, romantic side of Chaucer rather than in the comic naturalism for which he is perhaps best known today. No one dramatized 'The Miller's Tale' or 'The Reeve's Tale,' for example, which might seem more stage-worthy to a modern writer than 'The Knight's

Tale' or 'The Clerk's Tale.'" But no remotely faithful dramatization of either the "Miller's Tale" or the "Reeve's Tale" would have passed the censor, and even today such a production would be somewhat scandalous—witness the warnings which accompany screenings of Pasolini's disappointing *Canterbury Tales*.

40. Gerald Eades Bentley, *The Profession of Dramatist in Shakespeare's Time, 1590–1642* (Princeton: Princeton University Press, 1971), pp. 186–87. But see also pp. 146, 148, and 167, where Bentley leaves ribaldry off a list of reasons why a play might be censored. This is clearly a mistake for Herbert, given his consistent interest in eliminating ribaldry as well as profanity and sedition; it is harder to tell about Tilney, but the initial Act of Common Council on regulating plays of 1574, according to Chambers, took account of the "unchaste and seditious speeches" which, among other ills, had troubled Londoners (Chambers, 1: 283).

41. Chaucer, *Works*, Speght, ed., p. 27.

42. Needless to say, there is none of this in the accepted source passages. See Bullough, *Sources*, pp. 406, 410, 417. For "stones" as testicles, see Eric Partridge, *Shakespeare's Bawdy* (New York: Everyman, 1960), pp. 195–96.

43. For "hole" as female genital orifice, see Partridge, *Shakespeare's Bawdy*, p. 128, and *OED Supplement*, "hole," sb. 8. See *OED*, "hole," sb. 8 and *Supplement*, "hole," sb. 8 for "hole" as anus. "Crannied hole" offers rich possibilities to the imagination, visual and tactile. On "cranny" as a standard Elizabethan translation of Ovid's "rima," found in grammar-school dictionaries, see Anthony Brian Taylor, "Golding's Ovid, Shakespeare's 'Small Latin', and the Real Object of Mockery in 'Pyramus and Thisbe,'" *Shakespeare Survey* 42 (Cambridge: Cambridge University Press, 1990), p. 58; Taylor points out in a note that "crannied hole" is not an expression used in Golding (but the contextually obscene redundancy is a very odd translation of Ovid). Taylor's overall point is that Shakespeare's parody is not aimed at Golding, but is, by way of Peter Quince as well-meaning and industrious but incompetent poet, a piece of genial self-mockery—this too is rather Chaucerian, in fact, though Taylor believes that Chaucer has nothing to do with it.

44. The verbal connections here to Alison's "naked ers" are hard to document (though the comic grotesquery of the misdirected kiss remains): in contemporary English, "ass" is an American pronounciation, and "bottom" a more polite synonym, for "arse," but neither word is easy to link to "arse" in Elizabethan English. According to Spevack's *Concordance* (Marvin Spevack, ed., *The Harvard Concordance to Shakespeare* [Cambridge: Harvard University Press, 1974]), Shakespeare never uses the word "arse," uses "bum" only four times, "buttocks" only twice, "posterior" never explicitly in this sense (though jokes in *LLL* 5.1 seem to depend on it), "fundament" never, "backside" never, "fart" never—in general this anatomical region and the comic or erotic possibilities associated with it get surprisingly little mention. A census of such words in Marlowe or Jonson would surely yield very different results, given that the opening scene of *The Alchemist* alone approaches Shakespeare's modest total.

Chapter Seven

1. On the rise of historiography in the late 1500s and its relation to the history play as a competing (as well as partly derivative) genre, see Phyllis Rackin, *Stages of History: Shakespeare's English Chronicles* (Ithaca: Cornell University Press, 1990). "Beginning and ending in a sense of anachronism, the Renaissance revolution in historiography was impelled by a desire to recuperate an older, better world. Confronted with the destabilizing forces of rapid social change, Shakespeare's contemporaries took refuge in nostalgic historical myths of a stable, Edenic past. But these very efforts produced their own frustration." (p. 142).

2. See Elizabeth Freund, " 'Ariachne's Broken Woof': The Rhetoric of Citation in *Troilus and Cressida*," in Patricia Parker and Geoffrey Hartman, eds., *Shakespeare and the Question of Theory* (New York: Methuen, 1985), pp. 19–36.

3. Jonathan Dollimore, *Radical Tragedy: Religion, Ideology and Power in the Drama of Shakespeare and His Contemporaries* (Brighton: Harvester, 1984), p. 44. Norman Rabkin, without criticising time's surrogacy, sees it as the determinant of value to which the play points: "Value exists not in the subjective will of the valuer, or, as the play's rationalists would have it, in the object he sees, but only in that object as time disposes of it" (*Shakespeare and the Common Understanding* [New York: Free press, 1967], p. 53). Dollimore and I would agree, I suspect, that Rabkin should substitute "successive human societies" for "time," here.

4. While endorsing (for humans) the importance of survival through time after death by juxtaposing strong descriptions of nature's orderliness in differentiating species and strong descriptions of its chaotic contingencies for individuals, *Troilus and Cressida* anticipates a Darwinian outlook more thoroughly than any other play. But it is Darwin without progress.

5. *Radical Tragedy*, p. 45.

6. Quotations from the New Arden *Troilus and Cressida*, ed. Kenneth Palmer (London: Methuen, 1982), are incorporated parenthetically.

7. C. C. Barfoot, *"Troilus and Cressida:* 'Praise Us as We are Tasted,'" *Shakespeare Quarterly* 39 (Spring 1988): 49.

8. Linda Charnes, " 'So Unsecret to Ourselves': Notorious Identity and the Material Subject in Shakespeare's *Troilus and Cressida*," *Shakespeare Quarterly* 40 (Winter 1989): 434. I presume that some version of this essay, which I came upon after this chapter was substantially finished, will appear in Charnes' forthcoming book, *Materializing the Subject: Notorious Identity in Shakespeare* (Harvard).

9. On this see Charnes, "Notorious Identity"; Gayle Green, "Shakespeare's Cressida: 'A kind of self,' " in Carolyn R. S. Lenz, Gayle Greene, and Carol T. Neely, *The Woman's Part: Feminist Criticism of Shakespeare* (Urbana: University of Illinois Press, 1980), pp. 133–49 (an essay which, like Charnes's, also has excellent things to say about value markets); and Janet Adelman, " 'This Is and Is Not Cressid': The Characterization of Cressida," in Shirley N. Garner, Claire Kahane, and Madelon Sprengnether, *The (M)Other Tongue* (Ithaca: Cornell University Press, 1985), pp. 119–41.

10. One might compare the wound counting in *Coriolanus* for similar market valuation of the activity of fighting (see chap. 8).

11. René Girard, "The Politics of Desire in *Troilus and Cressida*," in Patricia Parker and Geoffrey Hartman, eds., *Shakespeare and the Question of Theory* (London: Methuen, 1985), p. 199.

12. "Is [Helen] worth keeping? Why, she is a pearl / Whose price hath launched above a thousand ships . . . " (2.2.82) Compare *Doctor Faustus*, in C. F. Tucker Brooke, ed., *The Works of Christopher Marlowe* (Oxford: Clarendon Press, 1910), p. 189, ll. 1328–29: "Was this the face that lancht a thousand shippes? / And burnt the toplesse Towres of *Ilium*?"

13. The hint of Matthew 13:46, the parable of the pearl of great price for which Troilus would "sell all the goods he has," to my mind largely confirms the mercantile image.

14. E.g., Dollimore, *Radical Tragedy*, p. 45.

15. For an argument that her value *does* tumble in Troilus's eyes, see René Girard, "The Politics of Desire in *Troilus and Cressida*," pp. 188–90.

16. This is a classic female double-bind; wanting both sex and respect, Cressida cannot have one without sacrificing the other.

17. *Bleak House* (1853; Boston: Riverside, 1956), p. 433.

18. In a term proposed by Girard, this is a crisis of "undifferentiation" or "no difference." See *A Theater of Envy: William Shakespeare* (New York: Oxford University Press, 1991), pp. 160–66.

19. I do not mean to suggest that concerns about maintaining one's value are unknown to the Homeric warrior; such concerns are in fact central in Homer. But they manifest themselves in angry insistence on receiving one's heroic due rather than anxiety about the system in which fame and honor are recorded and remembered. This system is on the whole trustworthy in both the *Iliad* and the *Odyssey*. Indeed, the *Iliad* and the *Odyssey* simply *are* this system. Odysseus's endorsement of the accounts of the Trojan War given by the blind bard Demodokos in book 8 of the *Odyssey* seems intended as a reflexive validation of epic reliability.

20. "Notorious Identity," p. 439. The final line is taken from the Beatles' "Penny Lane."

21. This is true of a number of books in Shakespeare: consider Ophelia's prayer book and the book Hamlet pretends to read from to Polonius, for instance.

22. Sonnet 94.

23. See, e.g., Frank Kermode, "Opinion, Truth, and Value," *Essays in Criticism* 5 (1955): 185–86.

24. H. P. Grice, "Logic and Conversation," in Peter Cole and Jerry L. Morgan, eds., *Syntax and Semantics*, vol. 3, *Speech Acts* (New York, 1975), p. 45. The emphases are Grice's.

25. Barbara Hernstein Smith, *Contingencies of Value: Alternative Perspectives for Critical Theory* (Cambridge: Harvard University Press, 1988), p. 109.

26. This makes Cressida unique among Shakespearean female leads; Miranda is a special case (and even she surprises Prospero by remembering that

she once had women tending her), but I cannot think of any others. Even Lady Macbeth has a woman watching her while she sleepwalks; and Octavia in *Antony and Cleopatra*, a minor character by comparison, also exchanged between men, enters to her brother "with her train" (3.6.38 s.d.), which probably includes women.

Chapter Eight

1. See Paul A. Rahe, *Republics Ancient and Modern: Classical Republicanism and the American Revolution* (Chapel Hill: University of North Carolina Press, 1992), p. 8, for argument that this transformation is one modern readers are programmed by their own polities to approve, even as their circumstances no longer force them to place a huge civic value on personal willingness to fight alongside fellow citizens.

2. "The Life of Caius Martius Coriolanus," from Plutarch, *Lives of Noble Grecians and Romanes*, trans. Thomas North, 1579; reprinted in the Arden *Coriolanus*, ed. Philip Brockbank (London: Methuen, 1976), p. 318. For the Midlands Rising and the play, see E. C. Pettet, "*Coriolanus* and the Midlands Insurrection of 1607," *Shakespeare Survey* 3 (Cambridge: Cambridge University Press, 1950), pp. 34–42.

3. Quotations from the play are taken from the Arden *Coriolanus*, ed. Philip Brockbank (London: Methuen, 1976), and citations are given parenthetically throughout.

4. See E. P. Thompson, "The Moral Economy of the English Crowd in the Eighteenth Century," *Past and Present* 50 (1971): 76–136. On the essay's influence, see Paul Slack, *Rebellion, Popular Protest, and the Social Order in Early Modern England* (Cambridge: Cambridge University Press, 1984), p. 3; and Annabel Patterson, "The Very Name of the Game: Theories of Order and Disorder," *South Atlantic Quarterly* 86 (Fall 1987): 532. Patterson shows how Thompson's article precipitated a conflict among historians of early modern England over the nature and scope of popular protest.

5. "Moral Economy," pp. 78–79.

6. Ibid., pp. 108–109.

7. Ibid., p. 113. Thompson adduces further examples on subsequent pages: "the poor knew that one way to make the rich yield was to twist their arms" (p. 115).

8. I accept the arguments of Wilbur Sanders for the retention of the Folio speech assignments. See Sanders and Howard Jacobson, *Shakespeare's Magnanimity* (New York: Oxford University Press, 1978), pp. 139–40.

9. John Walter and Keith Wrightson, "Dearth and the Social Order in Early Modern England," in Slack, ed., *Rebellion*, pp. 108–28.

10. Walter and Wrightson, "Dearth and the Social Order," p. 127.

11. "Moral Economy," p. 126.

12. Brecht's analytic dialogue on the opening scene of *Coriolanus* is of great interest in this regard, since he and his players wish to see the plebeian-patrician relation as one of class conflict swept aside by nationalism when the

fatherland comes under attack, on the model of German workers' movements at the outsets of World War I and World War II. See John Willett, ed., *Brecht on Theatre* (New York: Hill and Wang, 1964), pp. 252–65.

13. "Dearth and the Social Order," p. 114.

14. See *Brecht on Theatre*, pp. 262–63.

15. The comparison is elaborated by Reuben Brower in *Hero and Saint* (New York: Oxford University Press, 1971).

16. Stanley Fish, "How to Do Things with Austin and Searle," in *Is There a Text in this Class?* (Cambridge: Harvard University Press, 1980), pp. 200–220; Janet Adelman, "'Anger's My Meat': Feeding, Dependency, and Aggression in *Coriolanus*," in Murray Schwartz and Coppélia Kahn, eds., *Representing Shakespeare* (Baltimore: Johns Hopkins Press, 1980), pp. 129–49; Paul Cantor, *Shakespeare's Rome* (Ithaca: Cornell University Press, 1976), pp. 55–124. The suggestion that, in exile, Coriolanus must come to be either a beast or a god originates with F. N. Lees, "*Coriolanus*, Aristotle, and Bacon," *Review of English Studies*, n.s. 1 (1950). See also G. K. Hunter, "Shakespeare's last tragic heroes," in *Dramatic Identities and Cultural Tradition* (Liverpool: Liverpool University Press, 1978). My chapter could be seen as an attempt to modify Hunter's summary of the late tragic pattern, and to be aimed specifically at his claim that "in none [of the late tragedies] does the individual hero succeed in creating a new world of value inside himself, finding the point of growth which will absorb and transmute the world as it is" (p. 255). W. Hutchings, "Beast or God: The *Coriolanus* Controversy," in C. B. Cox and D. J. Palmer, eds., *Shakespeare's Wide and Universal Stage* (Manchester: Manchester University Press, 1984), is a useful summary of criticism of *Coriolanus;* Hutchings is stronger on British than on American critics. Robert Miola, *Shakespeare's Rome* (Cambridge: Cambridge University Press, 1983), discusses the play in terms of its connection with Shakespeare's other Roman works and with the classics. Bruce King, in *Coriolanus: Critics Debate* (Atlantic Highlands, NJ: Humanities Press International, 1989), offers a recent summary of criticism and issues.

17. The family dynamic resembles that between Hal and Henry IV explored above.

18. He is a traitor to Rome if we assume that he owes loyalty to a city which has banished him; he is a traitor to the Volsces if we assume it is treachery not to pursue to the utmost the advantage of the nation one serves.

19. *Shakespeare's Rome*, p. 120.

20. For arguments which anticipate or parallel Fish, see D. J. Gordon, "Name and Fame: Shakespeare's Coriolanus," in G. I. Duthie, ed., *Papers Mainly Shakespearian* (Aberdeen: Oliver and Boyd, 1964), and Joyce Van Dyke, "Making a Scene: Language and Gesture in *Coriolanus*," *Shakespeare Survey*, vol. 30 (1977); for psychological discussions which draw on image patterns and anticipate, parallel, or draw on Adelman, see Maurice Charney, *Shakespeare's Roman Plays* (Cambridge: Harvard University Press, 1961), Coppélia Kahn, *Man's Estate: Masculine Identity in Shakespeare* (Berkeley: University of California Press, 1981), and Stanley Cavell, "Who Does the Wolf Love? *Coriolanus* and the Interpretations of Politics," in Patricia Parker and Geoffrey Hartman, eds.,

Shakespeare and the Question of Theory (London: Methuen, 1985), pp. 245–72;
for a political account of the play which anticipates Cantor in some ways see
A. P. Rossiter, *Angel with Horns* (London: Longman, 1961).

21. Thus Oscar Campbell, following hints from Bradley and Shaw, calls
the play both "a tragical satire" and "a history play" in *Shakespeare's Satire*,
excerpted in James Phillips, ed., *Twentieth Century Interpretations of Coriolanus*
(Englewood Cliffs: Prentice Hall, 1970), pp. 25–26. A. P. Rossiter comments
in *Angel with Horns*: "*Coriolanus* is the last and greatest of the Histories
. . . Shakespeare's only great political play; and it is slightly depressing, and
hard to come to terms with, because it is *political tragedy*" (p. 251). Paul Cantor
suggests that the play's power to disturb comes about because "Coriolanus's
banishment raises doubts about the assumption that to be a good citizen and
to be a good man are one and the same thing" (*Shakespeare's Rome*, p. 123); this
is near the Bradleyan view that Coriolanus's virtues are tragically *wasted* in the
play in a way that demonstrates inherent problems with the political process;
see A. C. Bradley's British Academy Lecture in the Signet *Coriolanus*, ed.
Reuben Brower (New York: New American Library, 1966), p. 257.

22. Signet *Coriolanus*, pp. 250–51.

23. *Coriolanus* is certainly the most concentrated instance of this; in a diffuse
way, there is a generational transfer of political role in the *Henriad*, where we
can see advice and potency passing from John of Gaunt to Henry IV to Hal.
On the first stage, and its psychological aspects, see Harry Berger, Jr., "*Ars
Moriendi* in Progress, or John of Gaunt and the Practice of Strategic Dying,"
Yale Journal of Criticism 1 (Fall 1987): 39–65, and also Berger's "Psychoanalyzing
the Shakespeare Text: the first three scenes of the *Henriad*," in Parker and
Hartman, *Shakespeare and the Question of Theory*, pp. 210–29.

24. The word "noble" in all its forms appears much more often in *Coriolanus*
than in any other Shakespearean play: Coriolanus himself is "noble," "all noble," the producer of "noble blows," "too noble for this world," "thou noble
thing," "a noble servant," "the most noble corse," and a man who "shall have
a noble memory" in the course of the play, to choose only the most prominent
examples. According to the Spevack *Concordance*, bringing together entries for
"noble," "nobler," "noblest," "nobly," "nobility," and "nobleness," *Coriolanus*
contains 85 instances; its nearest competitor, *Henry the Eighth*, has 55 (mostly
in modes of address); *Antony* and *Julius Caesar* 44 each; and *Hamlet* 20.

25. The argument that follows places me in the company of Terry Eagleton, who, in the process of declaring that Coriolanus, "though literally a patrician, is perhaps Shakespeare's most developed study of a bourgeois individual-
ist," comments also that neither Hamlet nor Coriolanus "will engage in
reciprocal exchange or submit to the signifier . . . But the paradox of such
private enterprise of the self is that although it regards personal identity as
private, autonomous and non-exchangeable, it is historically bound up with
the full-blown exchange economy of commodity production." See his *William
Shakespeare* (Oxford: Basil Blackwell, 1986), pp. 73–74. I think Eagleton is
completely wrong in asserting that Shakespeare identifies autonomy claims

with emergent capitalism in *Coriolanus;* I agree with him, however, that Shakespeare sees economies of circulation and exchange as a pervasive and ascendent modifier of ideas of personal value.

26. He does, as Fish points out, finally put his request to the people in proper form as a speech act (see "How to Do Things with Austin and Searle," p. 206).

27. "Of Glory," *The Complete Essays of Montaigne,* bk. 2, no. 16, trans. Donald Frame (Stanford: Stanford University Press, 1958), p. 477. Montaigne writes earlier in the essay: "We call it making our name great to spread and sow it in many mouths; we want it to be received there in good part, and to profit by this growth." (p. 474). For a collection of sixteenth and early seventeenth century English positions on "nobility," see Paul A. Jorgenson, *Redeeming Shakespeare's Words* (Berkeley: University of California Press, 1962). Jorgenson believes that the essential test of nobility which Coriolanus fails is that of "serving the public good" (p. 83).

28. Volumnia means "you make my dreams come true," but her words also convey her belief—a mistaken one—that she has succeeded in transmitting her own values and desires without alteration to her son.

29. Thus the plebeians' starvation and threats of violence in the opening scene are answered by a political concession, the creation of the tribunes, and this is evidently felt by the plebeians to be a generous and successful exchange.

30. The best guide to these is Annabel Patterson's *Shakespeare and the Popular Voice,* chap. 6. I regret once again, as I did in citing her chapter on *Hamlet,* that I came to her account of *Coriolanus* too late to incorporate it fully, the more so in that we disagree on several points.

31. His sword was out, and exceedingly active, on the London Road, and it did not rest after his arrival. See Lawrence Stone, *The Crisis of the Aristocracy, 1558–1641* (Oxford: Clarendon Press, 1965), pp. 76–77. Stone quotes *Eastward Ho!* (1605):

> I ken the man weel. He's one of my thirty pound knights.
> —No, no, this is he that stole his knighthood o' the grand day for four pound given to a page.

Stone continues:

> 'The grand day' was 23 July 1603, the day of the coronation, when 432 knights were dubbed at a single session . . . .
> For all of this confusion and ridicule, the title was still eagerly sought for. . . . the price kept up, and even rose, so that in March 1604 Sir William Stewart was asking £100 of a client for his recommendation. By now James was using the honour to reward anyone who took his fancy. For example, in 1605 he knighted his goldsmith, William Herrick, 'for makinge a hole in the great diamond the King doth wear'. Worse still was the fact that James had now forgotten his former indignation at the sale of knighthoods and was distributing the right of nomination among his courtiers. From them these rights passed, like stocks and shares, into

general currency among London financial speculators, so that in 1606
Lionel Cranfield bought the making of six knights from his friend Arthur
Ingram for £373.1s.8d.

Stone also records financial negotiations from the 1603–1608 period for knighthoods of the Bath, and for peerages, and he notes that the scheme for the
creation and sale of a new noble rank, baronetcy, originated with Bacon in
1606, though it was not acted upon until 1611. In sum, there is every reason
to think of the marketing of nobility as a topical, and indeed much talked-of,
process in the first five years of James's reign.

32. Conrad Russell, *The Crisis of Parliaments: English History, 1509–1660*
(London: Oxford University Press, 1971) p. 207.

33. See Adelman, " 'Anger's My Meat,' " p. 131, for the argument that this
passage offers a key to a metaphoric cluster of great importance: "the unspoken
mediator between breast and wound is the infant's mouth: in this imagistic
transformation, to feed is to be wounded; the mouth becomes the wound, the
breast the sword. The metaphoric process suggests the psychological fact that
is, I think, at the center of the play: the taking in of food is the primary
acknowledgement of one's dependence on the world, and as such, it is the
primary token of one's vulnerability. But at the same time as Volumnia's image
suggests the vulnerability inherent in feeding, it also suggests a way to fend
off that vulnerability. In her image, feeding, incorporating, is transformed into
spitting out, an aggressive expelling; the wound once again becomes the mouth
that spits 'forth blood / At Grecian sword contemning.' The wound spitting
blood thus becomes not a sign of vulnerability but an instrument of attack."

34. In Plutarch, after the Volsces break camp, the senate and the people
honor Volumnia, but there is no question of the quasi-military triumph which
she seems to get in Shakespeare.

35. Compare Coriolanus's homecoming in act 2, where he also is slow to
salute his mother and greets her with a reference to divine participation in
their relation:

COMINIUS: Look, sir, your mother!
CORIOLANUS: O,
    You have, I know, petitioned all the gods
    For my prosperity. (2.1.168)

36. See Van Dyke, "Making a Scene," p. 146, for an account of the end of
the play that resembles this one. Most critics, indeed, concur in describing the
nature of Coriolanus's capitulation, though they disagree markedly about its
significance.

37. Clifford Geertz, "Centers, Kings, and Charisma: Reflections on the
Symbolics of Power," in Joseph Ben-David and Terry Nicholas Clark, eds.,
Culture and Its Creators: Essays in Honor of Edward Shils (Chicago: University of
Chicago Press, 1977), p. 151.

38. "Centers," p. 167.

39. Anne Barton, "Livy, Machiavelli, and Shakespeare's 'Coriolanus,' "
Shakespeare Survey 38 (1985) 129.

40. Though see 1.9.77 where, after Coriolanus has refused the spoils of Corioli, he says "The gods begin to mock me: I, that now / Refus'd most princely gifts, am bound to beg / Of my lord general." Coriolanus associates situations in which he is forced to bargain with irony on the part of the gods.

41. Signet *Coriolanus*, p. 257.

42. A comment of George Hunter's on the contrast between *Julius Caesar* and Jonson's *Sejanus* parallels the claim I am making for Coriolanus: "To be good exempts one, in neither play, from the pains of history; but Shakespeare allows his stoical suicides to express for future times the free Roman values of a present moment and an individual outlook that is fixed forever by the escape from flux and decay that suicide offers." Jonson, Hunter observes, allows no such escape from historical judgment. See his "A Roman Thought: Renaissance Attitudes to History Exemplified in Shakespeare and Jonson," in Brian S. Lee, ed., *An English Miscellany Presented to W. S. Mackie* (Cape Town: Oxford University Press, 1977), p. 111.

Chapter Nine

1. Janet Adelman, *The Common Liar: An Essay on Antony and Cleopatra* (New Haven: Yale University Press, 1973), p. 170.

2. Janet Adelman, " 'Anger's My Meat': Feeding, Dependency, and Aggression in *Coriolanus*," in Murray Schwartz and Coppélia Kahn, eds., *Representing Shakespeare* (Baltimore: Johns Hopkins Press, 1980), pp. 129–49. The essay is discussed in chapter 7. Adelman's new book, *Suffocating Mothers: Fantasies of Maternal Origin in Shakespeare's Plays, Hamlet to The Tempest* (New York: Routledge, 1992), which I read after this chapter was completed, is strongly committed to psychoanalysis as a system but continues to see *Antony and Cleopatra* as "extraordinarily liberating" (see p. 191).

3. For two excellent recent essays which see *Antony and Cleopatra* reproducing and criticizing systems of constraint, see Linda Charnes, "Theatrical Practice *as* Critical Practice: Tactics vs. Strategies in Shakespeare's *Antony and Cleopatra*," SAA paper 1990, forthcoming in Charnes, *Materializing the Subject: Notorious Identity in Shakespeare* (Harvard), and Madelon Sprengnether, "The Boy Actor and Femininity in *Antony and Cleopatra*," in Norman Holland, Sidney Homan, and Bernard J. Paris, eds., *Shakespeare's Personality* (Berkeley: University of California Press, 1989). For a fine discussion of how race and gender collaborate as subordinating categories in Roman attitudes toward Cleopatra, see Ania Loomba, *Gender, race, Renaissance drama* (Manchester: Manchester University Press, 1989).

4. Roberto Mangabeira Unger, *Social Theory: Its Situation and Its Task* (Cambridge: Cambridge University Press, 1987), p. 13.

5. This relation is explicitly denied by Stanley Fish, who comments that "[t]he authority of contingent schemes of association is not shaken simply by an awareness of their contingency" (*Doing What Comes Naturally*, p. 432). I disagree, for reasons gone into in the Introduction, and I would add that whether or not the assertion of contingency shakes authority is itself contingent

upon what kind of legitimacy that authority claims. We do not really know what a society shot through with an endorsement of the contingency of its arrangements would be like: this is the kind of society Unger wants us to try to have.

6. Christopher Marlowe, *The Conquests of Tamburlaine, the Scythian Shepheard*, ll. 753 ff., in *The Works of Christopher Marlowe*, ed. C. F. Tucker Brooke (Oxford: Clarendon, 1910), lightly modernized.

7. See Stephen Greenblatt, *Renaissance Self-Fashioning* (Chicago: University of Chicago Press, 1980), chap. 5 and esp. p. 213: "We watch Tamburlaine construct himself out of phrases picked up or overheard: 'And ride in triumph through Persepolis' or 'I that am term'd the Scourge and Wrath of God'. Like the gold taken from unwary travelers or the troops lured away from other princes, Tamburlaine's identity is something *appropriated*, seized from others."

8. Christopher Marlowe, *The Jew of Malta*, prologue, ll. 14–21, in *Works*.

9. J. G. A. Pocock, *The Machiavellian Moment* (Princeton: Princeton University Press, 1975), pp. 36–37.

10. This seems to me to be a fair description of *Tamburlaine*, part 1, which ends with Tamburlaine conquering and then recrowning his future father-in-law, legitimizing his rule by marriage to Zenocrate (having chivalrously legitimized his suit by conquering Zenocrate's royal fiancé), "taking truce with all the world," and inviting his generals to doff armor and don the robes of lawgivers. Part 2, an unintended sequel written to meet public demand, perforce imparts a different shape to Marlowe's treatment of the whole career.

11. Machiavelli, *The Prince*, chap. 6, in *The Portable Machiavelli*, ed. Peter Bondanella and Mark Musa (New York: Viking Penguin, 1983), p. 93.

12. Hanna Fenichel Pitkin, *Fortune Is a Woman: Gender and Politics in the Thought of Niccolò Machiavelli* (Berkeley: University of California Press, 1982), p. 52.

13. Ibid.

14. Ibid., p. 109.

15. See Dollimore, *Radical Tragedy*, pp. 3–4; Cohen, *Drama of a Nation*, pp. 349–56; Leonard Tennenhouse, *Power On Display: The Politics of Shakespeare's Genres* (New York: Methuen, 1986), p. 15, p. 186. See also Rebecca Bushnell, *Tragedies of Tyrants: Political Thought and Theater in the English Renaissance* (Ithaca: Cornell University Press, 1990), p. 5; Franco Moretti, *Signs Taken for Wonders: Essays in the Sociology of Literary Forms* (London: New Left Books, 1983), p. 42: "Having deconsecrated the king, tragedy made it possible to decapitate him"; Gary Taylor, *Reinventing Shakespeare: A Cultural History, from the Restoration to the Present* (New York: Weidenfeld & Nicolson, 1989), pp. 7–9.

16. It might be added that Cruttwell's book is largely a skilled application of Eliot's "dissociation of sensibility" thesis, proposed in his essay "The Metaphysical Poets" in 1921. Although political history goes unmentioned by Eliot, the English Revolution turns out to coincide with the dissociation. After Charles I's head was cut from his body, English poets no longer felt thoughts as immediately as the odor of a rose. That Milton was, according to Eliot, a

culprit in the dissociation of sensibility and was in fact a defender of the regicide commonwealth may not be entirely coincidental.

17. Blair Worden, "Andrew Marvell, Oliver Cromwell, and the *Horatian Ode*," in Kevin Sharpe and Steven N. Zwicker, eds., *Politics of Discourse: The Literature and History of Seventeenth Century England* (Berkeley: University of California Press, 1987); see esp. pp. 162–68.

18. It was not published until the posthumous Marvell folio of 1681, and in most copies of the folio the ode was cancelled.

19. Prologue to *Tamburlaine*, part 1.

20. "An Horatian Ode upon Cromwell's Return from Ireland," *Andrew Marvell: The Complete Poems*, ed. Elizabeth Story Donno (Harmondsworth: Penguin, 1972), pp. 55–56.

21. *The Prince*, p. 93.

22. See Worden, "Andrew Marvell," sections 3 and 5.

23. Pocock, *The Machiavellian Moment*, p. 379.

24. Marvell's interest in this kind of mother-destroying birth is suggested by "The Unfortunate Lover" (*The Complete Poems*, pp. 42–43), which seems in some ways an allegory of events treated historically in the "Horatian Ode":

> soon these flames do lose their light
> Like meteors of a summer's night:
> Nor can they to that region climb,
> To make impression upon time.

℮

> 'Twas in a shipreck, when the seas
> Ruled, and the winds did what they please,
> That my poor lover floating lay,
> And, ere brought forth, was cast away:
> Till at the last the master-wave
> Upon the rock his mother drave;
> And there she split against the stone,
> In a Caesarean sectión. (5–16)

The mother disappears, and the baby is raised by cormorants who both feed him and feed upon him. The line "To make impression upon time" resembles "to ruin the great work of time" in the "Horatian Ode," and Cromwell himself is suggested both by the "orphan of the hurricane" (32) and by the "master-wave" which drove his mother on the rock, split her, and thus delivered a son who would owe no loyalty to the stability of nurture and be entirely fostered by the storm, which he fights against: "See how he nak'd and fierce does stand, / Cuffing the thunder with one hand . . . " (49–50)

25. "Marvell, Cromwell, and the *Horatian Ode*," p. 153.

26. See Donno's note, *The Complete Poems*, p. 241.

27. On this see Worden, pp. 153–7.

28. Unger, *Social Theory*, pp. 22–23.

29. Richard Rorty, *Contingency, Irony, and Solidarity* (Cambridge University Press, 1989), p. 39.

30. Adelman suggests this, in terms recalling Norman Rabkin's *Shakespeare and the Common Understanding*, in *The Common Liar*, chap. 1, passim and especially p. 30: "In order to be engaged in the movement of judgments, in order to see both the validity and the limitations of all perspectives, we must be able to accept each of the various judgments as true at least momentarily."

31. I quote from, the Arden *Antony and Cleopatra*, ed. M. R. Ridley (London: Methuen, 1954). Citations are given parenthetically.

32. The First World War began as a conflict between a kaiser allied with a Holy Roman Emperor on one side and a czar allied with a king-emperor on the other—all titles harking back to Rome and two of them harking back to the name Octavius gained by adoption from Julius Caesar.

33. "Life of Octavius Caesar Augustus" from North's *Plutarch* (1603), in Geoffrey Bullough, ed., *Narrative and Dramatic Sources of Shakespeare*, vol. 5 (London: Routledge and Kegan Paul, 1966), p. 323.

34. Herbert Marcuse, *An Essay on Liberation*, quoted in Christopher Hill, *The World Turned Upside Down* (New York: Viking, 1972), p. 336.

35. Though for the complexity of Machiavelli's position on this issue, see Pitkin, *Fortune Is A Woman*, pp. 73–74.

36. This difference shows in Antony and Octavius's positions in battle as well: Octavius leads from the rear, Antony from the front—when he is there at all. Cleopatra insists on being such a leader at Actium but cannot sustain the role.

37. On this see Adelman, *The Common Liar*, p. 141: "Even within the play, Shakespeare insists that we notice his new decorum, a decorum tolerant of excess."

38. Roberto Unger, *False Necessity* (Cambrige: Cambridge University Press, 1987), p. 569.

39. Jane Gallop, *The Daughter's Seduction: Feminism and Psychoanalysis* (Ithaca: Cornell University Press, 1982), p. 29.

40. Michael Grant, *Cleopatra* (New York: Simon and Schuster, 1972), pp. xiv–xv.

41. Stephen Booth discusses the problem this poses for actors in "The Shakespearean Actor as Kamikaze Pilot," *Shakespeare Quarterly* 36, no. 5 (1985). Plays in which actors playing lovers have more direct lovemaking to work with include *Romeo and Juliet*, all the romantic comedies, *The Winter's Tale*, and even *Troilus and Cressida* and *Othello*.

42. Michael Goldman, *Acting and Action in Shakespearean Tragedy* (Princeton: Princeton University Press, 1985), pp. 122–23.

43. Falstaff's death in *Henry V*, his heart "fracted and corroborate" for Hal, is the only other exception I can think of to Rosalind/Ganymede's dictum that "men have died from time to time, and worms have eaten them, but not for love" (*AYLI* 4.1.106), unless we count Mamillius in *The Winter's Tale* or Viola/Cesario's imaginary sister (*TN* 2.4.110). Lear and Gloucester may die of broken hearts, but only after physical ordeals fully sufficient to explain their deaths.

44. For references to such arguments, see *Antony and Cleopatra*, New Variorum Edition of Shakespeare, ed. Marvin Spevack et al. (New York: Modern Language Association, 1990), pp. 19 and 601–2.

45. But see Stanley Cavell, *Disowning Knowledge in Six Plays of Shakespeare* (New York: Cambridge University Press, 1987), p. 22: "I . . . tak[e] Shakespeare's reading of these famous events to contest the idea that Rome prepared for and will accede to Christianity, to suggest rather that the *final* victory may also be Caesar's—to pry open the issue whether the death of Antony (whoever that is) prepares the way for Christ (whatever that is) or prepares the way to contain and overcome Christ. If this is still Shakespeare's issue then it is still ours. And if this issue is the catastrophe or crisis before the Western world posed by the play, it is evidently not confined to a crisis in the authority of knowledge represented in skepticism." Although I read this nexus in quite the opposite way, my account of the play is indebted to Cavell's at a number of points.

46. "Redemption," in *The English Poems of George Herbert*, ed. C. A. Patrides (London: Dent, 1974), p. 60.

47. Graham Bradshaw, *Shakespeare's Scepticism* (1987; Ithaca: Cornell University Press, 1990), p. 34. The emphasis is Bradshaw's.

Coda

1. Quotations are from the Arden *Tempest*, ed. Frank Kermode (London: Methuen, 1954).

2. Richard Rorty, "Solidarity or objectivity," *Objectivity, relativism, and truth: Philosophical Papers*, vol. 1 (Cambridge: Cambridge University Press, 1991), p. 31.

3. *Objectivity, relativism, and truth*, p. 13.

4. That such associations should adhere to the writings of Rorty, Dewey, or James is outrageous, but familiar.

Index